THE
BRITISH ARMY

THE DEFINITIVE HISTORY OF THE TWENTIETH CENTURY

IMPERIAL WAR
MUSEUM

THE
BRITISH ARMY

THE DEFINITIVE HISTORY OF THE TWENTIETH CENTURY

INTRODUCTION BY
SIR MAX HASTINGS

C CASSELL
ILLUSTRATED

A CASSELL BOOK

An Hachette Livre UK Company

First published in Great Britain in 2007 by Cassell Illustrated,
a division of Octopus Publishing Group Limited,
2–4 Heron Quays, London, E14 4JP

Text, design and layout © 2007 Octopus Publishing Group Limited
Octopus Publishing Group is a division of Hachette Livre (UK)

A CIP catalogue record for this book is available from the British Library.

ISBN-13: 978-1-84403602-8
ISBN-10: 1-84403-602-2

10 9 8 7 6 5 4 3 2 1

Printed in China

CONTENTS

INTRODUCTION

LEFT Private Thomas Harry Evans of the 1st Battalion The Gloucestershire Regiment. He had completed 11 years of military service at the outbreak of war in 1914. He went to France with D Company of the 1st Gloucesters. He was reported missing, aged 27, during the First Battle of Ypres on 29 October 1914. He is commemorated on the Menin Gate at Ypres.

From its earliest campaigns to the present day, the British Army has been among our most successful national institutions. This book is designed to celebrate its achievement over the past century, and to honour the contributions of the fighting soldiers – volunteers and conscripts, professionals and amateurs – who have made its victories possible. Until 1914, though the Army often fought and conquered, the British people looked chiefly to the Royal Navy to defend them. But in the 20th century, the nation found itself for the first time obliged to send great armies to the Continent, to join conflicts in which huge numbers in the uniforms of many countries fought and died. By 1960, when conscription was finally abolished, millions of young men had served in the British Army. Some were more eager than others, to be sure, but on a hundred battlefields their achievements in the ranks of the great regiments won them the admiration of the world. The small volunteer force which has succeeded them, sustaining responsibility for Britain's defence for almost the past half-century, has become the most professional and accomplished in the nation's history.

Yet the Redcoat, the Tommy, the Squaddie has gained his glories and medals in the face of long periods in which the Army has been neglected. The British people enjoy celebrating the achievements of their warriors more than they like paying for them when their own safety is not immediately threatened. Kipling penned his splendidly cynical reflection on popular attitudes to Thomas Atkins in 1898:

While it's Tommy this an' Tommy that, an' "Tommy fall behind"
But it's "Please to walk in front, sir", when there's trouble in the wind, –

Since time immemorial, the soldier has paid in sweat and blood for failures of political and public will.

Nineteenth-century British victories over native peoples inspired complacency. Of these, Omdurman in September 1898 represented the apogee. Eleven thousand Dervishes died in the face of rifle, machine-gun and artillery fire from Kitchener's disciplined formations, which lost 48 killed. The Muslim masses were destroyed at ranges of over 800 yards, save where the 21st Lancers, accompanied by Lieutenant Winston Churchill, made a foolish and unnecessary charge.

RIGHT Lance-Corporal Harry van Tromp, of the 22nd Battalion The Royal Fusiliers. He was the son of the Mayor of Taunton, Somerset, and was killed in action, aged 34, at Vimy on 23 May 1916. This photograph was taken on his last day in England before leaving for the Western Front on 17 May 1916. He is buried in the Zouave Valley Cemetery, Souchez.

Yet, just over a year after Omdurman, the British suffered humiliations at the hands of the Boers in South Africa, which laid bare the limitations of their forces against white enemies armed with modern weapons. Private soldiers, drawn from the poorest section of society, had never been encouraged or even permitted to show initiative. Correlli Barnett has described the Victorian ranker as "a mindless brick in a moving wall of flesh". Their officers, careless sprigs of the landed classes, prided themselves on treating war as a game. The ballroom and polo pitch dominated the lives of young blades, who could afford commissions only if they possessed private means to supplement their pay. Kitchener observed sourly: "There appears to be a want of serious study of the profession by officers who are, I think, rather inclined to deal lightly with military questions of moment … Keenness is out of fashion … It is not the correct form."

Buller's army paid the price in a succession of bloody defeats that stunned the British people and delighted their jealous European rivals. Kitchener wrote crossly to a young relative: "The Boers are not like the Sudanese who stood up to a fair fight. They are always running away on their little ponies." To achieve the defeat of 50,000 farmers and secure South Africa from guerrilla insurgency, by 1901 the British Empire was obliged to field 450,000 men. When peace came, Kipling as usual caught the mood of the nation. He wrote that the Boer War had been "no end of a lesson".

Its consequences for the Army were dramatic and far-reaching. In the early years of the new century, a succession of official reports identified weaknesses, and ministers began to correct them. Fresh tactics were adopted, appropriate to the age of rifled weapons and smokeless powder. State-of-the-art artillery and machine guns were procured, though the full implications of modern firepower and barbed wire remained little understood. The War Office was reorganized, a general staff created. Efforts were made to broaden the social base from which officers were recruited, and to oblige them to study their profession.

Despite opposition from diehards, rankers were diverted from their traditional peacetime functions as mess waiters, beasts of burden, keepers of tennis courts and polo grounds, to address musketry and tactics. Cavalrymen learnt to fight on foot rather than flourish sabres or lances, to lead horses rather

LEFT A still from the British film *The Battle of the Somme*, probably filmed on the first day of the battle on 1 July 1916. A British Tommy is shown bringing a wounded man along a trench. Unfortunately, the wounded soldier died 30 minutes later.

than ride them, husbanding their mounts for action. Richard Haldane became Secretary of State for War in 1906, and proved the most effective peacetime military minister Britain ever had. A Lowland Scottish lawyer, in three years he conducted a massive reorganization. The old volunteers and militia were merged, to create the Territorial Army, 268,777 strong by 1914. As the shadow of conflict with Germany began to darken the Edwardian horizon, politicians as well as soldiers acknowledged that Britain must overcome the prejudice of centuries against European entanglements. The government adopted a strategy that required the dispatch of an army to the Continent in the event of war. Staff conversations were started with the French. It was assumed that any armed clash would be short, and thus that speed of mobilization would be decisive.

It was Haldane's achievement that, when war came on 4 August 1914, Britain's military machine slipped into action with unprecedented efficiency. The six divisions that comprised the British Expeditionary Force were the best the nation had ever sent to fight. Only a few years after the amateurishness of the Army had been laid bare in South Africa, the fit, bronzed battalions which marched the roads of northern France in August 1914 were supreme professionals. Most had sweated under Indian as well as Aldershot sun. They took just pride in their "mad minute" of rifle fire, which enabled each man to deliver 15 aimed rounds in 60 seconds. Their officers might still be gentlemen, but knew far more about their business than their predecessors who fought in the Sudan and Natal.

Picture them as they tramped the cobbled streets of those French and Belgian towns: service caps pushed back to reveal cheerful, fashionably moustachioed faces; pipes or fags drooping; backs bent under packs; Lee-Enfield rifles swung over shoulders. Here were Berkshires and Norfolks, Surreys and Shropshires, Yorkshires and Lancashires, units in which regional loyalties were now deeply rooted a generation after county names replaced the old numbered regiments of the line. Officers riding chargers led each company. The long, clattering columns of wagons, guns and limbers were likewise drawn by horses. This army was still overwhelmingly dependent on four-legged propulsion, possessed of only a few hundred motorcars and 15 motorcycles.

RIGHT A sergeant of the Lancashire Fusiliers in a flooded dugout opposite Messines near Ploegsteert Wood, Ypres, January 1917.

This was the old British Army on its way to die, possessed of a courage and fortitude matching those of the squares which stood at Blenheim and Waterloo. "We looked a ragtime lot," wrote that splendid old soldier Frank Richards of the Royal Welch Fusiliers, "but in good spirits and ready for anything. I never saw better soldiers or wished for better pals." At Mons and Le Cateau in late August 1914, British soldiers won undying fame. For all their small numbers, their fire devastated the advancing German masses, inflicting heavy casualties. Field Marshal Sir John French's formations suffered severely in the face of overwhelming enemy numbers, but resisted doggedly. British artillery has always excelled. Now, such actions as the stand of L Battery Royal Horse Artillery at Le Cateau, where its gunners fought almost to the last man, passed into legend.

But the French Army was falling back, and the little British contingent was obliged to follow suit. Through two weeks of frustration and confusion, heat and dust, the BEF trudged wearily westwards, struggling to keep pace with the French and just ahead of General von Kluck's advancing German divisions. The Germans, however, had their own difficulties.

Their men were exhausted, their right wing had been severely punished. They ran out of steam. The French and British armies seized the offensive, and won the critical victory of the Marne. As the Germans reeled, the Allies swept forward once more, regaining a foothold in Belgium. Through the autumn months of 1914, the rival armies battled in vain to achieve a breakthrough, with special ferocity around the Belgian town of Ypres. It was then that "Wipers" first entered the folk-memory of the British Army, in which it was to play a terrible part through the four years that followed. The rival armies vied to outflank each other in the "race to the sea". Each failed. By November 1914, the combatants were exhausted and had suffered huge casualties, without achieving a decision. Four years of trench warfare began, along 400 miles of what became known as the Western Front from Switzerland to the Channel, which introduced the British nation to a scale and type of warfare such as it had never envisaged. This inflicted losses much smaller than those suffered by Germany and France, but imposed a trauma that holds its place in our national psyche to this day.

LEFT A British Army corporal stands beside the camouflaged Mark V Tank "J18" in a cornfield near Albert, 9 August 1918.

The British people had always thought of war as a job for professionals, in faraway places. They took pride in rejection of conscription, for so long familiar in France and Germany. Few even among professional soldiers had heeded the lessons of the American Civil War, foremost of which was that mass mattered. For all its quality, the British Army was absurdly small – 247,000 strong – for a death struggle between great industrialized nations. By the end of 1914, it had already suffered 89,000 casualties. Imperial troops were hastily summoned to help hold the line in France, while Kitchener embarked upon the Herculean task of building a "New Army", millions strong, to meet the challenge of sustained conflict with Germany and its allies.

Its birth pangs were painful for 1,186,337 innocents who volunteered for service in 1914. Aged officers and NCOs were summoned from retirement to provide leaders. One unit was commanded by a 63-year-old colonel, and boasted only two other professionals – a subaltern whose leg had been badly broken in France, and a stone-deaf quartermaster who had retired in 1907. Most such officers knew nothing of modern war. Traditional two-battalion regiments were expanded ultimately to 12, 13, 14 battalions. Arms and equipment were lacking. In a thousand rainswept camps across England recruits fresh from civilian life suffered discomfort and privation, while old men taught them the rudiments of soldiering.

The New Army was marvellously keen. Its men possessed an intelligence and patriotism that carried them through those dispiriting early months. They displayed a willingness for sacrifice which commands the homage of posterity. But when the New Army's units deployed to France in the autumn of 1915 and spring of 1916, its leaders knew their unfitness for war. On 4 June 1916, just weeks before the Somme battle began, a battalion commander wrote wretchedly that his men were "still not PROPERLY TRAINED, although full of courage". They were deemed capable of only the simplest manoeuvres, advancing on the enemy in rigid lines. They were also, of course, asked to do the impossible.

The British people to this day cherish delusions about the First World War, much influenced by the poets of the Western Front, who understood suffering humanity better than industrialized warfare. The foremost "poets' myth" is that the conflict was futile. In truth, the Kaiser's Germany was an

RIGHT *The P.B.I.* by Henry Lamb (oil on canvas, 1941). The "poor bloody infantry" are shown marching in the rain along a country road.

aggressive and brutal military dictatorship, whose triumph would have been a catastrophe for Europe. There is also a popular belief that cleverer and more humane British generals could have avoided the slaughter in the trenches, and achieved victory at much less cost. In reality, in a war between powerful industrial nations of roughly equal strength, no easy breakthrough was attainable.

Science had reached a point at which the destructive powers of artillery and automatic weapons vastly outstripped available technologies of mobility and communication. Again and again between 1915 and 1918, at terrible cost, one side or the other seized its opponent's forward positions. Yet defenders proved able to reinforce threatened points more quickly than attackers could exploit local success. In the absence of portable radios, commanders lost control of their units once they left behind their trenches and telephones. It was a commonplace of those terrible battles that surviving attackers milled in confusion among captured trenches, doubtful what to do next, while their senior officers were likewise ignorant of where they had got to. Finally, because Germany in 1914 had seized vast tracts of Belgium and

France, it was always the Allies' responsibility to attack, to recover the lost ground. The Germans fortified and defended their line with skill and unflagging determination.

Neither the courage of the Tommy, nor any plausible initiative by Allied commanders, could alter these fundamentals. They became familiar to millions of British soldiers at Neuve Chapelle and Loos in 1915, on the Somme in 1916, at Passchendaele in 1917. The demand for men, always more men, proved unsustainable by voluntary means. In 1916 conscription was belatedly introduced. Thus did a military experience once known only to the relatively tiny armies of Marlborough and Wellington become the universal condition of a generation of young Englishmen. More than half the six million who passed through the British Army's ranks between 1914 and 1918 were pressed men rather than volunteers.

So much is said about the bungling of the First World War's generals, which were real enough, that their successes often go unnoticed. The development and management of the ragtag New Armies into the victorious fighting force of November 1918 was a remarkable achievement. Britain's first citizens' army suffered terribly, as did those of their allies and enemies,

LEFT *Sergeant Watts, 40 Battalion, Royal Tank Regiment*, by Henry Lamb (oil on canvas, 1941).

in four years of attempts to defy the realities of early 20th-century military power. But by the summer of 1918 Field Marshal Sir Douglas Haig's forces were trained, armed, equipped and supplied to the highest standard. In the last campaigns of the war, they inflicted a series of crushing defeats upon the Germans, taking 188,170 enemy prisoners – almost as many as the French, Americans and Belgians put together.

Technology had advanced dramatically: by Armistice Day, the British Army possessed 56,000 trucks and 34,000 motorcycles. Its Flying Corps had become a formidable fighting force, newly translated into the Royal Air Force. Hundreds of thousands of soldiers were necessarily employed not in shooting at the enemy, but in servicing and sustaining a multitude of fighting machines. Some 534 tanks supported the last British offensives. The proportion of manpower committed to various arms had shifted substantially: away from cavalry and infantry, towards engineers and artillery.

The generals were proved right about one big thing: victory could only be achieved by defeating the enemy on the Western Front. Politicians such as Winston Churchill, appalled by the stalemate, yearned to find ways round, to pursue a breakthrough in other theatres. At their behest, campaigns were launched against Germany's weaker allies, Turkey, Austria-Hungary and Bulgaria. Yet huge diversions of men, first to Gallipoli in 1915, then to Mesopotamia, Palestine, Salonika and Italy, contributed much less than their leaders had hoped to ultimate victory. Only by doing what Britain throughout its history had resisted – committing a mass army against the main forces of the enemy – did the nation decisively influence the outcome.

Some 702,410 British soldiers died. It is a popular myth that the men of the First World War suffered in a fashion otherwise unknown to human experience. In truth, war had always been terrible. Yet in the past, its sufferings fell upon small numbers of professionals. Now, instead, the British people were shocked to perceive the consequences of thrusting into the crucible of grief an entire generation of civilians. Butchers, bakers and candlestick-makers perished wholesale. A legion of highly articulate survivors recorded what they had seen in prose, verse and anger, foremost among them Siegfried Sassoon:

RIGHT *Sergeant B. Montague: One of the 'Desert Rats' (7th Armoured Division),* by Henry Carr (oil on canvas, 1943).

I died in hell –

(They called it Passchendaele). My wound was slight,

And I was hobbling back; and then a shell

Burst slick upon the duck-boards; so I fell

Into the bottomless mud, and lost the light.

An infantry officer wrote in November 1918: "Thank God! The end of a frightful four years … with the infantry, whose officers, rank and file have suffered bravely, patiently and unselfishly hardships and perils beyond even the imaginations of those who have not shared them." The conduct of the war, and its human price, created a mistrust and indeed mutual hatred between politicians and generals, "frockcoats" and "brasshats", which did little credit to either. Haig's dogged perseverance in attack, which professional warriors esteemed as stoical virtue, seemed to its victims callous folly. A victory won at such cost appeared to many people, civilians and conscript soldiers alike, not worth the purchase. Within a few years, there emerged the first trickle of what became a flood of bitter veterans' reminiscences, depicting the generals as blundering boobies. Both the cause for which the war had been fought, and those responsible for its conduct, became alike discredited – in many respects, unjustly so – in the minds of the British public.

With extraordinary speed, in the wake of the Armistice the wartime army was disbanded. Its 1918 strength of 3.5 million men shrank to 370,000 two years later. The rump reverted to its 19th-century function as a colonial gendarmerie. Whereas the years before 1914 were characterized by a rush to modernize, those which followed 1918 were defined by a drive for economy. The promotion of officers was frozen. A military career in Britain resumed its Victorian character, as a round of parties and hunting interrupted by occasional imperial skirmishes. By the mid 1930s, the average general was seven years older than in 1914.

Major-General J. F. C. Fuller and Captain Basil Liddell Hart, the retired officers who became Britain's leading proponents of mechanized warfare, possessed few admirers in

LEFT Private Phillip Johnson of the 2/6th Battalion The Queen's Royal Regiment (West Surrey) inspects the graves of British soldiers at Anzio, Italy, 1 March 1944.

their own country's senior ranks. In the memorably contemptuous phrase of the airman Arthur Harris, later Commander-in-Chief of Bomber Command: "The British Army will never take tanks seriously until they learn to eat hay and fart." The British people, profoundly pacifist in their instincts after the 1914–1918 experience, laid no charge upon their politicians to heed the welfare of their soldiers. The lesson of the Great War, as it was then known, was thought to be that Britain should revert to its old "blue water" strategy, and leave Continentals to indulge in murderous holocausts between themselves. Only in February 1939 did the British government belatedly recognize an obligation to send an army to France in the event of a new conflict.

The rush to rearm, in the face of Hitler, did much less for the Army than for the RAF and Navy, which gained priorities for cash. Leslie Hore-Belisha, as Secretary of State for War, has received less credit than he deserves for introducing reforms inspired by Liddell Hart. Thanks to Hore-Belisha, the British Army in 1939 was far more mechanized than that of the French or Germans. Its tanks were not inadequate: the problem was that commanders had no idea how to use them properly. Not

until 1944 did the British Army master tank–infantry cooperation. The RAF's determination to fight its own war as an independent service caused it to resist providing close air support for ground forces, such as the Luftwaffe gave the Wehrmacht. Anti-tank weapons were poor, and so was leadership. Infantry tactics were plodding and formal, based on set-piece attacks in stark contrast to the methods of the Germans, who emphasized local initiative and infiltration.

Yet, if the blindness of politicians and generals led to defeat in 1940, again and again British soldiers distinguished themselves during the May retreat. They displayed a dogged courage and will for sacrifice that enabled their comrades to get through to the sea.

Historians often celebrate the 1940 "miracle of Dunkirk", whereby a sudden German loss of grip enabled the British Army to evacuate 220,000 men from the wreckage of defeat, along with 118,000 French soldiers. In truth, this deliverance was even more far reaching. If the Allies had checked the German assault, the almost inevitable consequence would have been a sustained attritional struggle on the Continent, which might have cost Britain as dearly in the Second World

RIGHT With a Bren gun across his shoulder, Private J. George of the South Wales Borderers, 36th Infantry Division, looks tired and unshaven after nearly a week on patrol in the Pinwe area, Burma, 18–19 November 1944.

War as it did in the First. As it was, the British people were able to stand defiant for four years behind their Channel moat, training and re-equipping for the great day when once again they could engage the main forces of the enemy, this time as junior partners of the Americans.

Until June 1944, the Mediterranean proved the only theatre in which Churchill's ground forces could take on those of Hitler and Mussolini. The Desert War caught the imagination of the British public. British troops under Archibald Wavell inflicted decisive defeats on the Italians in Libya, Eritrea and Abyssinia. When the Germans entered the game, British troops were worsted in Greece, Crete and North Africa in 1941. In the late summer of 1942, however, at last the tide turned. Under the command of Montgomery, and re-equipped with American Sherman tanks and self-propelled guns, Eighth Army first threw back Rommel's offensive at Alam el Halfa, then in October launched the assault at El Alamein that marked the turning point of the Second World War in the west.

After 12 days of heavy fighting, the British broke through. At home, church bells were rung. The long chase across North Africa began, which ended 1,500 miles westwards in May 1943, with the surrender in Tunisia of the remnants of the Afrika Korps. Many of those who participated in the desert campaigns agreed afterwards that North Africa was the least repugnant theatre of war. Its battles were fought amid wastelands unencumbered by cities or civilians. The climate was relatively healthy. Both sides behaved as decently as conflict allows. The British Army retained fond memories of those years of brewing tea over fires made with petrol and sand; of the comradeship and intimacy of war between relatively small armies, each of which attained great *esprit de corps*; and of final victory.

By the end of the desert campaign, resources and techniques at last existed to make air support of the ground forces effective. Artillery was the British arm that commanded most admiration from the enemy. Armoured tactics had improved, as the army learned the vital importance of integrating the movements of tanks, infantry and anti-tank guns. Sappers produced many fine performances, as did the ever-growing technical support units, to which was now added a new corps, the Royal Electrical and Mechanical

LEFT Gunner J. Hinchcliffe, a Bren gunner of the 5th Battalion The Duke of Wellington's Regiment (West Riding) sets out on a "recce" patrol in the Dunkirk perimeter, 3 March 1945.

Engineers. The care of casualties improved dramatically, above all with the use of antibiotics, which saved many lives. Winston Churchill often fumed about the length of the Army's "tail". This, however, reflected the reality of modern high-tech warfare: riflemen bore the overwhelming burden of pain and casualties, but they could fight only with the support of hundreds of thousands of other soldiers servicing the support arms and a vast infrastructure.

The British Army that landed in Sicily and Italy in 1943, and then on D-Day in Normandy in 1944, was better equipped than any in the nation's history. At last, competent generals had been found, tactics refined, extraordinarily ingenious technology deployed and units trained to the highest standard. Some infantrymen in Normandy and Holland faced fighting as desperate and bloody as that which their fathers had known in the First World War. Hitler's Wehrmacht resisted with desperate courage, but was ground down in 11 months of bitter strife. The Army's greatest good fortune between 1941 and 1946 lay in the overall direction of Sir Alan Brooke, the dour, clever Northern Irishman who served as Chief of the Imperial General Staff. Brooke's contribution to victory, partly

by inspired chairmanship and partly by offering stubborn resistance to the Prime Minister's extravagances, is hard to overstate. His partnership with Churchill caused much exasperation to both men, but worked brilliantly.

Britain's most effective operational commander in the west was Sir Bernard Montgomery, the victor of Alamein. His record was marred by conceit and vainglory. But he earned the warm gratitude of the British Army for his care for the lives of his men, as well as for some impressive battlefield performances. He knew that, while the British people were committed to victory, they were also desperate to avoid any reprise of the sacrifices of 1914–1918. In this, he fulfilled their hopes. Though some units suffered terribly, Britain was able to celebrate its share in victory at a cost vastly smaller than that of the earlier "Great War".

Between 1940 and 1944, the British Army engaged in raids and amphibious operations performed by a completely new breed of "special forces". Churchill enthusiastically promoted Commandos, the Parachute Regiment, the Special Air Service and other "private armies", which especially flourished in the desert. Senior officers were sometimes sceptical that such

RIGHT Alan Rex of the 1st Battalion The Royal Fusiliers disembarks from the troopship *Empire Halladale* at Pusan, on arrival in Korea in 1952.

operations wasted resources and removed the best junior leaders from line units. Yet, despite the failure of the biggest raid of all against Dieppe in 1942, special forces gained important experience. Their operations, often wonderfully heroic, helped to keep the ground war alive through the years when most of Britain's soldiers were training in England for D-Day. They contributed much to British folklore of the Second World War.

The harshest combat theatre was Burma, where between 1942 and 1945 British and Indian troops sustained the longest single land campaign of the Second World War against the Japanese. Those who served with the "Forgotten" Fourteenth Army often complained how little notice was taken at home of their struggle against jungle, privation and disease, as well as a merciless enemy. Posterity, however, recognizes how remarkable their achievement was. For two years after the retreats of 1942, the Japanese retained the upper hand. But in the spring of 1944, Fourteenth Army achieved a decisive victory at Imphal and Kohima in Assam. Thereafter, British and Indian forces launched a superbly impressive advance into Burma, culminating in the May 1945 recapture of

Rangoon. Their commander, Sir William Slim, showed himself the most impressive British field commander of the war. His men displayed a fortitude in overcoming climate, terrain, as well as dogged opposition, which won the admiration of all who witnessed it. With nothing like the resources of Montgomery's forces in Europe, they crossed great rivers, scaled mountain ranges and covered huge distances supported only by air supply. In this last great shared endeavour between the British and Indian armies, they earned much glory.

By 1945, the British Army was proud and victorious, but desperately weary. For many months its numbers had been shrinking on the battlefield amid a national manpower shortage. The regimental system almost collapsed under the strain. It proved necessary to replace casualties with drafts from any unit to hand, heedless of cap badge. Britain had been bankrupted by the struggle to defeat Germany and Japan. Her servicemen, some of whom who had not seen their homes for years, were desperate to get back to civilian life. Yet the nation still possessed global responsibilities. The decade that followed victory was dominated by a struggle to sustain

LEFT Private John Rudd of the Middlesex Regiment sitting at the roadside in a Korean village with his dog, which has been trained for guard duties, *c.*1951.

Britain's military commitments in the face of huge financial difficulties. The armed forces shrank from 5.09 million men and women in 1945 to 700,000 four years later. Amid the new fears and tensions of the Cold War, conscription – now called National Service – was maintained. Large British contingents were deployed in the Middle and Far East, as well as in Germany. Yet their equipment was ageing, resources were stretched to the limits. To dispatch two brigades to Korea when war erupted there in 1950, it proved necessary to recall reservists and scrape the barrel for weapons and equipment. But through the three-year commitment that followed, British troops distinguished themselves again and again, most famously at the Imjin River in April 1951. The Commonwealth Division made an outstanding contribution to holding the line in Korea until the armistice of 1953.

Yet the 1956 Suez debacle showed that Britain could no longer sustain the commitments of the past. Its armed forces would have to shrink dramatically, as would its strategic burden. The government's 1957 Defence White Paper acknowledged that thenceforward, the nuclear deterrent must represent Britain's principal shield against a major enemy.

With the ending of National Service in 1960, the Army became once more what it had been a century earlier, a small force of professionals. While the British Army of the Rhine continued to train to meet a Soviet onslaught, its function was to serve as a tripwire. Even alongside the Americans and other NATO allies, there were no delusions that an all-out offensive could be halted by conventional means. Yet no one doubted that, if the Russians launched an attack, the British Army of the Rhine would fight to the death alongside the Americans. Deterrence worked. Successive generations of soldiers who endured years of boredom on the North German plain helped to win a new kind of victory, marked by the destruction of the Berlin Wall and collapse of the Soviet Union.

Between 1945 and the 1967 withdrawal from Aden, the British Army engaged in a long series of local actions around the world, a fighting retreat from successive outposts of empire. In this role, its soldiers displayed the courage, patience, skill and forbearance that have been their birthright through the centuries. They sustained this through more than 30 years of commitment in Northern Ireland, beginning in August 1969. Years of painful experience were required, to

RIGHT A Coldstream Guards sentry in position high in the mountains of South Arabia in April 1965 maintains a watch on the wadi below during the Aden confrontation.

master the specialized skills of peacekeeping and counter-terrorism – "low-intensity operations". But the Army progressively achieved remarkable proficiency, above all in junior leadership.

The Special Air Service, which became temporarily moribund after the Second World War, was first revived in Malaya, and thereafter committed to an increasing range of covert activities, notably in Oman in the 1970s. The rise of the Provisional IRA, together with the spread of international terrorism, prompted the SAS's development as the spearpoint of British counter-terrorist forces, regularly deployed all over the world. The 1980 storming of the Iranian Embassy in Kensington, following a hostage seizure by terrorists, promoted the regiment to iconic status. Through the past quarter-century, the SAS has gained unrivalled combat experience in Ireland, the Balkans, Iraq and Afghanistan, and today represents the Army's highest skills.

The 1982 Falklands War was dominated by the Royal Navy and Royal Marines, but the Army also contributed to the stunning British victory, achieved at a distance of 8,000 miles from home with the barest minimum of air support and radar capability. The South Atlantic conflict was a colonial throwback, more closely related to Kitchener's 1898 expedition up the Nile than to the core strategic purposes of modern Britain. The triumph of the Task Force laid to rest the ghost of failure at Suez, and caught the imagination of the British people. Their soldiers, sailors and airmen demonstrated that they still formed the finest fighting forces of their size in the world. The Parachute Regiment added lustre to its reputation as elite infantry, winning new battle honours at Goose Green and Mount Longdon. The war emphasized the vital message that, even in the electronic age, night-fighting skills can be decisive. The boldness and supreme professionalism displayed by British forces in a makeshift, immensely risky operation in the face of enemy air superiority, won the admiration of the world.

A senior British officer said in 1982: "The lesson of the Falklands is 'You Never Can Tell'." Again and again throughout its history, the Army has been called upon to fight local actions and full-scale wars in places, and against enemies, that nowhere featured in intelligence assessments or strategic planning. The unexpected happened yet again in

LEFT Men of the Black Watch in a Saracen armoured vehicle during border patrol duties in Northern Ireland in 1977. Saracens, armed with turret-mounted Browning machine guns, were often used as armoured personnel carriers.

1990–1991, when a British armoured division was mobilized alongside the Americans and French to expel Iraqi invaders from Kuwait. The Coalition achieved swift and overwhelming victory, assisted by its huge air forces. In order to deploy an undersized British division, it proved necessary to strip the Rhine Army of serviceable tanks and armoured vehicles. British military technology lags ever further behind that of the USA, the only world power that can afford to sustain a full range of military capabilities. But the British Army in the last decade of the 20th century and first years of the 21st displayed skills and commitment of the highest order.

By a notable irony, over the past 20 years the Army has continued to shrink in size, while being asked to fulfil worldwide commitments on a scale unimagined a generation ago. Its strength has declined from 170,000 in 1963 to barely 100,000 today. It has sustained counter-terrorist duties in Northern Ireland, while peacekeeping in the Balkans, defeating an insurgency in Sierra Leone and participating in major campaigns in Afghanistan and Iraq. Britain's involvement in the 2001 toppling of the Taliban was largely restricted to contributing air support and special forces. But in

2006, a major deployment began in the south of Afghanistan, especially Helmand Province, as part of NATO's commitment to provide internal security and reconstruction aid for the country.

The intensity of fighting in Helmand Province has matched anything that the Army has experienced since Korea. British battlegroups, handicapped by a shortage of helicopters and armoured vehicles, have engaged again and again with Taliban forces armed with rockets and plentiful automatic weapons, familiar with the terrain and enjoying local support. It is a tribute to British infantry skills that they have gained repeated tactical victories. Amid many decorations awarded, one posthumous Victoria Cross and one George Cross have been won. While political forces will be as important as military ones in determining the outcome in Afghanistan, British troops have achieved all and more than has been asked of them.

In eastern Iraq, during the Coalition's 2003 invasion, British forces carried out an almost textbook drive northwards from Kuwait, securing oilfields, encircling Basra and destroying Iraqi forces in their path. The Army's weapons, armour and

RIGHT After landing at San Carlos in the Falklands, a heavily laden paratrooper of the 2nd Battalion The Parachute Regiment heads south for Sussex Mountain on 21 May 1982. From there the battalion attacked Goose Green.

equipment performed better than in any conflict in its history. If operations had ended with the fall of Basra and the American seizure of Baghdad, they would have been regarded as spectacularly successful. Instead, of course, Coalition forces found themselves facing an ever more aggressive insurgency, which turned into near civil war between Sunni and Shia Iraqis. Since 2003, some 8,000 British troops in the south of the country have fought repeated bitter local battles against dissidents, while suffering attacks and casualties from suicide bombers, rockets, mortaring and ambushes. In 2007, the British began to reduce their presence in order to transfer forces to Afghanistan, and to reduce the Army's "overstretch". The future of Iraq remains highly uncertain, but almost every British regiment has contributed to the struggle to promote its security and suppress sectarian violence.

As technology grows ever more sophisticated, ever more men – and now also women – must be relieved of weapons and committed to monitor screens and operate specialized equipment. Yet "boots on the ground" remain the decisive factor in almost every theatre to which British troops are committed. Almost daily, on far-flung battlefields they display courage and skill of a kind Cromwell, Marlborough, Wellington, Kitchener, Montgomery and Slim would acknowledge with admiration. Again and again over the past century, British soldiers have shown that, while our people have thankfully never been militarists, they are splendidly martial. "The British are the last people left in Europe who like to fight," growled Dr Henry Kissinger with wry admiration in 2001. The Army in 2007 still represents one of our finest national institutions. But it will not remain so unless we, the British people, afford to it the attention, resources and respect which it so richly repays. We shall not deserve future military triumphs to add to those of the past, unless we provide those who secure them for us with means to sustain their great heritage.

1900–1914

A mule train stirs up the dust as it toils up a steep incline, in a photograph taken during the Second Boer War, 1899–1902.

THE SECOND BOER WAR

The shape of the British Army in the early 1900s was very much the legacy of the Cardwell and other reforms of the late 1800s. The Army's size had been increased with more battalions being added to each infantry regiment, service periods had been shortened, and infantry regiments had been renamed following geographical and territorial boundaries. Both the cavalry and artillery underwent reform too, so that by 1900 Britain possessed one of the most powerful regular armies in the world, totalling some 180,000 professional soldiers.

The turn of the 20th century saw the British Army engaged in the Second Boer War. It was a conflict that would tax the Army to the full in terms of manpower and logistical commitment, engaging vast numbers of troops. Tension had been growing for some time between the Boer republic of the Transvaal and the British government, stretching back to the inconclusive 1880–1881 First Boer War. The Boers felt threatened by increasing British interest in South African gold reserves, which had manifested itself in the acquisition of territory surrounding the Boer republic, as well as by the recent arrival of large numbers of British (and other nationality) prospectors known as "uitlanders" in the Transvaal. In October 1899 the mutual distrust erupted into armed confrontation, as thousands of settlers fled what they

LEFT A copy of the "Soldier's New Testament" associated with the service in South Africa of Private Arthur Wright in the 2nd Battalion The King's Own Yorkshire Light Infantry during the Second Boer War. The book was given to soldiers during the war.

Winston Churchill – prisoner of war

Hari Williams was a scout who served with the Natal Field Force and British Army in South Africa during the Second Boer War. Born in 1883, a Caucasian, he was brought up by a Maori family in New Zealand; his parents had died during the eruption of Krakatoa. He moved to Natal in South Africa at the age of ten, and thus when war came he knew the terrain, the language and the people intimately – equipping him well for his time as an Army scout.

"It's burned into my memory. You see, I was an impressionable mind at that time, and what I soaked in, remains to this present day. The British were very slow to come up. They had all landed in different parts ... On their way up country they met all kinds of obstacles, and the Boers were there waiting for them. So that by the second or third week of December, about five different armies had come to grief. It was called 'Black Week' ... None of them had got scouts that knew the country; they were fresh in the country, the men, the generals ... Stormberg was a junction between two railways, between one coming up from Port Elizabeth and the Natal Railway going to meet it. The Boers knew that, and that they'd have to come up through Stormberg, and they fortified it. They were almost annihilated ... At Magersfontein the Highland Division lost their general of wounds, General Wauchope ... The Scots were very proud of their uniform, all dressed up in plaid and topees. I said to one of them, 'You're an absolute target'. They were butchered at Magersfontein, they went straight into the trap the Boers had laid for them. The Boers had got plenty of guns, which could fire six or ten miles, and you never knew where they were firing from ... There was a great lack of scouts like me, I never met another one ... And I only met one war correspondent in the flesh, and that was Winston Churchill. And he'd already been captured ... Nobody had any idea of the size of the war. It wasn't just firing on a few stray Boer farmers ... The Boers were

RIGHT In November 1899, whilst working as a war correspondent for the *Morning Post*, Winston Churchill was captured by the Boers and imprisoned in Pretoria. He had been travelling in an armoured train, which was ambushed and destroyed by Boer commandos. Churchill can be seen here on the right, together with his fellow British-soldier prisoners.

determined to fight to the end, and they'd got the commanders to do it ... Although they didn't fight on Sundays, they moved about on Sunday, and they could cover a few miles, I tell you ... They were a horrible enemy, but once they were captured, they were docile. Even Cronje when he was captured with about 4,000 men, they just wiped their hands and said 'Well, that's that.' And away they came."

RIGHT This 9mm Lefaucheux pin-fire revolver was given to Winston Churchill after his escape from the Boers in December 1899. After making his escape, he was harboured by John Howard, a mine manager in nearby Witbank. Howard gave Churchill this revolver and made arrangements for him to be smuggled to Portuguese East Africa aboard a goods train. In 1901, with British control established in the Pretoria area, Churchill returned the pistol, in a box inscribed "Returned to Friends at WITBANK from W. S. CHURCHILL 1901".

RIGHT The Queen's South Africa Medal (1899–1901). On the obverse is the head of Queen Victoria and on the reverse is the figure of Britannia.

considered to be persecution in the Transvaal, and Britain moved to intervene on their behalf. The other Boer republic of the Orange Free State chose to support the Transvaal Boers in their struggle, and the Second Boer War began.

The Boers were organized into numerous "commandos", with service in these compulsory for all adult males. Their fighters were independent minded and wore no common uniform, but were hardy, and knew the terrain on which the conflict took place well. Their German-made Mauser carbine rifles were considered superior to the British Lee-Metford and Lee-Enfield rifles, being quicker and simpler to load, and they possessed artillery and machine-gun units. The British, too, could count on a certain degree of local knowledge, in the form of volunteer units raised among the fleeing uitlanders and British-supporting locals in Natal; these units, such as the Natal Field Force, were often mounted and were useful for intelligence gathering. Volunteer units from New Zealand, Canada and Australia also saw service on the British side.

The Boers began the war with an offensive aimed at causing the maximum damage to the British forces in the area before reinforcements could arrive from Great Britain. They attacked Kimberley and Mafeking, and pushed into Natal, laying siege to the garrison town of Ladysmith. British reinforcements began to arrive in theatre, and the two sides clashed at Modder River in November, a bloody but inconclusive engagement that saw the Boers pull back to a defensive position at Magersfontein. The last days of the 19th century were characterized by the events of "Black Week" (10–15 December 1899), which saw three separate defeats of the British: at Stormberg by Orange Free State forces, at Magersfontein, where the British suffered almost 1,000 dead, and at Colenso. January 1900 saw a further clash at Spion Kop – another disaster for the British – and in February the British (first under Lord Kitchener, and later Lord Roberts who

Care of the wounded

"I came across any amount of badly wounded men. There was nothing I could do to help them except give them general advice ... People would just have to put up with wounds. Each man, he had a little pocket inside his tunic, and in it was a first aid kit, bandages, you know, what they used for wounds. He would dress his own wounds, or his pal's – until help arrived, and in a good many cases, it never arrived. The doctors weren't sufficient. And those that were, were overworked until they dropped. I knew one or two men that worked themselves into an early grave. The Boer firepower was so great that doctors took the risk of being shot themselves. They couldn't see to everybody, so the stretcher bearers had to do what they could ... And they were suffering the same as the troops, the Royal Army Medical Corps, they went through the mill. They took a risk, going into the firing line ... I think the strongest stuff any of them carried was a bottle of rum ... You get very tired of war. Seeing all that suffering, seeing men die of ghastly wounds, simply because there was insufficient medical help. They did their best ... There were no Florence Nightingales up country, and that's where the damage was being done. The men were lucky to get down to base hospital and be properly treated."

Hari Williams, Natal Field Force

RIGHT Wounded men lying on the floor of a field dressing station probably immediately after the Battle of Modder River, in a photograph dated 28 November 1899. Modder is the Dutch for "mother".

retook command from Kitchener) managed to outflank and pin down Piet Cronje's large Boer force at Paardeberg on the Modder River, forcing him to surrender on the 27th. It was a turning point for the British, who remained on the offensive, relieving Ladysmith and Mafeking, and eventually capturing the Boer capitals of Bloemfontein and Pretoria. The war then degenerated into a bitter guerrilla campaign, with a large Boer force roaming the countryside, and the British adopting a scorched-earth policy (involving the internment of civilians in concentration camps) and the construction of a network of thousands of blockhouses. In May 1902, the last remaining Boer fighters surrendered. More than 20,000 British troops died during the course of the war.

Whilst the Boer War was the most significant and costly conflict to occupy the British Army during the opening years of the 20th century, Britain's global commitments saw the soldiers of the British Army in service in the Boxer Rebellion (1900), the Anglo-Aro War (1901–1902) in Nigeria, in Waziristan on the North-West Frontier (1901–1902), during the Tibetan Expedition (1903–1904), in the Zulu Rebellion (1906), and during the Abor Expedition (1911–1912) on the North-West Frontier.

The Battle of Paardeberg

Sir Clive Morrison-Bell served as an officer in the Scots Guards attached to the 2nd Battalion The Royal Canadian Regiment during the Second Boer War. In a letter home to his mother from Kimberley dated Monday 26 February 1900, he describes the aftermath of the fighting at the Battle of Paardeberg prior to Cronje's surrender:

"Got here yesterday from Paardeberg, where we are still round Cronje, having ridden across about 30 miles. Came to get some provisions for the mess ... I saddled up a pony and started. It then came on to rain in torrents, so I lay under a wagon, till I got drowned out. The rest of the night I passed on the floor of one of the field hospitals, having put back to camp. It was not pleasant. Men were groaning, gasping, crying out all night long. However, it was out of the rain ... Grub is still very short here, and the people are on rations ... The men have been simply starving, living on half rations, and lying about in the wet. They get flooded out every night now, and sometimes during the day ... I hope old Cronje will cluck it soon, he can't be very comfortable either. Last Sunday's battle (Paardeberg) was a pretty big thing, as no doubt you are aware by now ... It's a marvel I wasn't hit, the bullets were so thick. I hope to get through this alright, I want to see the end of it, and want it to be something to look back upon ... The cavalry have had an awful time, and these rains will bring on the sickness ... It's awfully cold at nights now ... The Boers walk about their trenches, and are getting used to the shells, I think, which seems wonderful. I located a gun the other day, and went round about two miles to get the howitzer battery to fire on it. I had to go back to my kopje [small hill] first, and then signal by flag where their shots were firing, as being low down it was entirely out of sight of them. The second and third shots burst on it, or within a few yards, you should have seen the men skip out. But after six shots they stopped, and I have no doubt by now, they have got it under cover, and will soon start it on us."

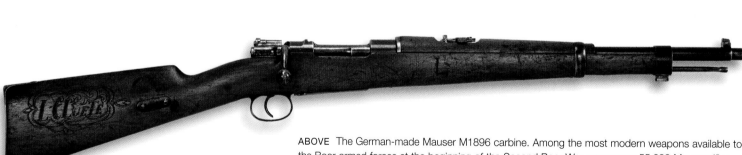

ABOVE The German-made Mauser M1896 carbine. Among the most modern weapons available to the Boer armed forces at the beginning of the Second Boer War were some 55,000 Mauser rifles. These had been purchased from the German company Deutsche Waffen-und Munitionsfabriken by the governments of the Transvaal and the Orange Free State. These bolt-action magazine rifles proved highly effective in the hands of the Boers, and caused questions to be raised in Britain about the efficiency of British musketry in comparison. Most of these weapons were lost to the Boer cause upon the surrender of their field armies in 1900. Thereafter the Boer commandos were obliged to fight their guerrilla campaign with captured British weapons. The name of the man to whom this rifle was issued, L. Cloete, is carved into the butt.

ABOVE General Piet Cronje (in the broad-brimmed hat) seated in the shade with British officers after his surrender at the Battle of Paardeberg, February 1900.

RIGHT The King's South Africa Medal (1901–1902). On the obverse is the head of King Edward VII. On the reverse is a helmeted Britannia, with a party of soldiers advancing on a coastal march.

1914–1918

A soldier looks down at a comrade's grave, Pilckem Ridge, Ypres, 1917.

1914

MOBILIZATION

Late in the evening of 4 August 1914, the ultimatum issued by the government of Great Britain to Germany to withdraw from Belgium expired and war was declared. The following day the British Army began to mobilize in order to form the British Expeditionary Force (BEF) of six infantry divisions and five cavalry brigades. The BEF was to take its place on the left wing of the French Army near to the Channel ports on which it depended for its supplies. In the event, two of the six infantry divisions, the 4th and 6th, were kept at home in case of German invasion or civil disturbance in Ireland. They followed later, joining the rest of the Expeditionary Force by 15 September.

At its full strength, the 80 divisions of the French Army dwarfed the BEF; however, the political significance of the commitment of British troops to the war was vast. It emphasized Great Britain's commitment to the "entente cordiale" with France. The BEF became considerably larger throughout 1914 and early 1915 with the commitment of Territorial units, as well as Imperial and Dominion forces. It was eventually divided into two armies towards the end of December 1914.

The first four divisions to move to France – the 1st, 2nd, 3rd and 5th – were organized into two army corps, I and II, commanded by Lieutenant-General Sir Douglas Haig and Lieutenant-General Sir James Grierson respectively; Major-General Edmund Allenby led the cavalry forces of the BEF; and Field Marshal Sir John French commanded the BEF as a whole as it crossed over the channel, landed to a rapturous reception in France and marched forward to take its part in what became known as the "Battle of the Frontiers".

The journey to France and Belgium

The British Army at the beginning of the First World War was unique amongst major European armies in that it relied for its manpower upon volunteers who enlisted to serve for a fixed period. European armies relied upon large numbers of conscripts to fill the ranks alongside a professional cadre. The advantage of the British system was that it provided a highly trained professional army, qualitatively superior to its Continental allies and opponents; its major disadvantage was its size.

Even at full strength, the peacetime regular army was not on a war footing and had to be reinforced through the mobilization of men and the requisitioning of horses, stores and supplies to bring units up to their wartime establishments. Reservists, men who had served at least two years on active service and were part of the Army Reserve, were called up to rejoin their units, men such as John McIlwain who recollects the atmosphere of re-joining his regiment, the Connaught Rangers:

"Left Newcastle at 10.30am. At all stations on the way crowds of reserve men like myself, keen and alert, promptly mounting the trains ... Years after, my wife spoke of the morning of the 5th August – 'You seemed so eager to get away.'"

Once the units had been assembled they were shipped across the Channel, landing at ports like Le Havre, where they received a rapturous reception from the French civilian population.

RIGHT 1st Battalion Irish Guards leaving Wellington Barracks to join the British Expeditionary Force, which was due to leave for France.

Lieutenant T. S. Wollocombe describes the reaction when his battalion landed in France on 14 August 1914:

"We got to our place of disembarkment by 1.15pm and disembarked moving to an open square along a road, by companies, which was lined by French Reservists who were keeping back a tremendous crowd of cheering spectators. These people, unlike our own, were so excited by the entry of the British into their town that it was hard to make oneself heard by our men at all. They were doing all they knew to get 'souvenirs' in the shape of cap badges and Regimental title plates etc. from our men. I saw one of our soldiers give a man a title plate and the thanks he got were in the shape of a kiss."

ABOVE Reservists of the Grenadier Guards, re-called up for service on the outbreak of war, queue for a medical inspection at Wellington Barracks, Chelsea.

RIGHT Upon the declaration of war the government took over the running of the railways in order to ensure that the large numbers of reservists for the armed forces could be mustered as quickly as possible.

LONDON & NORTH WESTERN
RAILWAY.

NOTICE TO STAFF.

The Government has decided to take over the control of the Railways of Great Britain in connection with the Mobilization of the Troops and general movements in connection with Naval & Military requirements.

The management of the Railway and the existing terms of employment of the staff will remain unaltered, and all instructions will be issued through the same channels as heretofore.

Euston Station, *August, 1914.*

ROBERT TURNBULL, *General Manager.*

LORD KITCHENER AND SIR JOHN FRENCH

Two forceful characters dominated the early days of the BEF, Lord Kitchener and Sir John French. Both men were very much products of the 19th-century army of Queen Victoria. Herbert Horatio Kitchener was born in Ireland in 1850 and joined the Royal Engineers in 1871, before serving extensively throughout the Middle East. He rose to national prominence through his service in Egypt and the Sudan, where he took part in the ill-fated mission to rescue General Gordon of Khartoum in 1884/1885. Kitchener was later appointed Governor-General of Eastern Sudan in 1886 before becoming Commander-in-Chief (Sirdar) of the Egyptian Army in 1892. It was as commander of the Egyptian Army that he undertook the re-conquest of the Sudan, culminating in the victory at Omdurman in 1898. Following this Kitchener was created Baron Kitchener of Khartoum and Aspall as well as governor of the Sudan. Kitchener's next major imperial role was as chief of staff to Lord Roberts during the Second Boer War (1899–1902) and, following Roberts' return to England in 1900, he took command of the British and Imperial forces and crushed the Boer guerrillas through the wholesale destruction of Boer farmsteads and the controversial relocation of the civilian population into "concentration camps", where large numbers died from disease and neglect. Following the Treaty of Vereeniging of 1902 which ended the Second Boer War, Kitchener was created Viscount Kitchener of Khartoum and the Vaal and of Aspall before being appointed Commander-in-Chief of the Indian Army, a position he remained in until 1909 before

34

RIGHT Lord Kitchener of Khartoum in his field marshal's dress uniform.

LEFT A souvenir tea caddy decorated with portraits of Lord Kitchener and Sir John French.

returning to Egypt as British Agent and Consul-General. Kitchener was on leave in Britain and about to go back to Egypt in August 1914 when, on the outbreak of war, he was appointed Secretary of State for War.

Sir John French's career had followed a very similar pattern. He too had served in the Sudan in 1884/1885 and also in South Africa in the Second Boer War. This was where French's reputation was made as commander of the British cavalry forces. Following the conclusion of the war French was appointed Commander-in-Chief of Aldershot in 1902, Inspector-General of the Forces in 1911, Chief of the

BRITONS

"WANTS"

YOU

JOIN YOUR COUNTRY'S ARMY!

GOD SAVE THE KING

Reproduced by permission of LONDON OPINION

ABOVE The famous, and much-imitated, recruitment poster featuring Kitchener. One of his prime responsibilities as Secretary of State for War was to raise ample forces to reinforce the BEF.

RIGHT Field Marshal Sir John French, Commander-in-Chief of the British Expeditionary Force in 1914, reviews a force of 10,000 over-age volunteers for home defence assembled in Hyde Park, London.

Imperial General Staff in 1912 and Field Marshal in 1913. Appointed to command the BEF in 1914, French found himself immediately in conflict with Kitchener over its deployment. Kitchener wanted the BEF deployed around Amiens, whilst French insisted it advance into Belgium. French won this round, but their relationship was further damaged during the retreat from Mons when Sir John was determined to fall back upon the Channel ports to protect his lines of communication and retreat back to the British Isles. As this would have opened up a potentially fatal gap between the British and French lines Kitchener came over to France to instil some confidence into French and get the BEF back into place in time for the Battle of the Marne. Their relationship never recovered and French was relieved from command in 1915.

Kitchener's star was also on the wane in 1915; he was relieved of his responsibility for munitions output following a crisis of production, whilst his association with the costly Gallipoli campaign tarnished his reputation. However, his death following the sinking of the cruiser HMS *Hampshire* whilst undertaking a mission to Russia caused an outbreak of national mourning.

THE BATTLES OF MONS AND LE CATEAU

On 20 August 1914 Sir John French issued his Operation Order No. 5 for the BEF, with instructions to move north into Belgium in order to support the attack of the French Fifth Army. Unfortunately the French forces had realized the strength of the German assault and they did not advance; instead they started to retreat on 21 August to avoid being overwhelmed by German assaults. This left the BEF in a precarious position just outside the Belgian town of Mons, with II Corps under General Sir Horace Smith-Dorrien holding a 21-mile-long position along the line of the Mons–Condé Canal while I Corps under General Sir Douglas Haig held a salient to the east of the town. Their flanks were unprotected and they faced an onslaught by a German force that was vastly superior in numbers. On the morning of 23 August the German First Army under General von Kluck began to launch piecemeal attacks on the British positions. Although the initial infantry assaults were beaten back with heavy losses, by 1400hrs the BEF was beginning to be forced from its positions in the face of overwhelming odds. By the evening the BEF had suffered 1,642 killed, wounded and missing, but German casualties totalled as many as 10,000 – largely due to the accurate, sustained rifle fire of the British regulars. The morning of the 24th saw the BEF start a withdrawal, with II Corps under

The retreat from Mons

The retreat from Mons was a haphazard affair. Some units became cut off between the German cavalry spearheads and the main force, and were compelled to travel by night to avoid capture. Others fought a series of confused encounters with German advance units as they sought to cover the retreat.

Trooper William Clarke from the 2nd Dragoon Guards (Queen's Bays), 1st Cavalry Brigade, the Cavalry Division, captures some of the confused nature of the encounters in the following description:

"Somewhere around this area we had a little set-to with an advance patrol of German cavalry, we lost two or three men and some horses. We crossed the Canal, I think we were headed for Bailly … We ended up at Nery. About this time a rumour had been going round that the Germans had been asking for peace. I wondered if we'd won, drawn or lost!"

The BEF did not only have to put up with constant probing by German forces, but the relentless nature of the marching and the porr weather conditions also played their part.

John McIlwain, a sergeant in the Connaught Rangers, 5th Brigade, I Corps, describes the conditions on 26 August:

"The sky lit up. Then rain, rain!, and I, in the stress of the retreat, like many others who were trained by Kitchener always to travel light, had thrown away my great-coat … General Spears [liaison officer with French Fifth Army] records in his diary 'I shall never forget the penetrating quality of that rain of August 26th.' But he had, as a staff officer, a shelter, waterproof carried for him, coffee on the boil and stronger liquors available. Amongst the French that night I saw Algerian troops hurried across from Africa on the outbreak of war, in their long cotton robes, then rags, soaked and clinging to their bodies. Many of these poor fellows had malaria, and many died, I daresay, soon after that night."

The 4th Division had arrived in France later than the rest of the BEF, arriving on 22 August. It had rushed to the front in time to play a part in the defence of Le Cateau before joining the rest of the British force in the long retreat to the Marne.

The divisional commander, Major-General Thomas D'Oyly Snow, CB, recalled the difficulty of getting the men to dig in properly during the arduous retreat.

"I rode round the troops who were supposed to be entrenched. In spite of what troops had learned during the Boer War, in spite of what they had been taught, all they had done was to make a few scratchings of the nature of what was called, fifty years ago, a shelter pit, of no use whatever against any sort of fire. I came to the conclusion then and never altered it during the war, that unless driven to it by his officers, the British soldier would sooner die than dig."

LEFT Soldiers of A Company of the 4th Battalion The Royal Fusiliers, part of the 7th Brigade, 2nd Division, in Smith-Dorrien's II Corps are shown here at rest in the Grand-Place at Mons on the afternoon of 22 August 1914.

RIGHT British cavalry on the retreat from Mons.

Smith-Dorrien fighting a major delaying action at Le Cateau on 26 August against the direct instructions of Sir John French. However, this action, which cost the British over 8,000 casualties and the Germans between 15,000 and 30,000 dead, successfully disengaged the BEF from the pursuing German forces and allowed it to retire beyond the Marne to the outskirts of Paris in relatively good order.

RIGHT British First World War medallion struck to commemorate the move of the British Expeditionary Force (BEF) to Belgium and France in August 1914. The medallion's reverse text is an extract from King George V's message to embarking troops.

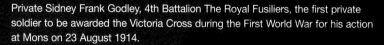

Private Sidney Frank Godley, 4th Battalion The Royal Fusiliers, the first private soldier to be awarded the Victoria Cross during the First World War for his action at Mons on 23 August 1914.

Lieutenant Maurice James Dease, 4th Battalion The Royal Fusiliers, who also won the Victoria Cross in the same action as Godley.

The first major military operations of the war led to the first acts of heroism and the first awards and decorations. There exists no higher award for valour in the British Army than the Victoria Cross, which was instituted following the Crimean War as an award "For Valour" for officers and men in front-line service.

The first Victoria Crosses of the First World War were awarded to an officer and private of the 4th Battalion The Royal Fusiliers, for bravery in combat at the town of Nimy on the Canal du Centre just to the north of Mons itself. The battalion was retreating in the face of sustained pressure from the German troops of IX Corps at about 1400hrs on the afternoon of 23 August 1914. As the battalion started to retreat, Lieutenant Maurice Dease, the machine-gun officer of the battalion, held up two advancing German battalions despite being repeatedly wounded. Eventually unable to continue, he was taken to a dressing station where he died of his wounds. Following Dease's withdrawal Private Sidney Godley, also of the machine-gun section, took up the fight and continued to operate his weapon, despite being badly wounded, until the battalion had withdrawn. He finally succeeded in dismantling the gun and threw it into the canal to prevent its capture by the advancing Germans. Godley was assumed by his battalion to have been killed in the action, but was in fact rescued by Belgian civilians and taken to a hospital in Mons where he became a prisoner of war. He spent the remainder of the First World War in the POW camp at Doberitz in Germany.

Dease and Godley's exploits were recognized in the *London Gazette*, the newspaper of record of the British government, in November 1914, with Godley's award being described as: "For coolness and gallantry in fighting his machine gun under a hot fire for two hours after he had been wounded in action at Mons on 23rd August". Though these were the first awards there were many more to come, in total 634 awards were made during the First World War, including two to one medical officer, Captain Noel Chavasse of the 10th (Liverpool Scottish) Battalion The King's (Liverpool) Regiment. His first award was for his actions during the Battle of Guillemont, part of the Somme battles, on 8 August 1916, the *London Gazette* describes his action as follows:

"During an attack he tended the wounded in the open all day, under heavy fire, frequently in view of the enemy. During the ensuing night he searched for wounded on the ground in front of the enemy's lines for four hours. Next day he took one stretcher-bearer to the advanced trenches, and, under heavy fire, carried an urgent case for 500 yards into safety, being wounded in the side by a shell splinter during the journey. The same night he took up a party of trusty volunteers, rescued three wounded men from a shell hole twenty five yards from the enemy's trench, buried the bodies of two officers and collected many identity discs, although fired on by bombs and machine guns. Altogether he saved the lives of some twenty badly wounded men, besides the ordinary cases which passed through his hands. His courage and self-sacrifice were beyond praise."

In 1917, Captain Chavasse was again awarded the VC during the Third Battle of Ypres, though this time posthumously. He was the only man to be awarded two Victoria Crosses during the First World War.

RIGHT The Victoria Cross awarded to Captain Edward Kinder Bradbury of L Battery, Royal Horse Artillery, 1st Cavalry Brigade, for his bravery in action at Néry during the retreat from Mons. The award was made posthumously and Captain Bradbury is buried in Néry Communal Cemetery, France.

RIGHT The cap badge of the Royal Fusiliers, the unit with which both Godley and Dease served.

THE FIRST BATTLE OF YPRES

Following the German withdrawal after the Battle of the Marne, both sides sought to exploit the open flank between the River Oise and the Channel in what became known as the "race to the sea". The BEF moved once again to the left flank of the Allied forces, taking up positions in Flanders where it would remain for the next four years. In doing so it found itself pitted against the German Fourth and Sixth Armies under von Falkenhayn in the First Battle of Ypres. The battle, which can be divided into the four distinct actions of La Bassée, Armentières, Messines and Ypres, began on 20 October, when 14 German divisions attacked along a 20-mile front. Despite breaking through the Belgian defences to the north they suffered heavy losses, particularly within their war-raised volunteer divisions, which proved no match for the BEF rifles in the central sector.

On 24 October, progress was halted when the Belgians blew up the sea dykes, flooding the region. Six German divisions of the Gruppe Fabeck renewed the offensive on a narrower front on 31 October, breaking through Haig's I Corps at Gheluvelt before hastily assembled reinforcements pushed them back.

The final offensive came on 11 November with Ypres as its objective. Breaking through at Nonne Boschen (Nun's Wood) at the southern end of the line, the Germans were held off by a group of cooks and batmen and the crisis passed.

The First Battle of Ypres officially ended on 22 November 1914 as the Allies entrenched themselves along what would become known as "the Salient", a triangular-shaped projection into the German front line that was to prove an uncomfortable home for British troops over the following years.

Amongst the battle's dead were an estimated 41,000 of Germany's ill-prepared volunteer forces, victims of what became known as *Der Kindermord bei Ypern*, the massacre of the innocents at Ypres, as well as over 58,000 British and Empire forces. First Ypres proved to be the graveyard of the pre-war professional British Army, and a great deal of reinforcement was required before the BEF could go over to the offensive in 1915.

Blooding of the Territorials

The First Battle of Ypres saw the first operational deployment of British Territorial Force soldiers, the "Saturday night soldiers" who volunteered en masse for foreign deployment even though their terms and conditions ensured they could not be compelled to serve outside Great Britain. One such territorial was J. K. Wilson, who was a private in the London Scottish, the first Territorial battalion to see action:

"On 29th October the move to the front began: the CO had received a hurried call to Ypres, we were to be rushed up to the front on motor busses ... A desperate fight was now going on all along the front from the Flemish sand dunes to the heights of Arras, but in the centre the full force of the German onslaught was directed against Ypres, which the 1st Corps, the 7th Division and Byng's Cavalry Division held precariously ... It proved to be one of the most critical days of the whole war. Skirting the village of Wytschaete on our front line we suffered our first casualties.

"Heavy shells were bursting among the roofs of the houses scattering showers of tiles and bricks, wounding and killing many of the poor people preparing to leave ... I was to fight in the company of many troops as the war proceeded, but never again did I witness the superb professionalism of these young veterans of Mons with their young officer so ably directing their fire, quite fearless in their dedicated efficiency."

BELOW A detachment of the London Scottish in Kemmel after their action in defending Messines Ridge, 31 October 1914.

ABOVE British troops resting in a Belgian village, 13 October 1914.

LEFT On 14 October 1914, Princess Mary, only daughter of King George V and Queen Mary, launched a fund to provide a Christmas gift for "every sailor afloat and every soldier at the front". This is one of those gifts, specifically for smokers.

PRISONERS OF WAR

The battles for Mons, Le Cateau and the Marne saw the first large-scale capture of British soldiers as prisoners of war. The First World War was the first major conflict where the treatment or prisoners of war was governed not by unofficial deals of local conventions, but by the force of international law. The Hague Conventions of 1899 and 1907 had laid down basic requirements for the treatment of prisoners, insisting that they be treated humanely, fed and housed in a manner equivalent to the soldiers of the country that captured them, and not forced to contribute to the capturing power's military effort, though they could be put to other work. The International Committee of the Red Cross,

founded in 1863, also played a valuable role in recording the status of prisoners of war, distributing letters and parcels and inspecting prisoner-of-war camps. Even with all these safeguards, being taken as a prisoner of war was fraught with danger. There were numerous occasions right from the start of the war when men were killed whilst trying to surrender, or even after they had surrendered. There is little direct evidence of official orders for units to "take no prisoners", but it is clear that, particularly where a unit had suffered heavy casualties or in the face of some innovation such as the use of gas, enemy prisoners could expect little sympathy.

42

GERMAN CRUELTY TO BRITISH PRISONERS

LORD KITCHENER says:-

The Germans have stripped and insulted British Prisoners and have shot some in cold blood.
The Germans act with the same barbarous savagery as the Sudan Dervishes.

THE PRIME MINISTER says:-

We shall not forget this horrible record of calculated cruelty and crime and we shall exact reparation against the guilty Germans.

JUSTICE CANNOT BE DONE WITHOUT YOUR HELP

TAKE UP THE SWORD OF JUSTICE

ENLIST TO-DAY

LEFT In the same way as the ill-treatment of Belgian civilians proved to be a spur for recruitment right at the start of the war, the perceived savagery of the Germans towards British prisoners of war proved another source of material for the recruitment posters, such as this one dating from June 1915.

ABOVE A British prisoner of war captured by the Germans during the March offensive of 1918.

It was certainly true that prisoners could expect a certain degree of rough treatment, as W. F. West describes following his capture outside Mons:

"Taken prisoner by the Germans on Sunday 23rd August 1914 on the south of Mons, Belgium, searched and stripped of our uniform buttons and cap badges with a few kicks here and there, marched four deep back through Mons to a temporary compound surrounded by electrified barbed wire. Most of us were exhausted through want of food, water and wounds and consequently could not keep up the pace the German Soldiers set who marched in front and when we fell out the Germans who marched by our sides and rear, kicked us, spat at us and used the Butt End of their Rifles on us even bayoneting some of us who were more dead than alive and leaving them on the side of the road."

This rough treatment could also extend beyond the point of capture all the way through to the prisoner-of-war camp, as J. P. Rush, company sergeant-major of 2nd Battalion The Duke of Wellington's Regiment, describes following his capture on 24 August 1914 near Wasmes, he was taken to Mons and held till mid-September before being shipped to Germany:

"Before leaving the station we were searched and our Greatcoats were taken away from us, and many German Officers fitted themselves with a coat in our presence, the remainder were taken away by the German Soldiers ... The number of prisoners in the camp varied up to about 11 or 12 thousand by the end of 1914. The English prisoners numbered about 1500 or 2000, many cases of stabbing, with bayonet, hitting with the butt end of the rifle ... for no reason whatever ... It was practically a Reign of Terror. An Englishman was hardly ever safe in the presence of a German soldier. I also witnessed an Englishman suffering from dysentery pushed off a latrine and knocked back to his tent by a German sentry who kept prodding him with the rifle butt."

RIGHT The tunnel at Holzminden prisoner-of-war camp, taken after the tunnel was discovered and dug up following its use for an escape attempt.

1915

THE BATTLE OF NEUVE CHAPELLE

Following the long winter in the trenches, the BEF was still too weak to undertake offensive operations at the beginning of 1915, but plans began to be made for an assault on the German salient around the village of Neuve Chapelle in order to capture the strategically dominant Aubers Ridge and to threaten the railway junction at Lille.

This was to be the first major attack against a German fortified position and the date for the assault was set for 10 March 1915. The First Army under Haig was chosen to carry out the attack and a large amount of artillery ammunition was provided to enable a heavy bombardment of the German lines immediately prior to the attack.

At 0730hrs on the morning of 10 March the guns opened up in an attempt to cut the wire in front of the German lines. Ten minutes later a "hurricane" bombardment devastated the majority of the German front line and the eight assaulting battalions went forward. Five of these met with success, taking the German trenches; the other three battalions either lost their way or found the German defences intact and suffered heavy casualties.

The first British offensive

Philip Neame served as an officer the 15th Field Company, RE, during the preparations for the battle:

"The chief work was the preparation of assembly trenches for the infantry to shelter in immediately before the battle, because the whole infantry of the division had to crowd into the forward area on a narrow front and the result was there had to be lines of breastwork or narrow trenches owing to the waterlogged nature of the ground and these were laid out and constructed under the supervision of the sappers ... Another was the provision of approach tracks leading up to the front, of course that had to be done with due thought as to concealment, a certain amount of duckboard approaches had to be put over ditches and so on ... The bombardment was the most impressive that I heard throughout the war; it was quite brief and only had a limited amount of heavy artillery, it was nearly all field gun fire, but in the short period that it took place the guns were firing at such a rapid rate that the noise was absolutely shattering and where it was accurate against the German breastworks it had a most decisive effect and kept the Germans down and our advancing infantry suffered only minor losses ... On the left part of the brigade on which I was working the artillery bombardment failed. I believe it was due to the fact that the batteries operating there had only come into their positions at the last moment and had not been able to register properly beforehand ... The result was the German trenches opposite the left part of the attack were not damaged and the left battalion of the infantry brigade I was concerned with was decimated when they got up and clambered over our breastwork. To my horror I saw them practically mown down."

LEFT *A Ration Party of the 4th Black Watch at the Battle of Neuve Chapelle, 1915* by Joseph Gray. The ghostly scene shows a ration party moving through a battlefield at night. The figures of the soldiers are obscured by the light, but they are all laden with boxes and sacks. They make their way through terrain littered with debris, their path lit by the fires of the battle on the left of the painting.

The assaulting battalions achieved a limited success and occupied Neuve Chapelle itself; however, in a pattern that would repeat itself over the following years, they were incapable of exploiting their successes before the Germans managed to bring up reserves. They were thus unable to break through the German second line. The assault was called off on 12 March 1915.

RIGHT Sword bayonet for SMLE Lee-Enfield Mk 3 and Pattern 1907, third type rifle.

LEFT A general scene showing damage to several buildings in Neuve Chapelle immediately after its capture by 8th Division. This amply illustrates the destructive power of the "hurricane" artillery bombardment.

THE SECOND BATTLE OF YPRES

Fought between 22 April and 25 May 1915, the Second Battle of Ypres was the only German offensive of the year on the Western Front. It is infamous for being the first occasion that poison gas was used on the Western Front.

Von Falkenhayn, the German Commander-in-Chief, intended to move divisions to support the effort against Russia and the offensive was at least partly designed to cover this redistribution of manpower.

On 22 April 1915, the German Fourth Army attacked supported by 160 tons of chlorine gas. French forces were overwhelmed by the new weapon and the Germans came close to breaking through, only to be held up by determined resistance by Canadian forces. Desperate measures were taken to protect the defending troops from the effects of the chlorine, and rudimentary gas masks were rushed to the front. These proved effective enough for the line to be held in most places, though the Allies were forced to withdraw, against Sir John French's wishes, surrendering the highest ground of the Ypres Salient and losing up to three miles of front by the time of the final German gas assault on 25 May 1915. This withdrawal proved controversial and led to the dismissal of Sir Horace Smith-Dorrien as commander of Second Army and his replacement by Herbert Plumer, commander of V Corps.

ABOVE British casualties of the gas attack on Hill 60 (near Ypres) receiving treatment at No. 8 Casualty Clearing Station, Bailleul.

The birth of chemical warfare

The use of gas came as a surprise to the men in the trenches; there was a great deal of shock, anger and resentment at what was perceived to be an underhand way of waging war.

Captain Barnett of the Indian Medical Service describes the initial reaction on 22 April 1915:

"Saw gassed men – blue faces choking and gasping. How we hate the German – I want to kill many slowly. Never heard the Tommies curse so – never cursed so hard myself. Canadians taking no prisoners – good job too. Exterminated two German battalions with bayonet. Shelling dreadful – it rains shells – day & night ... Cannot see how we can survive."

One of the battalions that suffered most at the Second Battle of Ypres was the 1st Dorsets who defended the notorious position Hill 60 from a determined German assault on 1 May. The Dorsets held their ground and became the first unit to successfully protect their positions against an attack supported by gas, but they suffered fearful losses.

Sergeant-Major Ernest Shepherd of the 1st Dorsets recalled:

"The scene that followed was heartbreaking ... had we lost as heavily while actually fighting we would not have cared so much, but our dear boys died like rats in a trap ... the Dorset Regiment's motto now is, 'No Prisoners'."

RIGHT Vickers .303-inch Mk I machine gun. The standard heavy machine gun used by the BEF.

RIGHT *The Ypres Salient at Night* by Paul Nash. A night scene showing three soldiers on the fire step of a trench surprised by a star shell lighting up the view over the battlefield. On the left there is a flooded shell-hole, beyond which stand three other soldiers. The men are wearing steel helmets, dating the painting from after the 1915 battle.

GAS WARFARE

Although it was banned by the Hague Convention of 1899, all the major combatants in the First World War experimented with chemical warfare before the Germans became the first to use gas in anger at Bolimov on the Eastern Front in January 1915, followed at Ypres on the Western Front on 22 April 1915. The principal agent used was chlorine, which caused injury and death through stimulating the lungs to overproduce liquid and thus drowning the victim. The Germans introduced phosgene gas in 1916, which proved more lethal, and finally "mustard" gas in July 1917. The Allies quickly followed suit, with the first British gas attack taking place in September 1915, and the remainder of the war saw each side seeking to develop more lethal strains and methods of delivery, whilst at the same time improving their soldiers' defences against the inevitable chemical attacks.

The first defences against gas were primitive in the extreme, and Gunner Heraty, a gunlayer with an 18-pounder battery, explains the difficulties of using one of the early-style gas helmets in the Ypres Salient:

"It was the first time I had been in a gas attack and it was early in December, 1915, and our respirators were really old fashioned ... [they] were made like a hood, similar to those worn by the Ku Klux Klan, they had two circular eyepieces let in, and a rubber tube with a mouthpiece leading through the material, which appeared to be made of flannelette, to the outside, where the rubber tube was flattened which would enable the wearer to breathe outwards but would not allow any air to be breathed in, the whole hood which was saturated with a chemical liquid had to be pulled over your head and tucked into your tunic around the neck, and believe me, if you were not gassed within half an hour due to the stench of the chemicals it was saturated with, you were lucky."

The advent of chemical warfare on an industrial scale brought a whole new range of problems for the medical staff on all sides. New methods of treatment had to be devised, whilst casualty evacuation was also a major problem

RIGHT *Gassed* by John Singer Sargent RA. The scene is the aftermath of a mustard gas attack on the Western Front during the First World War as witnessed by the artist. Mustard gas was an indiscriminate weapon causing widespread injury and burns, as well as affecting the eyes. It offered the possibility of making a significant breakthrough but in practice, defences were usually prepared, soldiers replaceable and the land could be contaminated for lengthy periods.

48

LEFT A gas sentry ringing an alarm at Fleurbaix, 15 miles south of Ypres. Various warning devices were used in the trenches, bells, rattles, empty shell cases among them. The soldier in the photograph is wearing the P helmet which was used from November 1915 until the end of 1916. The P helmet replaced the earlier and similarly shaped "Hypo" helmet, and was impregnated with hyposulphite of soda and phenate so as to protect the wearer from both chlorine and phosgene gas. The P helmet had glass eyepieces and a mouthpiece outlet valve.

"I took off my coat, put on my gas helmet – P.H.[sic] – and went down. Well inside the entrance at the top of the stairs I found two people. We brought out the first and found him alive and went back for the next. He was lying with his head on the top step and was dead. He was very pale with blue lips ... I found the next man at the bottom of the stairs ... It took a long time to get this man up, as the stairs were very narrow and very steep and very low. In the struggle, about halfway up I think, my helmet got pulled out from under my shirt ... almost immediately I felt something was going wrong with me – I was breathing very heavily with the exertion and found it impossible to hold my breath. I smelt nothing. I hung on without knowing much of what I was doing till I fell just at the entrance."

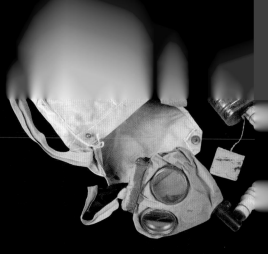

ABOVE A British Small Box Respirator and haversack.

Wounded by phosgene gas, Major Burt Hamilton recovered and was later awarded the Military Cross for the rescue under fire of three men from another collapsed dugout on 1 September 1916.

THE GALLIPOLI LANDINGS

The stalemate on the Western Front led to the development of many stratagems to inflict decisive blows on the enemy elsewhere. Notably, this search for an indirect approach to the issues on the Western Front led to the decision to force the Dardanelles, seize Constantinople and knock Turkey out of the war, thus easing the pressure on Russia. This plan was very much the brain child of the First Lord of the Admiralty, Winston Churchill, and was designed as a naval operation with very limited support from the Army, which feared the potential drain on manpower that another front would provoke. In the end Kitchener was prevailed on to provide forces and he allocated the Australian and New Zealand

Army Corps (ANZAC), which had recently arrived in Egypt, along with the regular 29th Division and the Royal Naval Division. Two French divisions bolstered this force, which was to be commanded by General Sir Ian Hamilton.

The naval attack started in late February with a number of bombardments and assaults by Royal Marines, and the grand advance began on 18 March with a force of 16 battleships. Unfortunately the assault failed with the loss of three ships, and a further three badly damaged. On 22 March, it was decided that the troops would be landed to take control of the peninsula and help ease the passage of the fleet.

The troops landed on 25 April at three different locations: the 29th Division at Cape Helles at the tip of the peninsula, the ANZACs further up the coast at what became known

On the beaches

George B. Horridge was a 2nd Lieutenant, serving with the 1/5th Battalion The Lancashire Fusiliers during the landing at Helles, Gallipoli in May 1915.

"We landed at 'W' Beach, afterwards known as 'Lancashire Landing', at Gallipoli ... We were transferred from the big ship to small, lighter craft. It was very cold, about 11 o'clock at night. When we got ashore, we were marched inland, up W Beach, and there were some sort of shallow holes, and we stayed there the night ... On 7 May 1915 we moved from where we had been the night before, D Company leading, followed by C, B and A. We moved across a small stretch of open land, down a sort of path now called Artillery Road, which led down to Gulley Ravine ... We then crossed over the gulley, being nearly dry, and wound our way up a narrow path on the further side of the gulley. When we got to the top of this path, which was about 300 yards from the cliff leading down to the sea, we were told to extend our platoons, turn right, and keep going ... There were a few hisses of bullets, and the further we went on they got more and more. We came to a trench, and then advanced still further. I began to lose control of my platoon as I simply couldn't see them in the scrub. All I could do was blow my whistle ... Eventually I got into the front-line trench ... The order was given to advance. I couldn't see the

Turks, they seemed to be hidden by bush, but the firing was very heavy; the Turkish bullets were hitting our trench just like on a rifle range. We didn't get more than about 10 or 15 yards until it became quite obvious that if we didn't lie down we were going to be hit. So we lay down, and you could see the bullets were cutting the grass in places ... I ended the day more or less under the cover of the cliffs. By

the end I wasn't in touch with any of my platoon, they'd stopped at various places on the way up ... After that we marched back to the beach. The battalion lost 180 casualties on that day ... What was my first impression of military action? I thought it would be a very good plan if the war were to end there and then. Unfortunately, it was to go on for another four years."

LEFT Royal Fusiliers returning from the trenches through Gully Ravine.

RIGHT Landing of the 1st Battalion The Essex Regiment at W Beach on 25 April 1915.

as ANZAC Cove, and the French across the other side of the straits at Kum Kale.

The ANZACs were the first ashore, at dawn, and made good progress towards the Sari Blair Ridge before being aggressively counter-attacked by Turkish forces under Mustapha Kemal. The 29th Division landed in broad daylight at five separate beaches – S, V, W, X and Y. The landings at S, X and Y were largely unopposed, but the landings at V Beach were a disaster, with the surviving troops having to be evacuated, while W proved costly to take with the 1st Battalion The Lancashire Fusiliers winning six Victoria Crosses in the process. There was no breakthrough and the fighting at Gallipoli rapidly settled into the trench warfare pattern all too familiar from the Western Front.

RIGHT The "Malta" Grenade was the result of an urgent request for 10,000 grenades in July 1915 by Sir Ian Hamilton, Commander-in-Chief of the Mediterranean Expeditionary Force, to make up crucial deficiencies in weapons and stores for British frontline troops fighting at Gallipoli. As its name suggests, this cast-iron, ball-type grenade was produced in Malta.

FORCES OF DOMINION AND EMPIRE

The opening year of the First World War saw the near destruction of the pre-war Regular Army. The battles of Mons, Le Cateau and First Ypres had bled the six regular divisions of the BEF dry. The Territorial Force divisions had filled the gap to a degree, but the New Army formations raised in 1914 would not be ready for action until mid 1915.

Among the troops used to fill this gap were those from the British Empire and the Dominions who fought alongside of the British Expeditionary Force on the Western Front and on other fronts. Among the first to arrive were formations of the Indian Army, whose Expeditionary Force A consisted of the 1st and 2nd Cavalry Divisions, and the 3rd (Lahore) and 7th (Meerut) Divisions. This force arrived in October 1914 and was sent straight into line during the First Battle of Ypres, serving in the La Bassée area. The 7th (Meerut) Division later formed part of the main assault force at the battle of Neuve Chapelle in March 1915. The Indian troops suffered cruelly on the Western Front and were withdrawn in October 1915, later seeing action in the African and Mediterranean theatres.

The Canadian Expeditionary Force, 30,000 strong and made up of volunteers, sailed for England on 3 October 1914. Following its arrival and training in England it formed one infantry division and a cavalry brigade, which left for France in February 1915. Their first major action took place during the Second Battle of Ypres when they resisted the first German gas attacks. Three further Canadian divisions followed: the 2nd in September 1915, the 3rd by March 1916 and the 4th by August 1916, and a Canadian Corps was formed in September 1915.

The Australian Imperial Force was raised in much the same way and initially consisted of the 1st Australian Division and the 1st Light Horse Brigade. These troops were deployed to Egypt in January 1915 where the 2nd Light Horse Brigade joined them and formed into the Australian and New Zealand Army Corps (ANZAC) to serve in the assault on Gallipoli. Australian troops later served in both the Mediterranean theatre and on the Western Front, where five Australian Divisions eventually served as the Australian Corps, the strongest British and Empire army corps on the Western Front. The Australian troops gained a reputation for courage and fighting spirit. However, relations were not always cordial. Many British officers complained about the lack of discipline in the Australian ranks, and tension was often present.

ABOVE VCOs (Viceroy Commissioned Officers) and other ranks of 129th Baluchis take aim in the trenches on the outskirts of Wytschaete, Belgium, in October 1914.

BELOW Eight ANZAC soldiers wearing sheepskin jackets and a mixture of slouch hats and steel helmets, resting on their way up to the trenches at the Somme, December 1916.

Captain Lowe, a cavalry officer, relates the following story of a friend's encounter with Australian soldiers:

*"In the summer of 1917 when I was with my Regiment in Picardy we had an officer, 'Daddy' Grant by name, who was a first class boxer. If the War had not intervened he would undoubtedly have boxed for Britain in the Olympics. One day he was riding along a country lane, past an orchard, on his way to Corps Headquarters. All of a sudden an apple hit him a hard smack on the back of his neck. He looked over the fence and saw three Australian soldiers roaring with laughter. 'Daddy' dismounted, tied up his horse and climbed into the orchard. 'Which of you fellows threw that apple?' he asked. 'I did', said one 'and you can go and f**k yourself. What's more I'm going to say that to every goddamned Imperial officer I see today!' Daddy Grant took off his Sam Brown belt and his tunic and in no time the Australian was flat on his back in the grass. 'Who's next?' asked Daddy and proceeded to do the same to the other two. This done they all shook hands, finished off the whisky which Grant always carried in a hunting flask on his saddle, and parted the best of friends."*

BELOW Canadian artillerymen on the Somme chalking a seasonal message onto a shell for loading into a 60-pounder gun – the message reads "Xmas Greetings from Canada".

THE BATTLE OF LOOS

In the summer of 1915, the commander of the French armies, General Joffre, planned an offensive for the end of September to attack each flank of the German positions on the Western Front. To help do this, he requested the assistance of Sir John French and the BEF. Sir John was unwilling to cooperate, partly due to a lack of artillery shells, but Kitchener ordered him to assist Joffre and so the new offensive came about. It was decided that the assault should take place just to the north of Lens near the small village of Loos, after which the offensive was named. It was also decided that the offensive should be entrusted to Sir Douglas Haig and his First Army, though Sir John French kept close control of the reserve formations of XI Corps and the 21st and 24th (New Army) Divisions.

Haig's plan was to attack on a broad front with six divisions and, due to the lack of artillery shells, he resolved to use chlorine gas on a large scale to overwhelm the Germans, the first time the British had used this weapon. The attack was launched on 25 September and rapidly ran into difficulties, which were partly due to the presence of British gas in no man's land. However, there was progress in the south and Loos was taken. But, due to the fact that the reserves had been held too far back and that the Germans had constructed a second line of defensive positions, these successes were not exploited the following day when the attack was renewed. The battle carried on until early November and resulted in a butcher's bill of over 60,000 casualties for the BEF.

As a direct result of the battle, particularly his handling of the reserves, Sir John French was removed from his post as commander of the BEF and replaced by the commander of First Army, Sir Douglas Haig.

ABOVE Welsh Guards moving off from Vermelles for the attack on Hill 70, 27 September 1915.

The "Big Push"

Captain Owen Morshead commanded the brigade signal section, 20th Brigade, 7th Division, at the Battle of Loos and describes the build up to the battle on 25 September and the initial assault:

"It was curious to see the assault; such an anti-climax it seemed. The gas ceased, saving for a beastly hissing leak in every fire-bay – and up went the men, up the ladders and over the parapet into the whistling cloud. No Aldershot charge, no wild and exhilarating haroosh; but a cautious, peering creep behind the slow-moving pall of gas, which slowly receded before a whiff of wind and hung about on the wet ground leaving a rank odour which never left the field. All night long messages had been passing over my wires from the gas expert in the front line back to G.H.Q. giving

BELOW Scots Guards at Loos.

half-hourly reports on the direction and strength of the light breeze: it must have been a nasty touch-and-go decision, and as far as our little frontage was concerned the issue must have hung by a hair. For as I thrust my way along the front line, after seeing Bridestone out, the bottom of the trench was encumbered with our own men overcome by the heavy fumes, their distended purple faces exposed where they had torn off odious masks. Many of them were the luckless gas operators. For no-one was the helmet more maddening than for my signallers in their fumed dugout, for they neither heard nor spoke with their telephones."

Trooper William Clarke of the 2nd Dragoon Guards (Queen's Bays) witnessed the aftermath of the battle:

"During the terrible battle at Loos when all those thousands of men were slaughtered, it had proved impossible to bury them all. They lay in trenches where they'd fallen or had been slung and earth had just been put on top of them. When the rains came it washed most of the earth away, you'd go along the trenches and you'd see a boot and puttee sticking out, or an arm or a hand, sometimes faces. Not only would you see, but you'd be walking on them, slipping and sliding. The stench was terrible because of all that rotting flesh. When you think of all the bits and pieces you saw ... If ever you had to write home about a particular mate you'd always say that he got it quickly and cleanly with a bullet and he didn't know what happened."

BELOW British troops advance to the attack through a cloud of poison gas as seen from the trench which they have just left: a remarkable snapshot taken by a soldier of the London Rifle Brigade on the opening day of the Battle of Loos, 25 September 1915.

SIR DOUGLAS HAIG

ABOVE *Field-Marshal Sir Douglas Haig, KT, GCB, GCVO, KCIE, Commander-in-Chief, France, From December 15th 1915. Painted at General Headquarters, May 30th 1917 by Sir William Orpen RA.*

Douglas Haig is certainly the most controversial figure in the British Army during the First World War. It is indeed arguable that he is the most controversial figure in the history of the British Army. Few commanding officers divide opinion in the same way. To his supporters he is a "great captain", the architect of victory in 1918 who shaped the BEF into the war-winning army that it became. To his detractors he is the "butcher of the Somme", the epitome of the "chateau general" and a justification of the argument that the BEF were "lions led by donkeys".

He was born in 1861 in Edinburgh the son of a scotch whisky distiller. He was educated at Oxford University, which he left without taking a degree, and entered Sandhurst before being commissioned into the 7th (Queen's Own) Hussars. His experience of life in the 19th-century British Army was similar to that of his superiors, in that he was part of

Kitchener's expedition to Sudan and later served at Omdurman, while he came to Sir John French's attention through his service in the Second Boer War. Returning to England he commanded the 17th Lancers before becoming aide de camp to King Edward VII, establishing royal connections that would serve him well later in his career. He was then appointed Inspector-General of Cavalry in India under the command of Kitchener, before returning to England as Director of Military Training in 1906, assisting with the Haldane reforms. At the outbreak of war he was GOC Aldershot, which ensured he commanded I Corps of the BEF once it moved to France.

Haig commanded I Corps during the Battle of Mons and the retreat to the Marne, before successfully holding off the German assault at Ypres during the closing months of 1914. Following the establishment of two armies in the BEF, Haig took command of First Army with the rank of full general. It was in this position that he planned the Battle of Loos, the fall-out from which was to cost Sir John French his position and lead to Haig's elevation as C.-in-C. of the BEF.

It was his decision-making in this role, specifically with regard to the Somme and Passchendaele offensives, that has caused so much controversy over the years. Many believe that Haig's approach was deliberately attritional, seeking to wear the Germans down through heavy losses at the expense of his own men's lives. Indeed, he is quoted as saying before the Somme offensive of 1 July 1916 that:

"The nation must be taught to bear losses. No amount of skill on the part of the higher commanders, no training, however good, on the part of the officers and men, no superiority of arms and ammunition, however great, will enable victories to be won without the sacrifice of men's lives. The nation must be prepared to see heavy casualty lists."

It is certainly true that the Prime Minister of the day, David Lloyd George, believed that his strategic approach was flawed and even went so far as to try to withhold reinforcements from the BEF.

However, it was Haig's army that won the great victories of 1918 in a series of battles of manoeuvre and open warfare far removed from the attritional slaughters of the Somme and Third Ypres, and he remained a popular figure with the ex-soldiers of the BEF in the post-war years, as, until his death at the age of 66 in 1928, he played a large role in the formation of the British Legion and the Haig Fund for the financial assistance of ex-servicemen

ABOVE A formal portrait of Field Marshal Sir Douglas Haig on horseback at Poperinghe, 1917.

RIGHT Service dress cap worn by Haig.

SALONIKA

Whilst the vast majority of the British Army was serving on the Western Front, other British troops were fighting elsewhere in Europe, in particular in the Balkans. Following the outbreak of the war, the Austro-Hungarians had invaded Serbia but had been pushed back by the end of 1914, and an uneasy stalemate prevailed. Germany sought to knock Serbia out of the war and, to that end, enlisted the support of Bulgaria and Austria-Hungary for a three-pronged attack. Alarmed by this development, the Allies decided to dispatch a force to Salonika to assist the Serbs, but they were too late. The Serbian Army was driven out of their country, through Montenegro and Albania, before being eventually evacuated

to Corfu on French transport ships whilst the first Allied forces landed in Greece. By December 1915 there were five British and three French divisions located in Salonika. In August 1916, there was a joint Austro-Bulgar assault on the position, followed by an Allied advance later in the year, but it was not until 1917 that a major assault on the Bulgarian positions around Lake Dojran was launched and repulsed with the loss of over 14,000 men.

1918 saw a change of leadership at the highest level, with the French general Franchet d'Esperey taking command in June, and a major offensive was launched in September. Having suffered heavy casualties in the Lake Dojran sector once more, the Allies finally broke through and the Bulgarian position collapsed. An armistice was signed on 30 September.

The Balkan expedition

Terence Trevor Hamilton Verschoyle was a British officer serving with 5th Battalion The Royal Inniskilling Fusiliers, at Salonika:

"The battalion knew before it left Gallipoli it was off to Salonika, but it didn't know when. We'd heard nothing of Salonika. We arrived at Salonika on 16 October in the morning ... Eventually we had to march out to a camp, which was pitched in a sea of mud, you couldn't get any tent pegs to stick in ... To make things worse the local populace tried to ply the platoon with drink on the line of

march. One of my platoon sergeants was virtually dead drunk and had to be carried along ... The rain went on for about three days ... We knew that the Allies had sent a small force to assist the Serbs, of which we would form part, and that was as much as we knew ... We were in camp for about three weeks and did a certain amount of training, then we entrained for the front on 8 November... We moved up across a very high ridge almost onto the Bulgarian border to a place called Mimishlee. We got the full force of the 27 November great blizzard,

which did so much damage at Gallipoli. We were about 3,000ft up ... Hostilities weren't really practical in that sort of weather. The Bulgars were overlooking us, but they were as cold as we were ... Nothing happened until the Bulgars developed their attack on 8 December. They advanced in considerable strength. My company was ordered to counter-attack, but fortunately the order was countermanded, because they were far too numerous for one company to do anything about. We beat a retreat back down the ravine behind us and up the other side ... It was the one occasion I recall when the rear, instead of saying 'Go slow in front', kept saying 'Can't you get a move on?' ... Eventually we marched back to Salonika, took us nearly a week, it was very bad going, nothing but marshes and ploughed fields. There were a lot of refugees streaming past us all the time ... Then we moved up to a pleasant site at Hortiac, a few miles outside Salonika, where we spent the next three months making roads, providing the donkey labour. I went back on a cruise tour about 15 years ago, and was delighted to find that my road still existed!"

LEFT Infantry manning part of the 10th (Irish) Division's position on Kosturino Ridge in Serbia, December 1915.

RIGHT *The Battle of 'The Pips', 24th April 1917* by William T. Wood, showing a battle on the Dojran Front.

LEFT Officers and men of 26th Divisional Ammunition Train playing football in Salonika, 25 December 1915.

THE END AT GALLIPOLI

After the initial assault on Gallipoli there followed a period of stalemate from May to the end of July while the Allied troops, particularly the ANZACs, desperately hung on in the face of repeated Turkish attacks. At the beginning of August, Kitchener sought to break the stalemate by reinforcing Hamilton's troops with five new divisions, the 10th, 11th, 13th, 53rd and 54th, formed into IX Corps. Hamilton planned to make the main effort of his new offensive with the ANZACs towards the Sari Blair Ridge, whilst the British VIII and French Corps attacked at Cape Helles and the newly arrived IX Corps made a landing at Suvla Bay to the north. The new offensive started on the night of 6/7 August, but the attacks at Sari Blair and Cape Helles failed with great loss of life. The inexperience of the troops and the timidity of the generals ensured that the new landings at Suvla Bay were not exploited to the extent they might have been. A final attack at Suvla Bay on 21 August failed to break through and the position on the peninsula settled into stalemate once more. Hamilton returned to England to be replaced by General Monro, who recommended that the force be evacuated. Kitchener travelled to Gallipoli in November and, seeing for himself the desperate nature of the position, agreed. The troops at Suvla Bay and Anzac Cove were evacuated on 19 December whilst the remainder of the troops at Cape Helles left on the night of 8/9 January. Unlike the rest of the campaign, the evacuation was a success and not a single man was lost.

Evacuation of the peninsula

Private Robert Loudon of the 1/4th Battalion The Royal Scots (Queen's Edinburgh Rifles), 156th Brigade, 52nd (Lowland) Division, joined his battalion in Gallipoli as a replacement on 1 December 1915 and reflected on the dismal conditions they were suffering:

"The conditions for the men on the Peninsula were most unpleasant. There was continuous dust stirred up by high explosive bursting, and by the movement of men and mules. Myriads of flies, crawling over everyone, gave the men no peace. When they were eating, one hand had to be waved continuously to prevent flies settling on the food. Many men got dysentery. Lice and fleas were prevalent."

It was not just the living conditions. The fighting on the peninsula was tough enough to compare with anything experienced on the Western Front. In an entry to his diary, Sergeant John McIlwain of the Connaught Rangers describes the outcome of a confused action on 27 August 1915 during the month of bitter battles that cost so many lives for so little territorial gain:

"Turks bomb us from front and left flank, also snipe us from along the trench to the left. My men with few exceptions panic-stricken. My rifle red almost with firing ... Turks but ten yards away drive us back foot by foot. I have extraordinary escapes. Two men killed beside me ... and I am covered head to foot in blood. Casualties alarming and we would have fought to the very end but for the 18th Australian Battalion a party of whom jumped in amongst us and held the position until reinforced. When able to look about me I find but two Rangers left with me. The rest killed, wounded, or ran away ... The most awful night of my life ... I was reported killed of course. Receive congratulations but wish that I could change my bloody clothes."

LEFT Stores burning on the beach after the evacuation at Suvla, photographed from HMS *Cornwallis*.

RIGHT Evacuating guns and personnel from Suvla Point on rafts in daylight.

RIGHT An Arab *Jambiyah*
with scabbard – taken from
a dead Turk at Gallipoli.

**Robert Loudon desrcibes on the evacuation
of the Gallipoli Peninsula, 8/9 January 1916:**

*"The third and last contingent left the
front-line trenches about 11.30 p.m.,
reached the beach, and embarked. By
3.30 a.m. on the 9th of January, 1916,
the evacuation of our forces from
January had been completed without
the loss of a single man.*

*Time fuzes to magazines, dumps,
etc., had been lit, and in a short time
abandoned tents and heaps of stores
and supplies burst into flames. At 4
a.m. the two magazines under Cape
Helles were blown up. At last the
Turks realized that something unusual
was happening."*

1916

ENLISTMENT AND CONSCRIPTION

At the beginning of the war it was quickly realized that Britain's peacetime army, even bolstered by reserves and the Territorial Army, would not have the strength of numbers to participate for long in a war between the great Continental powers and would need considerable reinforcement. So on 25 August Lord Kitchener called for 30 divisions of volunteers. In the first month over 300,000 came forward, and in total over 2.5 million men volunteered for service throughout the course of the war. But this was not enough. By May 1915

there was a need for more men than were coming forward and the Derby Scheme, named after the Director-General of Recruitment, Lord Derby, was instituted. Men were to register their names voluntarily, but would only be called up when the need arose. Not enough came forward and, in January 1916, the first Military Service Act passed through parliament. This Act specified that men from the ages of 18 to 41 were liable to be called up for service unless they were married or else served in one of a number of reserved professions. A further five variants of the Act were passed before the end of the war, culminating in conscription for

Conscientious objectors

Men became conscientious objectors for a number of reasons: religious beliefs and political affiliations were two of the major ones. Tribunals decided their fate and many took up non-combatant roles either at home or in the BEF. Those who did not cooperate with the tribunals could expect to be imprisoned or even threatened with execution. H. Steele was one of those conscientious objectors:

"I was an 'Absolutist' Conscientious Objector in the First World War – of the brand or variety which refused to appeal to, or before, any Tribunal for the purposes of securing any form of Exemption from Military Service or other Alternative service within the framework of the Military Service Act.

"Arrested (by the civil police) in April 1916, and 'handed over' to the Military by a Police Court Magistrate. Tried by Court Martial on five occasions. Sentenced to a total of 7½ years imprisonment with hard labour.

"Experienced confinement in guard rooms – experiences in guard rooms were more exciting than in prison – in Warley Barracks (Essex), Chatham Great Lines, Chatham Lower Barracks, Chatenden Camp (Kent), Canterbury Barracks: Prison (Chatham) Maidstone Gaol, Canterbury Gaol, Preston Gaol – with brief spells in Wormwood Scrubs and Wakefield Gaol. Most of my 'time' was 'done' in Maidstone. Released from prison in April 1919 – from Preston. Discharged from the Army (for 'Misconduct') in April 1919."

MEN OF MILITARY AGE WHO HAVE PROMISED TO ENLIST IN THEIR GROUP WHEN REQUIRED are informed that IT IS ABSOLUTELY NECESSARY for them to BE ATTESTED NOW And that enlistments under the Group System will close on SATURDAY, DECEMBER 11th THEY CANNOT APPEAL To be placed in a later Group unless they have been attested by that date MARRIED MEN will not be called upon to serve until the Single Men have been summoned to the Colours SINGLE MEN ENLIST VOLUNTARILY AND AVOID CONSCRIPTION

LEFT By mid 1915 the number of volunteers enlisting had tailed off and new methods of recruiting, such as the Derby Scheme, were instituted.

those between the ages of 17 and 51 extending throughout the British Isles, including Ireland, though it was never exercised there for fear of civil disorder. In total some 2.5 million men were conscripted after 1 January 1916 with fewer than 20,000 becoming "conscientious objectors".

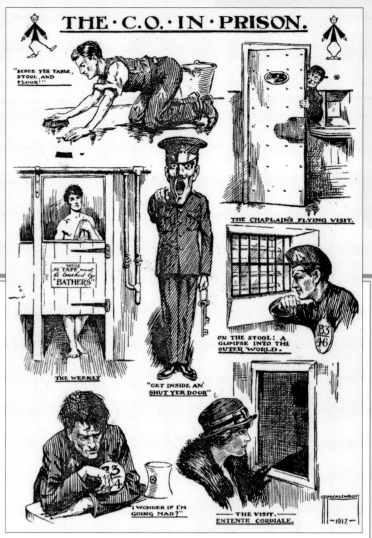

THE · C.O · IN · PRISON.

RIGHT An illustration portraying the routine of an imprisoned conscientious objector.

LEFT Conscientious objectors in prison during the First World War.

ABOVE Young British conscripts at the base depot of Étaples in 1918.

THE EASTER RISING

The outbreak of the war caused the postponement of the establishment of Home Rule in Ireland until the cessation of hostilities. The mainstream Irish parties accepted the assurances of the government of the day and encouraged their supporters to enlist in the British Army. However, there were more strident nationalist voices in Ireland, including the Irish Republican Brotherhood, and this organization infiltrated a number of other nationalist and militia outfits and sought to instigate an armed uprising to win Irish independence. On the morning of Easter Monday, 24 April 1916, armed men began to assemble at a number of pre-arranged meeting points in Dublin.

The rebellion was launched from the steps of the General Post Office building (GPO) and it was from there that Patrick Pearse proclaimed the existence of an Irish Republic and the establishment of a Provisional Government. Meanwhile the rebels occupied other key Dublin buildings.

It took the surprised British authorities the better part of a day to organize a military response. Martial law was declared throughout Ireland and troops were rushed to Dublin. The rebels were slowly driven back in vicious street fighting until only the GPO remained in rebel hands. On 29 April, the Provisional Government decided to seek surrender terms, and by 0345hrs, the fighting was all but over with central Dublin in ruins.

In accordance with their "tough policy" the British had the leaders of the rising tried by court martial under the Defence of the Realm Act: 15 of them, including the signatories to the Declaration of Independence, were summarily executed in Kilmainham Gaol and a further 3,500 "sympathizers" imprisoned.

Dublin in flames

Captain Lowe was the son of Brigadier-General Lowe who coordinated the initial British response to the Rising, and he also served as his father's aide-de-camp. He described the apocalyptic scenes that filled central Dublin:

"By Tuesday night the centre of the city was a sea of flames. The Post Office, an imposing building recently modernised by the British, was gutted. It was an awful and never to be forgotten sight. The Irish fought fanatically. They would occupy a

BELOW A contemporary photograph showing Sackville Street, where the GPO was located, taken on either 27 or 28 April 1916.

ABOVE British soldiers holding a street against Irish rebels.

whole street at a time and bash holes in the walls dividing the houses, thus making a self-contained fortress of each city block. The women would run the gauntlet of heavy fire from both sides to carry messages. Although my father issued strict orders that no women were to be fired at under any circumstances whatsoever, many were killed. A dead woman lying in the street with her skirts bunched up around her waist is a truly horrible and unforgettable sight, the worst I ever saw in the whole war."

Captain "Mickey" Martyn of 2/8th Battalion The Sherwood Foresters remarked on the fighting in Dublin:

"I found that a bullet in Dublin was every bit as dangerous as one in no man's land ... In some ways fighting in Dublin was worse – In France you had a fair idea of where the enemy was and where the bullets were going to come from. In Dublin you never knew when or from where you were going to be hit."

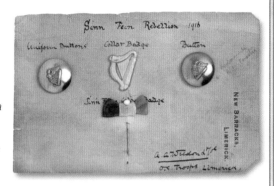

ABOVE Sinn Féin badges and collar buttons.

THE MESOPOTAMIA EXPEDITION

At the beginning of the First World War a small force of British troops landed at the top of the Persian Gulf to protect the interests of the Anglo-Persian Oil Company against a potential Turkish threat. The Indian government controlled the forces in the region, and by the time General Sir John Nixon took command in March 1915 an improvised corps of two infantry divisions and one cavalry brigade had been assembled. This force was split into two with one column advancing up the River Tigris under Major-General Sir Charles Townshend and the other advancing up the River Euphrates under Major-General George Gorringe. Townshend advanced rapidly and took the town of Kut Al Amara on 28 September 1915, though his logistical chain from his supply base at Basra was now becoming dangerously extended. He pressed on towards Baghdad and reached as far as Ctesiphon, 24 miles south of the city. An attack against Turkish positions failed on 22 November and Townshend was compelled to retreat back to Kut, which he fortified. Surrounded by Turkish troops he held out here and waited for relief. Despite the best efforts of the Allied troops this relief never came and Townshend and his men were compelled to surrender on 28 April 1916. After this debacle, General Sir Frederick Maude took over from Nixon in August 1916 and, heavily reinforced, advanced up the rivers once more. Kut was retaken in February 1917 and Baghdad finally fell on 11 March 1917. The remainder of the campaign was spent consolidating Mesopotamia and ended with the seizing of the oilfields at Mosul in early November 1918 after an armistice with the Turks had already been agreed.

The fall of Kut Al Amara

Captain Barnett of the 34th Sikh Pioneers, 3rd Division, wrote of the wealth of Mesopotamia that awaited the victor:

"How this country became the desert it is one cannot imagine for the soil is the richest in the world & it only needs the engineer here & the canal builder to turn it into the finest country in the world. It will be one of the richest prizes we have gained in the war. The burning question at present is who is to get to Bagdad first – the Russians or us."

He also took part in the relief expedition to Kut Al Amara. Four times the force tried to break through the Turkish lines to relieve the British defenders of Kut, but each time they were beaten back with heavy losses, which totalled over 23,000 by the end of the campaign. On 18 April 1916 Barnett wrote:

"Stood to arms all night as Turks are countering most violently. Fought all night and stuck to most of captured ground. At least 3,000 Turks killed – two whole divisions out of action. Keary wanted to push on but Gorringe [GOC Tigris Corps] said no – obstinate mule. I think – so do most that Kut is doomed & this was our last chance."

Kut indeed fell ten days later and its garrison of over 12,000 men was taken into captivity. Of these, over 4,000 perished due to the harsh treatment meted out to them by their Turkish captors.

RIGHT An aerial view of Kut, a Turkish town on the banks of the River Tigris, to which Major-General Sir Charles Townshend (Commander of the 6th Indian Division) retreated after his failure to advance into Mesopotamia. The subsequent siege by the Turks lasted 147 days, all attempts to relieve the British forces failing.

BELOW Major-General Sir C. V. F. Townshend.

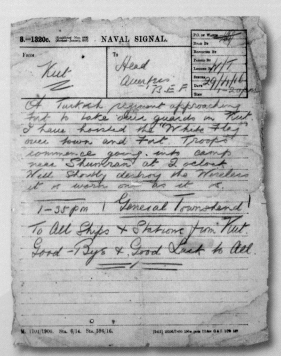

LEFT Townshend's signal prior to surrender.

RIGHT The embroidered decoration on this wallet relates to the service of W. A. Bullock of the 7th Battalion The Gloucestershire Regiment in the Mesopotamian campaign.

THE BATTLES OF THE SOMME

Following the German offensive at Verdun, the French desperately needed the BEF to take the pressure off their lines and draw German reserves away. It was therefore decided to launch a major offensive on the Somme. The preliminary bombardment began on the morning of 24 June 1916, with the systematic shelling of barbed-wire obstacles and a programme of counter-battery fire. Two days later, the attempt to destroy fortified positions began in earnest. However, it rapidly became clear that the bombardment was not having the desired effect and the wire remained uncut. As a result, on 28 June Haig delayed the start of the infantry attack for two days, with the main assault starting on 1 July 1916.

There were some successes, notably the 36th Ulster Division at Thiepval, but overall the day was a disaster for the BEF with nearly 60,000 casualties – just under 20,000 killed. Particularly hard hit were the New Army battalions, many of which had not been in battle before.

Despite the losses of the first day the fighting on the Somme persisted until 18 November, with 12 separate battle honours awarded. Over a million men became casualties during the course of these battles: the British lost 415,000, the French 200,000 and the Germans anything between 250,000 and 600,000. Captain von Hentig of the German General Staff called the Somme "the muddy grave of the German Army" and the battle certainly fulfilled its aim in drawing off the German reserves.

Slaughter of the New Armies

Gunner Heraty served on one of the 18-pounder batteries that supported the assault:

"A ceaseless shelling of Jerry's trenches and barbwire entanglements was kept up until 'zero hour' which was 7.30 a.m,. 1st July 1916, in broad daylight ... I saw hundreds of young lads who had only just got their heads above the parapets killed before they could even get out of the trenches. I turned several of them over, thinking that I might be able to recognize any of them, and several of them could not have been more than 17 years of age, and to make matters worse the German barbwire [sic] defences we were supposed to have blown to pieces were practically untouched, I actually saw them when we went through with our guns, after we had been strafing them from the middle of June, 1916."

Major-General Thomas D'Oyly Snow, CB, commanded VII Corps, part of General Allenby's Third Army. He wrote in his diary on 15 July 1916:

"Of course the advance is a tremendous success not a bit a false one. The enemy has got to be fought everywhere very hard. It's not a bit of good sitting down and saying you are wearing him out. The gain in land matters little as long as you can inflict damage on him. Everything is going very well indeed – no one minds the losses as long as we are moving."

LEFT *Dead Germans in a Trench* by Sir William Orpen, RA. The bright white chalk spoil immediately behind the wattle-revetted German trench suggests the Somme front.

The Reverend T. Guy Rogers was a chaplain to the 2nd Guards Brigade, Guards Division, during the later Somme battles and describes the effect of the continuous casualties:

"It is the most melancholy thing in the world to walk round the battalions recognising scarcely one familiar face. No one at home can understand what it is suddenly to miss all the bright faces – one day every one full of life and hope, and the next day no one left – just blankness and a pain at the heart."

ABOVE Still from the British film *The Battle of the Somme*. The image is part of a sequence showing a reconstruction of British soldiers moving forward through wire at the start of the battle, 1 July 1916.

RIGHT British gunners firing an 18-pounder gun at St Leger aux Boise on 3 August 1916.

MEDICAL SERVICES

In common with many parts of the British Army prior to the First World War, the Royal Army Medical Corps (RAMC), which had been formed to care for British sick and wounded in the late 19th century, was completely unprepared for the scale of the task they were about to undertake. During the course of the war, the RAMC treated some 2,700,000 casualties whilst increasing its ration strength to over 145,000 officers and men.

Right from the very beginning of the war the medical services were under constant pressure in dealing with the level of casualties, not to mention the severity of their wounds. Major Eben Stuart Burt Hamilton of the RAMC served with the Royal Irish Regiment during the retreat from Mons, when all manner of logistic and organizational support networks came under the utmost pressure:

"Retreating soldiers especially the Royal Irish but others from other regiments – Gordons – Middlesex – RFA –

Cavalry on foot etc. were there too, were pouring along the road back towards Hyon, while shrapnel was bursting above our heads all the time – wounding a man here and there. A fair number of retreating men had slight wounds which we bound up. There were of course no serious cases – these had to be left in the trenches or in the fields up by Obourge where our line had been."

The first major offensives also proved traumatic, as Major Burt Hamilton was to find at the Battle of Loos on 30 September 1915:

"Just after this our first convoy arrived and we started work. By 5.30 we had admitted 572 ... the whole thing was a sort of long nightmare with the only thing clear being the necessity for dressing more and more people every minute."

The standard procedure for dealing with a casualty remained the same throughout the First World War and was

LEFT *The Wounded At Dover*, 1918, by Sir John Lavery, RA, RSA. A scene of the platform at Dover railway station. Wounded soldiers are boarding a hospital train. A group of wounded stand in the foreground, to the right lie others on stretchers, one tended by a nurse. There are khaki-clad figures running the length of the platform, pushing wheelchairs and carrying stretchers.

RIGHT The gas ward at Netley Hospital, Hampshire. Patients with mustard gas burns undergo salt bath treatments.

divided into three principal stages: collection, evacuation and distribution. In the first stage casualties were treated initially at the Regimental Aid Post by the battalion medical officer, though this often only involved the dressing of wounds, before passing them along the line to the Advanced Dressing Station managed by the Field Ambulance attached to the brigade. This unit could deal with more serious cases, but generally most major medical treatment was carried out at the next link of the chain, the Clearing Hospital or Casualty Clearing Station. These units, generally at a divisional level, treated the majority of battlefield casualties, stabilized them and sent them into the evacuation stage of the process when they were passed onto the more permanent hospitals either in France or Great Britain. This system worked well during normal circumstances, but could be overwhelmed by sheer numbers of casualties such as on the first day of the Somme, whilst the nature of the battlefield conditions at Third Ypres also made the collection of casualties extremely difficult.

Battlefield casualties also proved only a proportion of the work carried out by the RAMC. Illness, particularly in unhealthy climates such as East Africa and Salonika, proved a major factor. In fact in East Africa battlefield casualties only formed three per cent of admissions to hospital. The medical services of the British Army also had to cope with new forms of casualty: artillery caused the majority of the wounds inflicted during the First World War, whilst the advent of gas warfare introduced a whole new range of techniques to the medical spectrum. By the end of the war huge advances had been made in the fields of blood transfusion, fluid replacement, prevention of wound infection and reconstructive surgery.

ABOVE *Indian Army wounded in hospital in the Dome, Brighton* by Douglas Fox-Pitt.

BELOW Wounded men of the 1st Battalion The Lancashire Fusiliers, being tended in a trench in 29th Division area near Beaumont Hamel on the morning of 1 July 1916.

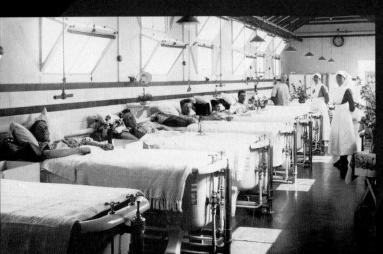

1917

THE ARAB REVOLT

Following the stalled offensives against Turkey at Gallipoli and in Mesopotamia, fresh impetus for the campaign came from within the Ottoman Empire itself, specifically in its territories on the Arabian Peninsula. The Ottomans had ruled these lands since the 16th century and the local Arab population of some six million people was growing increasingly disaffected with the regime and looked for both a leader and a means to expel the Turkish Army. An Arab independence movement grew in popularity in the Hejaz region of the Red Sea coast and Hussein Ibn Ali, the Sherif of the holy city of Mecca, proved a natural leader for this movement.

The Hejaz region also proved well suited for launching the revolt as, despite the construction of a railway across it, it remained a fairly inaccessible region. The difficult terrain made the movement of large numbers of troops a difficult process. The region's location on the Red Sea also allowed for communication with the British command in Egypt, and, following intense negotiations, throughout 1915 the Royal Navy shipped rifles into the region. The Turks were well aware that trouble was brewing and began to mass troops in Damascus to put down the revolt.

On 5 June 1916 the revolt broke out in the cities of Medina and Mecca. The Medina venture failed, but Mecca was taken, giving the nascent revolt a secure base from which to operate. Once their base was secure, the Arabs began a series of attacks on the Hejaz railway to prevent Turkish reinforcements being moved from Damascus, as well as launching small-scale assaults on local Turkish garrisons.

The Arabs proceeded to secure the coastal towns of Jeddah, Yenbo and Wajh, which allowed for the re-supply and support of the Arab Army by the Royal Navy. By late 1916 a number of British and French advisors, including T. E. Lawrence, later immortalized as "Lawrence of Arabia", had arrived in Arabia, initially to assist in the logistical arrangements, but, increasingly, they took an active role in the direction of the revolt. The seizure of Aqaba in July 1917 opened a major new supply route to Egypt, thus allowing the Arab Army to support General Allenby's operations in Palestine and Syria. From 1917 onwards the Arab Army played a major role in the British strategic thinking, taking part in the offensives at Gaza, Jerusalem and Megiddo, before reaching Damascus on 1 October and Aleppo on the 25th.

Lawrence of Arabia

The most famous individual figure involved in the Arab Revolt, immortalized in print and on screen, is T. E. Lawrence, "Lawrence of Arabia". Born in 1888 he studied history at Oxford, writing his undergraduate thesis on the Crusader castles of Syria, before becoming involved in archaeological excavations in Arabia. Lawrence joined the British Army in October 1914 and was posted to the intelligence branch in Cairo. With the outbreak of the Arab Revolt, Lawrence was one of a number of British and French advisors sent to the Hejaz to assist in the uprising. Lawrence became close friends with the Emir Feisal, whom he describes in glowing terms in his book the *Seven Pillars of Wisdom*: "I felt at first glance that this was the man I had come to Arabia to seek – the leader who would bring the Arab Revolt to full glory."

Lawrence proved an important figure in the revolt, urging closer cooperation between the various Arab factions and being involved in the planning for the capture of Aqaba in 1917 as well as the Arab advance on Damascus. After the end of the war Lawrence promoted the cause of Arab independence, becoming part of the Emir Feisal's delegation at the Paris Peace Conference. Although British and French treatment of the Arabs embittered him, he returned to government service to assist in the setting up of the kingdoms of Iraq and Transjordan in the early 1920s. In an effort to avoid the publicity that dogged him following the publicizing of his exploits in Arabia, he enlisted in the RAF under an assumed name in 1925. T. E. Lawrence died in a motorcycle accident in Dorset in 1935.

BELOW The *agel* (headrope) worn by T. E. Lawrence.

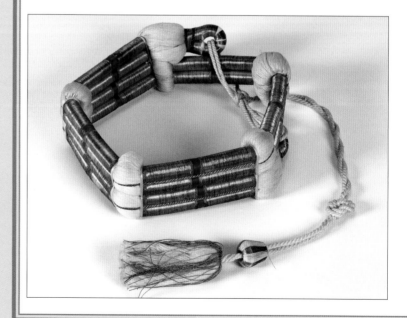

LEFT The Mk 3 Lee-Enfield rifle carried by T. E. Lawrence during the Arab Revolt.

RIGHT *Lieutenant-Colonel T. E. Lawrence, CB, DSO*, by James McBey, 1918.

BELOW A snapshot taken by Lawrence in 1917 showing Emir Feisal and Sherif Sharraf.

THE BATTLES FOR GAZA

With the entry of Turkey on the side of the Central Powers, British forces in Egypt, anxious to secure the Suez Canal from assault, undertook a defensive posture, and when the assault by Turkish forces came in February 1915, it was driven back to Beersheba with heavy losses. However, following the evacuation of Gallipoli, large numbers of men became available to what was now called the Egyptian Expeditionary Force under the command of Lieutenant-General Sir Archibald Murray. This force began a painstaking crossing of the Sinai Desert, supported by the construction of a railway and a fresh-water pipeline. The infantry divisions advanced down the coast and the cavalry, notably the Australian Cavalry Division and Imperial Camel Corps, protected the desert flank.

Convinced that they were about to be subjected to a major British offensive, the Turks launched a number of spoiling attacks at Romani in August 1916, before withdrawing altogether from Egypt to Gaza in January 1917. Sir William Robertson, the Chief of the Imperial General Staff (CIGS), now approved a British offensive against Gaza and, once his railhead and pipeline had caught up, Murray launched the First Battle of Gaza on 26 March 1917. However, the direct assault failed, due in part to a loss of nerve by British commanders at a critical moment in the battle. The Turkish commanders and

The First Battle of Gaza

Donald Penrose was an officer with the 1/7th Battalion The Essex Regiment during the First Battle of Gaza and recalled the state of confusion that existed in the lines:

"It was a very sad affair. We lost a number of our men, our reserve was called in and I think one night we actually were going to be withdrawn because the brigadier told us afterwards that he had to give an order he had never had to give before in his life, 'get out of it as best you can'. Our company were forming what was called an outpost line. During the night our company commander said to me to get in touch with the people on our right if I could find out where they were, which I did. Then he told me to find the people on our left and I tried and tried but couldn't find anybody anywhere or any sign of anything, and, finally, I got lost myself, and I thought I would wait till dawn came up, which wouldn't be long, and go and have a look see. Well, dawn came up and I still saw no sign of anyone, there should have been people between us and the coast, and then I saw a column coming up in fours headed by a brigadier on a horse. I dashed across to him and said 'I don't know whether you know sir but the Turks are just over that ridge'. 'Are they, by God!' he said, and wheeled round and went away. They were the people who should have been on our left at that time. I reckon I saved a real slaughter, if they had got up any higher they would have been machine-gunned by the Turks all over the place."

ABOVE The Hong Kong and Singapore Battery (the "Bing Boys") in action during the First Battle of Gaza.

their German advisors were given a critical breathing space to reinforce their forces and fortify the Gaza–Beersheba line.

Murray tried again on 17–18 April, in the Second Battle of Gaza, and this time reinforced his assault with tanks newly arrived from France. However, again the assault failed with heavy casualties, leading to Murray's replacement by General Sir Edmund Allenby.

ABOVE Four British sergeants pose with their camels in front of the Sphinx and Pyramids during a sightseeing visit in Egypt.

RIGHT Hotchkiss Machine Gun Mk 1*. The "Portable" version of the French-designed Hotchkiss machine gun was manufactured in Britain during the First World War for issue to cavalry units. The Mk I* version was produced for use in tanks. The Mk I* replaced the original wooden butt with a pistol grip, and could feed cartridges from "belts" made from short, linked strips, each containing three cartridges, as well as from the standard Hotchkiss 30-round strip.

THE BATTLE OF ARRAS

The British assault at Arras, launched on Easter Monday, 9 April 1917, was designed to divert German attention and reserves away from the main Allied effort that was to be carried out by the French Army under General Nivelle a week later further to the south. At the beginning of February 1917, the Germans launched Operation *Alberich*, the withdrawal to the newly constructed Hindenburg Line in order to shorten their line and conserve troops. This withdrawal had an immediate effect on both the British and French plans, as their offensive was now aimed at empty positions. Artillery now had to be re-positioned and plans redrawn. The British attack involved troops from First, Third and Fifth Armies, under Horne, Allenby and Gough respectively, while a prominent role was given to the Canadian Corps under Lieutenant-General the Hon. Sir Julian Byng.

The initial assault went well for the British, particularly in the Third Army sector. Between 9 and 12 April the Canadian Corps also managed to capture Vimy Ridge in one of the most successful set-piece attacks of the war. However, the situation was less favourable for Fifth Army, and the 4th Australian Division was badly knocked about around Bullecourt on 10 April. As the battle dragged on the British advance lost momentum and became increasingly difficult to control, due in part to the problems of communication on the battlefield. Meanwhile German reserves arrived and started counter-attacking to win back the lost ground. The offensive was halted on 15 April, before being resumed on 23 April and again on 23 May. Neither of these attacks gained much ground and instead resulted in heavy casualties, over 159,000 up until 17 May. The end of the battle saw Allenby replaced by Byng as commander of Third Army.

Care of the wounded at Arras

Private Frank Cooper of the 5th Battalion The Oxford and Buckinghamshire Light Infantry fought in the struggle for Telegraph Hill, part of the Battle of Arras:

"Now it was early morning on 9.4.17 and still dark. We all got ready to move out of the deep underground Christchurch cave. We then marched in single file to the trenches ... I saw our 18-pounder guns wheel to wheel; our heavy guns were further back from the line. Now our bombardment had started and the creeping barrage was on. The boys had their tot of rum, but I did not drink mine.

"At 9.30am the order was 'go', every soldier was out of the trench and in no man's land. The battle was on. I just glanced to right and left and there were English soldiers all in a line, going forward to the German lines. The tanks were with us, but they seemed to be bogged down and slow. The trouble was the large shell holes and the mud and water. We'd just got to the German trenches when Captain Higgins' servant came to my officer to tell him the captain had been killed. Then I was knocked down, hit by a piece of shrapnel.

"Another wave of soldiers was coming on. One of them told me to roll into a shell hole, or else I would get hit again, so I did ... It was not long before the stretcher bearers came to bandage me up."

Private Cooper was taken back to a dressing station before being moved to the British base camp at Etaples and then back to England.

RIGHT *The Manchesters, Arras 'Just out of the trenches near Arras. Been through the battles of Ypres and Somme untouched. Going home to Sheffield to be married.',* by Sir William Orpen, RA. A young British soldier is portrayed in full kit.

LEFT A battery of 60-pounder guns in action during the Battle of Arras, April 1917.

ABOVE One of the few photographs of an actual attack; an officer of the 9th Battalion The Cameronians (Scottish Rifles) leads the way out of a sap during the Battle of Arras, 11 April 1917.

THE WAR IN AFRICA

Far away from the war in Europe the First Word War had a profound impact in Africa, where the colonial forces of Germany and Great Britain fought through until 1918. At the outbreak of the war Germany possessed four colonies in Africa: Togoland (modern Togo), Kamerun (Cameroon), German South-West Africa (Namibia) and German East Africa (Tanzania, Burundi and Rwanda). The first of these territories fell quickly, overrun by troops of the West African Frontier Force on 27 August 1914. Kamerun proved harder to conquer, and three British columns advancing from Nigeria were beaten back with heavy losses in late August 1914. Reinforcements, particularly naval forces, enabled the British to take the capital Douala at the end of September and they pushed on into the interior, where the final German forces surrendered in February 1916. Whilst dealing with German South-West Africa, there was also a substantial Boer rebellion. However, the majority of the Boers remained loyal and fought on the British side, ensuring that both the revolt and the German colony were defeated by July 1916. It was only in German East Africa that the British forces faced severe setbacks in their campaigns against the German colonies. The first British assault at the port of Tanga on 3 November 1914 ended in a disaster for the attacking forces, and the campaign was not taken up until March 1916 when a largely South African force under J. C. Smuts pushed southwards from Kenya, supported by a Belgian advance from the Congo and a Portuguese one from Portuguese East Africa. The South African force pushed southwards, reaching Dar es Salaam on 3 September 1916, but never managed to trap the German main force under its commander General Paul von Lettow-Vorbeck. The South African troops also suffered terribly in the conditions, particularly from malaria, and in 1917 African troops from Nigeria began to replace them. Despite the numerical odds against him, von Lettow-Vorbeck continued to escape his pursuers, first slipping over the border into Portuguese East Africa and then Northern Rhodesia, where he learned of the Armistice in Europe and surrendered his forces on 25 November 1918.

RIGHT A fez belonging to a German colonial Askari.

The landing at Tanga

Major-General Arthur Aitken was the original commander of the IEF (Indian Expeditionary Force) sent to East Africa and he was tasked with the initial British assault of the campaign, the seaborne attack on the German port of Tanga. His forces consisted of two Indian and one British infantry brigades, while the German defenders consisted of a single company of native troops, though the German commander von Lettow-Vorbeck with around 1,000 men rapidly reinforced this force. The British force landed on 3 November 1914 and, as Major-General Aitken relates:

"Up to this it had been clearly proved that so far from Tanga not being held, or only being lightly held, it was very strongly prepared for defence with a very adequate force to hold it. Every house had been prepared for defence with two, three, and even four tiers of fire and plenty of machine guns. There was also a railway cutting just in front of the town which was completely enfiladed by machine guns and rifle fire.

In spite of all this I am absolutely certain that had the whole of my force consisted of reliable troops, or had the bad units put up any resemblance of a fight, we should have captured Tanga and been able to hold it."

Unfortunately his troops could not hold it and the Indian forces broke and ran. The whole force had to be re-embarked and shipped back to Kenya, leaving behind rifles, machine guns and over 600,000 rounds of ammunition, which proved invaluable to von Lettow-Vorbeck's campaign.

RIGHT A patrol of the 4th Battalion The King's African Rifles regroups after a fight in the bush. A wounded German Askari lies in the foreground. c.1914.

BELOW General Paul von Lettow-Vorbeck, second from right, 1916.

THE BATTLE OF MESSINES RIDGE

Following hard on the heels of the disappointing outcome to the Arras offensive came Haig's offensive in Flanders. This offensive was split into two distinct phases: the first was an attack on the Wytschaete–Messines Ridge, and the second, which was to start a few weeks later, was aimed at taking the Passchendaele Ridge. Collectively these actions are known as the Third Battle of Ypres.

The first part of this two-pronged operation was entrusted to the Second Army of the BEF commanded by General Sir Hebert Plumer. He had started to plan an operation in the Messines area in 1916 by ordering the digging of tunnels under the German lines, into which enormous land mines were to be placed. Plumer took this meticulous attitude towards planning into every detail of the operation, which included the construction of an enormous scale model of the ridge. A methodical artillery bombardment began on 21 May designed to crush the German depth defences. The attack started at dawn on 7 June 1917 following the detonation of 19 (out of 22) enormous mines that had been dug beneath the German lines. These decimated the front-line defenders, killing as many as 10,000 of them, and the initial British assaults went smoothly, achieving all of the admittedly limited objectives within three hours. The initial German counter-attack launched on the 8th was beaten back with heavy losses.

Blowing the mines

Private V. E. Fagence, a Lewis gunner with the 11th Battalion The Queen's Royal Regiment (West Surrey), 123rd Brigade, 41st Division, describes the opening of the battle at Messines Ridge on 7 June 1917:

"Zero hour (3.10 a.m. 7th June) arrived and the comparative quiet that had previously reigned, was broken by the noise of a 15-inch gun a few miles to the rear of us firing a single shell. This seemed to be the signal for nineteen huge land-mines (which had been placed under the enemy lines), to be exploded with a shattering roar, and with the earth shaking as in an earthquake. Simultaneously with this, at the back of us, about a thousand guns of all calibres from 15-inch down to 18-pounders, opened up and with the reports from these and the explosions of the shells bursting on the enemy positions in front the noise was pandemonium."

The attack was a complete success and the battalion only suffered 198 casualties, light numbers for a set-piece attack of this magnitude. There were actually 22 land-mines in all in tunnels dug under the German lines. Nineteen exploded, as described above, causing a shock wave felt as far as London; one was discovered and neutralized by the Germans; one exploded in 1955 following a lightning strike; whilst one remains unexploded (and its location unknown) to this day.

Commenting on the mines the night before the battle, General Sir Hebert Plumer said to his staff: "Gentlemen, we may not make history tomorrow, but we shall certainly change the geography."

LEFT German prisoners taken in the Battle of Messines Ridge, 8 June 1917.

RIGHT *The RAMC at Messines during the 1917 Offensive*, by Gilbert Rogers, MBE. Two medical orderlies carry a wounded man on a stretcher through a trench. Another two orderlies attend to a wounded man at the top of the trench wall.

Further German counter-attacks continued until the 14th, but failed to win back any of the lost ground. The Battle of Messines Ridge stands as the pre-eminent example of how an attack was conducted with a limited objective during the First World War, and was also the first occasion in the war in which the Allied attacking force lost fewer men than the German defenders (10,000 compared to 25,000).

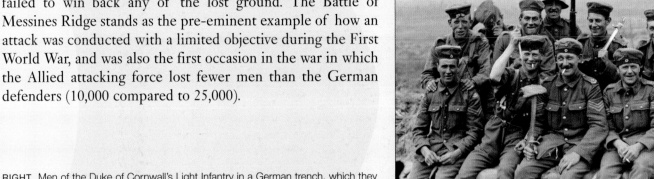

RIGHT Men of the Duke of Cornwall's Light Infantry in a German trench, which they have captured, sporting a German helmet, caps and other spoils of war.

THE THIRD BATTLE OF YPRES

Following the success at Messines Ridge, Haig launched the northern part of his Flanders offensive on 31 July with a series of separate actions known collectively as the Third Battle of Ypres. Gough's Fifth Army took the principal part in the early offensives to the north of Ypres in the Battles of Pilckem Ridge, Gheluvelt and Langemarck. The ten-day bombardment prior to the assault had the dual effect of forewarning the German defenders of the forthcoming offensive and churning up the ground in the salient, making both offensive movement and the extraction of casualties extremely difficult. Despite some initial success, such as the capture of Pilckem Ridge, Gough's Fifth Army became bogged down and, towards the end of August, Haig decided to try again with Plumer's Second Army. Having prepared his men and plans for three weeks, Plumer launched a series of attacks against the Menin Road Ridge and Polygon Wood, culminating in the Battle of Broodseinde from 4 October, which finally drove the German defenders from Polygon Wood. At this point the weather once again intervened, with heavy rain making the battlefield impassable.

Haig was still determined to push on and launched his final set of offensives, aimed at securing Passchendaele Ridge, on 12 October. On 6 November, Canadian troops finally captured the village of Passchendaele, thus ending the battle. Over 250,000 men had died on each side in conditions that have since become a byword for the suffering endured by the front-line infantryman in the First World War.

Slaughter in the mud

The night before the start of the Third Battle of Ypres, 20 July 1917, Gunner Heraty was selected as one of a party of 24 gunners who were to follow the infantry after the main assault and construct a new battery in the captured positions:

"The time was now 3.45 a.m., 31st July, and our officer said 'Now lads you can creep up to the surface' ... We had no sooner popped our heads up when we saw two gun flashes and in seconds the whole sky was lit up behind us and the thunder of guns firing was terrific. I had never seen or heard anything like it before in my life. I had been in the battle of Ypres and the battle of the Somme but this was greater than any of the above and as far as one could see for miles the whole front was lit up.

"Well we were now struggling through the shell holes and the black mud which stuck to us like glue, until we reached a point near to where our first line trenches used to be before the attack opened out. Our officer decided that our new gun position was to be at this spot, so each gun place was marked off and it was now hard graft with gun, spades and trenching tools, filling sand bags, with tunics and shirts off and the rain coming down like hell,

BELOW A silhouetted file of men of the 8th Battalion The East Yorkshire Regiment, going up to the line near Frezenberg.

and a thick mist covering the ground like a November morning.

"We commenced to build a double row of sand bags to form a gun pit and a certain amount of protection from shell fire, which we were getting plenty of at the time being, and we could see the sappers and engineers laying 'Duck boards' and plank roads along the shell shattered roads and fields which became the only places you could move along, for if you slipped off into the mud you were doomed. Jerry was shelling us with his 5.9 Howitzers, and as they landed among parties of infantry men and sappers working on the duck boards, arms and legs flew into the air like lumps of mud. If any-one had told us before the war that we should have witnessed such slaughter and loss of life and still kept our sanity I would have told them they were talking a load of 'Bull Shit'."

LEFT Stretcher-bearers, struggling in mud up to their knees, carry a wounded man to safety near Boesinghe on 1 August.

BELOW
The Battlefield of Ypres, by Sir D. Y. Cameron, RA, RSA. A view across the desolate battlefield of Ypres. Small islands of mud surround flooded bomb craters.

83

ENGINEERS

The advent of positional warfare and the entrenchment of armies towards the end of 1914 ensured a pivotal role for the men of the Royal Engineers. At the outbreak of the war the Corps of Royal Engineers consisted of just over 25,000 men; one year later the number stood at just over 126,000, while by the end of the war the Corps numbered nearly 315,000 officers and men. As a proportion of the BEF the Royal Engineers made up nearly 12 per cent in November 1918. In August 1914 it had been 6 per cent.

The first major responsibility for the Royal Engineers was in the traditional realm of military engineering. The field and fortress companies attached to the divisions, corps and armies of the BEF carried out this role. The field companies built and improved roads and bridges, dug field positions, strengthened captured positions and generally carried out the standard military engineering works required by infantry units. Fortress companies carried out a similar role, but were also trained in all aspects necessary to man fixed permanent fortifications. On the Western Front they were used to maintain the secondary positions that lay behind the front lines, which included a line of defence, as well as storage facilities, gun emplacements, workshops, observation posts, aeroplane hangars and water-supply systems. Throughout the course of the war Royal Engineers also took on responsibility for gas warfare, mining and tunnelling, not to mention being heavily involved in the development of new weapons such as the Stokes mortar and the tank.

The other major responsibility that the Royal Engineers had during the First World War was for signalling and communications in general, later transferred to the Royal Corps of Signals. Their methods included wireless and cable telegraphy, voice telephone, motorcycle and mounted dispatch riders, semaphore and carrier pigeons. At no time was communication more difficult, or more vital, than when an attack was underway. Major Owen Morshead, RE, was awarded the Distinguished Service Order during the Battle of Broodseinde, one of the few success stories of Third Ypres. The *London Gazette* citation noted his "conspicuous gallantry and devotion to duty in making his way forward with a supply of pigeons to clear up a situation and sending back clear information. He also conveyed important orders to the leading battalion. It is impossible to speak too highly of his conduct."

Major Morshead himself describes the events of the morning:

"Our great attack was launched at 5.50 am, and was uniformly successful along our front and that of all the divisions operating to the north of us ... The situation being very obscure at noon, I was sent forward to ascertain and report, so I issued from the ark with an orderly and a pair of pigeons, and made my way across a pestilential waste to the Butt, and thence despatched my doves, which duly arrived. I found the situation quite well in hand, and remained up there co-ordinating the work of the battalions."

BELOW *Sappers at Work: Canadian Tunnelling Company, R14, St Eloi*, by David Bomberg. An intense scene of sappers from the Royal Canadian Engineers constructing a tunnel. The men are digging, moving earth and using pulleys and levers to erect support timbers on the interior.

ABOVE Royal Engineer motorcyclists prepare to set out on their bikes with baskets on their backs, 2 June 1918. The baskets each contained four pigeon compartments and were used to transport pigeons from the breeding lofts at Sorrus to the line.

ABOVE A group of Royal Engineers at work on a light railway line near Boesinghe.

BELOW *Road Menders* by Adrian Hill. Eight sappers moving across an empty landscape. They walk over muddy and flooded terrain. Each carries a ladder to be used as a duckboard.

THE THIRD BATTLE OF GAZA

Following the failure of the first two battles of Gaza, the new commander of the Egyptian Expeditionary Force, General Sir Edmund Allenby, decided to try a different approach. His force had been heavily reinforced and he now possessed three corps: the Desert Mounted Corps, which contained the Australian Mounted, ANZAC Mounted and Yeomanry Divisions; XX Corps with four infantry divisions; and XXI Corps with three infantry divisions. Allenby decided to concentrate his cavalry against Beersheba, while XXI Corps made a feint frontal attack against the Gaza positions; once Beersheba fell XX Corps would roll up the Turkish defences. In the event, this plan worked better than all expectations. Not only did Beersheba fall to an assault by the Australian and ANZAC Mounted Divisions on 31 October 1917, but the diversionary attack at Gaza, supported by a force of eight tanks, broke through the Turkish lines and forced them into a retreat on 1 November. Allenby immediately launched an aggressive pursuit in an attempt to cut off the Turkish Army in southern Palestine. However, delaying actions at Huj and El Maghar, though beaten back by Yeomanry attacks, served to delay Allenby enough to allow the bulk of the Turkish Army to withdraw. The Turks withdrew from Jerusalem on 9 December and Jaffa fell to XXI Corps on 16 December. The offensive cost 18,000 Allied and 25,000 Turkish casualties.

The fall of Jerusalem

J. Wilson was part of the 179th Company, Machine Gun Corps (part of the 60th Division), and was sent up the line on 12 November 1917 as a replacement, arriving before Jerusalem on Sunday 9 December:

"In the afternoon we again moved forward along the road that had been the previous day's fighting line. A little way along the road we came upon a ghastly sight. Three Turkish field guns and their ammunition wagons had been caught by our rifle fire and then shelled by the Turks to prevent our using them.

Men, mules and guns were lying all over the road just as they had fallen. I noticed one poor animal with its head and forelegs blown away, I should not have liked to have seen that sight; the remains of it were fearful enough.

"But even as we passed this ghastly mess, away in front of us Jerusalem stood in sight. And so it is also, that in all the ghastly blunderings and bloody tragedies of our poor human story, there is always in front of us, clear and plain beyond the wreckage of our lives, the view of a City of God, which all the

wreckage is only the outcome of our blundering eagerness to attain.

"We entered Jerusalem about 4 o'clock, our Division being the first within the city. The people received us with a heartiness quieted by a real sense of the greatness of the event. They did not shout much, but on their faces there was a great welcome. The departing Turks had looted them as thoroughly as haste would permit, so it is not exactly surprising that their affection for us should be very fresh and strong."

The crisis developing on the Western Front meant that Allenby would not have the manpower to undertake any more offensives until late 1918.

FAR RIGHT A direction sign indicating the way to Jerusalem.

RIGHT General Allenby's formal entry on foot into Jerusalem. The leading figure is that of Borton Pasha, the British Military Governor of the city, followed by his two aides de camp. Further behind, reading from left to right are Colonel de Piepape, commanding the French Detachment, General Allenby, whose head is visible between the shoulders of the officers preceding him, and Lieutenant-Colonel D'Agostino, commanding the Italian Detachment.

LEFT *The Camel Corps. A Night March to Beersheba*, by James McBey. A column of soldiers on camels rides through the desert at night.

DEVELOPMENT OF THE TANK

From the beginning of the stalemate of trench warfare on the Western Front, all sides sought a breakthrough weapon to transform the situation, and the British came up with the "tank". One of the first spurs towards its development came from Winston Churchill in his role as First Lord of the Admiralty who, after witnessing the demonstration of a tracked vehicle in June 1915, formed the Landships Committee to investigate the potential of the weapon. The name "tank" was adopted as a codename to disguise the project's true intention. The first prototype, "Little Willie", was produced under the direction of Colonel Swinton of the Royal Engineers. He established that the vehicle should have a minimum speed of four miles per hour, be able to climb a five-foot high obstacle, successfully span a five-foot trench, and be immune to the effects of small-arms fire. Although "Little Willie" did not meet these requirements its successor, "Big Willie" (also called "Mother"), proved more successful and formed the basis for the Mark I tank that went into production in January 1916. Two variants were produced, a "male" version fitted with 6-pounder guns and "female" versions armed only with machine guns.

LEFT A British Army steel helmet (with chain-mail visor) as worn by tank crews.

ABOVE The Reverend C. Lomax served as a chaplain with the 151st Infantry Brigade and witnessed one of the very early tank attacks: "The tanks were a great success. I did not see them in action, but our men were full of them. They certainly put the wind up the Bosch. His favourite strong places were as nothing and they crossed trenches with ease. An R.A.M.C. man said to an upstanding wounded German who knew the vernacular 'Well, we've got you properly beat this time'. The reply was 'What can you expect, when you come over in bloody taxis'."

ABOVE A Mark I tank (C19, "Clan Leslie") at Chimpanzee Valley. The original caption states that tanks first went into action on this day, 15 September 1916.

INSET The cap badge of the Machine Gun Corps.

The new machine needed a new unit to man it and, in keeping with the aura of secrecy that surrounded the development of the new weapon, the new unit received a name that did not reflect its actual role. Instead it was known as "Heavy Branch" of the Machine Gun Corps. This secrecy extended to not telling new recruits what was involved. J. K. Wilson was originally in the 1/14th (County of London) Battalion The London Regiment (London Scottish) before being commissioned into the Heavy Branch:

"We were sent home to be kitted out as 2nd Lieutenant Machine Gun Corps, Heavy Branch and as we were mounted riding boots with spurs.

"Our instructions were to travel from Waterloo to Wool and report to Bovington Camp in Dorset. About a dozen or so met at Waterloo, all looking very spruce, and in due course reported to the Camp Commandant only to find ourselves in the Tank Corps, booted and spurred, such was the secrecy of the new arm."

Officers and men worked side by side under extreme conditions in the new tanks, and these circumstances inspired a collective approach that would certainly have been out of tune with the pre-war British Army, as J. K. Wilson recognized:

"To be a successful tank officer one had to have or cultivate the common touch, you lived so close to your men it was more communal than other commissions.

"Minor breaches of discipline would have to be condoned that would not be tolerated in the Infantry. Officers' Messes were much larger and their servants or batmen would do the waiting on. I remember one voracious young officer diving too deeply into the tureen of vegetables being rebuked by one florid faced cockney butcher with: 'Hi, go easy with them greens.' I wonder what would have happened to him in the Guards."

The first tanks went into action on 15 September 1916 at Flers-Courcelette during the Battles of the Somme, ushering in a new era of armoured warfare.

THE BATTLE OF CAMBRAI

Although the Third Battle of Ypres had descended into a bloodbath in a quagmire, there was still one more British assault in 1917: the Battle of Cambrai.

Cambrai saw the first use of massed armour and was originally planned by the chief of staff of the Tank Corps, Colonel J. F. C. Fuller, as a showcase for tanks whose tactical potential had hitherto been squandered by lack of concentration or unsuitable terrain.

Taken up by General Sir Julian Byng, the plan evolved into an Army-level offensive supported by 376 tanks, with the seven divisions of III and IV Corps aiming to break the German defences of the Hindenburg Line, with the Cavalry Corps standing by to exploit any success.

The attack began at dawn on 20 November 1917 and by 1130hrs all the initial objectives had been taken bar one, with gains of up to six miles. The second day saw the lines consolidated, but further British attacks up to the 27th gained little more.

On 30 November the Germans counter-attacked, regaining much of the land the British had taken. Byng managed to shore up the British line and, on 4 December, Third Army withdrew to a defensive position that closely matched its start line of the 20th. Although the battle ended in stalemate, it heralded the arrival of the tank as a weapon capable of breaking the impasse of the Western Front, a role it would assume throughout 1918.

ABOVE An aerial view of Bourlon Wood, part of the Cambrai battlefield.

Dawn of an armoured age

Captain J. K. Wilson was originally a private in the London Scottish before being commissioned into the Heavy Branch of the Machine Gun Corps and posted to the 26th Company, 9th Battalion The Tank Corps. He served in the battle of Cambrai, where he was wounded in the face:

"Field Marshal Haig was first and foremost a cavalryman and until the first day of that battle ended he had always hoped to employ his cavalry en masse in a major engagement. With this hope in view he placed five divisions under one commander with the object of pushing them through the gap if the early morning tank attack proved successful.

"Some half dozen tanks had been used singly on Sept. 15 1916, during a major battle on the Somme, but they were not a conspicuous success. They were not used again until November 1917, at the Battle of Cambrai.

BELOW A Mark IV ("male") tank of H Battalion held up in the German second line at the side of the road, one mile west of Ribecourt. Some men of the 1st Battalion The Leicestershire Regiment rest in the trench.

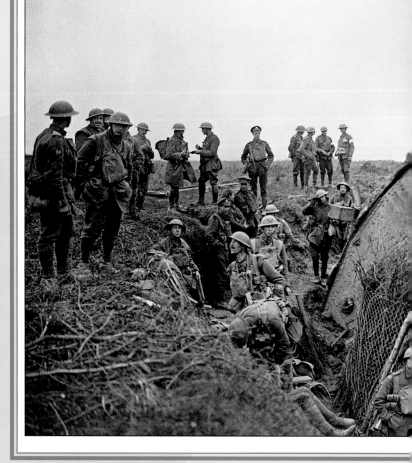

"On this occasion a large number in close formation, profiting by a misty dawn, charged the German position on a front of a mile or more. Never was there a greater success. The enemy line collapsed in width and depth: front-line, supports and reserves were completely surprised and over-run. For once the Germans ran like rabbits, leaving intact more than one bridge over the canal.

"Behind the tanks came three infantry divisions, and behind the infantry stood five splendid divisions of cavalry, the cream of the British Army, superbly mounted and as keen as mustard, with nothing between them and Cambrai but a demoralized enemy.

"At one of the bridgeheads a fuming cavalry brigadier was asked by a general staff officer of an infantry division who had crossed and recrossed the bridge himself, when the cavalry was going to advance. The angry brigadier replied: 'Not until I get orders from corps in writing – I am not allowed to advance a yard'.

"Orders to advance never came out and the finest force of British cavalry ever assembled returned in the evening to its billets in the back area. There was no pursuit, the infantry were exhausted and too slow, and the tanks could not do it alone, so the Germans were given time to regain their morale."

BELOW A British Mark IV tank at Wailly. This shows how it would have appeared to occupants of the German trenches during the Battle of Cambrai. This was the first occasion on which tanks were launched en masse in a surprise attack and it clearly demonstrated the potential of the armoured vehicle.

1918

THE GERMAN OFFENSIVE

The collapse of Russia meant that the German commander, General Erich von Ludendorff, would finally be able to have numerical superiority on the Western Front. He planned a major offensive for the spring of 1918 to break the Allied lines decisively before the Americans, who had joined the Allied side in 1917, could move a substantial number of troops across the Atlantic.

Ludendorff hoped to exploit the rifts he saw emerging between the Allied armies, driving a wedge between the French and British forces, whilst simultaneously severing Allied rail communications with the northern front.

Kaiserschlacht – the Emperor's battle – opened with Operation *Michael* on 21 March with the German Seventeenth, Eighteenth and Second Armies lined up against British Third and Fifth Armies. Sixty-five German divisions launched a five-hour artillery assault until, under partial cover of gas and smoke and with the misty conditions on their side, the troops advanced across the 60-mile front.

Gough's Fifth Army soon collapsed, exposing Third Army's flank and forcing it to withdraw, abandoning Peronne and the Cambrai Salient that had been fought so hard for the previous year. The German Eighteenth Army drove the shattered remnants of Third Army headlong across the Somme before British and French units were able to plug the gap. Paris itself came under fire on 25 March, and the following day Foch was nominated Allied Commander. He would become official Commander-in-Chief of all Allied forces in France on 3 April.

With the momentum of the German advance beginning to ebb away Operation *Michael* was closed down on 5 April for the loss of 163,000 British, 77,000 French and 250,00 German casualties. Immediately, a second offensive was launched in Flanders, Operation *Georgette*. On 9 April Horne's First Army came under severe assault by the German Sixth Army while Plumer's Second Army lost almost all the ground won at Third Ypres the year before. Despite these setbacks, with French assistance the British line stabilized and the German offensive ended on 29 April without achieving the desired decisive breakthrough.

Ludendorff attempted three further offensives from May to July: *Blücher-Yorck*, *Gneisenau* and *Friedensturm*. These assaults were aimed at the French line south of the British. The Germans managed to reach Chateau Thierry and the Marne, but again failed to break the line decisively.

Kaiserschlacht

Private Frank Cooper of the 5th Battalion The Oxfordshire and Buckinghamshire Light infantry was in the front line when the great German attack started:

"On 21st March, at 4.30am, the Germans opened out on about 50 miles of our front line. It was one of the largest bombardments in the Great War, with 5.9-inch German guns and 6-inch shells. You knew approximately where they were going to fall, and you took cover if you could. With the German 77mm gun, which we called 'whizz bangs', the safest place was well down in the trench, but the soldier who was on look out didn't have a chance. The high velocity shells were impossible to dodge. I was near to one soldier when one of these high velocity shells came over and burst just above his head. It caught him and the wounds were all over his body. He died of the wounds ...

"We had lost our front and support trenches and now the fighting was in the open. The first few days we were retiring fairly well, keeping in touch and the line not broken, but we had casualties all the time, killed and wounded. We had 106 divisions against us ... and we had lost most of our Officers and our soldiers too. Our ranks were very thin indeed."

ABOVE *Waiting for the German Offensive: An advanced machine-gun post on the Broodseinde Road, Ypres Sector, March 1918*, by Adrian Hill.

LEFT Men of the 51st Division in a hastily dug trench in a ploughed field, 10 April 1918. One soldier sleeps beneath a patterned blanket, the others have their equipment scattered around them.

RIGHT The Lewis gun was the brain child of US Army officer Colonel Isaac Newton Lewis. It was a light machine gun operated by gas tapped from the barrel at the moment of firing. The barrel was cooled by a patent system of aluminium fins within a jacket. The muzzle blast of the gun was supposed to draw air through the jacket and over the fins. It was this apparatus that gave the gun its distinctive shape.

THE ROYAL FLYING CORPS

As late as 1907 no heavier-than-air flying machine existed in Great Britain, so for such a formation as the Royal Flying Corps (RFC) to exist only five years later was a considerable achievement. It was created in 1912 as a replacement for the Air Battalion of the Royal Engineers and operated balloons as well as aircraft.

By the time of the mobilization of the BEF in August 1914, the RFC had a strength of around 64 operational aeroplanes in seven different squadrons. Four of these, Nos. 2, 3, 4, and 5 (No. 1 was a balloon squadron), accompanied the BEF to France with a further seven following by mid 1915. These squadrons were initially divided into wings of three or four squadrons, with each wing supporting an army.

The aircraft of the RFC were designed for reconnaissance and communication, but within days the pilots and observers had equipped themselves with a variety of weapons and, gradually, different specializations evolved: air-to-air combat, aerial bombing, artillery observation and reconnaissance. The organization of the Corps reflected these developments and, on 30 January 1916, a "brigade, Royal Flying Corps" was established in each field army consisting of two wings. One of the wings was assigned to support the troops at a corps level, while the other was used at an army level for air superiority and bombing missions. Other wings were assigned directly to the General Headquarters of the British Expeditionary Force.

When originally formed, the RFC consisted of two distinct Naval and Military Wings and, with the support and encouragement of the First Lord of the Admiralty, Winston Churchill, the Naval Wing finally became the separate Royal Naval Air Service in July 1914. This branch of the Royal Navy focused more on the long-range offensive potential of the aircraft and developed the first British strategic bomber, the Handley Page 0/100. It also pioneered the use of aircraft aboard ship, with the first successful landing on the deck of a ship taking place in August 1917.

In the summer of 1917, Jan Smuts recommended the formation of a new aerial service independent of the Army and the Royal Navy. This was proposed because of the present and future potential significance of air power. The proposal also had the added benefit of making the 67,000 officers and men of the RNAS available for service on the Western Front. An Air Force and Air Council were established by an Act of Parliament on 29 November 1917 and, on 1 April 1918, the RFC and the RNAS were amalgamated to form the Royal Air Force. One of its first actions as an independent force was in support of the Battle of Amiens, where it played a major role in suppressing the German defences and achieving operational surprise for the offensive. By the end of the war the RAF was the largest air force of all the combatant powers, consisting of over 4,000 aircraft and 114,000 men.

LEFT Sopwith F1 Camel, single-seat scout. One of the most successful aircraft used by the Royal Flying Corps.

BELOW The Mk I flying mask.

ABOVE With aircraft came anti-aircraft fire, as illustrated here in the diary of the Reverend C. Lomax.

RIGHT The distinctive pattern of tunic was first introduced in 1912 and known as the "maternity" jacket. Although the RFC originated from the Royal Engineer Balloon Sections, the ethos of the new corps may be summarized as owing much to the idea of a "Cavalry of the Air". The pattern of tunic worn by other ranks and those officers commissioned into the RFC bears more than a passing resemblance to the so-called "Lancer" tunics worn by officers and men in cavalry regiments.

ABOVE Lieutenant (Temporary Captain) Albert Ball, VC DSO** MC (1896–1917), 7th Battalion The Sherwood Foresters (Nottinghamshire and Derbyshire Regiment) and Royal Flying Corps. Albert Ball, one of the most famous of the First World War flying "aces", was born in Nottingham. He enlisted as a private in the 2/7th Battalion The Sherwood Foresters in September 1914. He learned to fly in 1915 and transferred to the Royal Flying Corps early in 1916. From May 1916, first with No. 11 Squadron and then with No. 60 Squadron, he established himself as one of the RFC's outstanding fighter pilots, winning the Military Cross in June. By October he had been awarded the Distinguished Service Order and bar and was credited with 30 victories. Already a national hero, he was awarded a second bar to his DSO in November 1916, making him the first triple DSO in the British Army. Ball joined No. 56 Squadron as a flight commander on 7 April 1917, soon increasing his official score to 44 victories. On 7 May he failed to return from a patrol. Though he was last seen in combat with an Albatross DIII piloted by Lothar von Richthofen, brother of the famous "Red Baron", the exact cause of Ball's death remains a mystery. He was awarded a posthumous Victoria Cross in June 1917. Ball is buried in Annoeullin Communal Cemetery, France.

THE BATTLE OF AMIENS

By the summer of 1918 the strategic balance had swung very much in the favour of the Allies, and it was their turn to mount a major offensive. Haig, with the approval of Foch, favoured an assault by Rawlinson's Fourth Army, supported by the French First Army, to push back the German Second and Eighteenth Armies that threatened the vital railway junction of Amiens.

Having disguised his intentions through a variety of deception measures, Rawlinson launched his attack at dawn on 8 August 1918. A combination of a thick mist and lack of artillery registration ensured that the opening barrage fell on German positions that were taken completely unaware. The infantry of the Fourth Army, ably supported by tanks and protected by an effective creeping barrage, advanced for five miles across a front of 12 miles, inflicting 27,000 casualties in the process.

The battle extended southwards on 9 August with a French assault. Ludendorff sanctioned the withdrawal of the German Eighteenth Army, now threatened with envelopment between the British in the north and the French in the south.

Later assaults between the 9th and the 11th failed to match the successes of the first two days, and the battle ended on 11 August partly because of the exhaustion of the troops involved. The cost had been high with the British suffering losses of around 22,000 against German 75,000 casualties.

Breaking the Hindenburg Line

Private V. E. Fagence of the 11th Battalion The Queen's Royal Regiment (West Surrey) took part on the assault on the Hindenburg Line in September 1918:

"Shortly before Zero hour, which was fixed for 5.40 am, Lieutenant Whittaker and Sgt Randall [respectively platoon officer and sergeant] came round with the rum jar and gave us each our ration, which was very welcome as the night had been rather cold. That was the last time we were to see them alive. Zero hour arrived and our artillery fire commenced, augmented by overhead covering fire by the machine guns of the MGC. I remember feeling quite exhilarated by the thought of once more being in an attacking role, instead of the defending one to which we had necessarily been assigned, for the past five months. Also there was the prospect that the war was coming to an end, and perhaps after a few more battles (provided that we were fortunate enough to come through each of them without being killed or wounded), we would be going home. But this feeling soon ended."

Once through the much-vaunted defensive line, the fighting broke out into the open, a new experience for those who had spent the previous four years embraced in the deadlock of trench warfare. Private Fagence relates his feelings on fighting in open country around Clary and Bertry on 9 October 1918:

"When it was light enough for us to see we found that we were now in inhabited country with people living in the houses, but not showing much of themselves as the territory had been occupied by the Germans until only a few hours previously. It was strange to see green fields and meadows, and trees with leaves on them, and houses undamaged and with glass in the windows, after the desolated acres which we had been used to for the last six months. In fact for a short time it was almost like being in fairyland. But we were soon to be fetched up sharp by realities."

The first day of the Battle of Amiens was described by Ludendorff as "the Black Day of the German Army", less because of the material losses suffered by the Germans, but more because of the attitude shown by the troops, some of whom were reported to have abused reinforcements as "strike breakers".

RIGHT British infantry, artillery and tanks waiting for the second stage of the attack.

LEFT A crowd of German soldiers taken prisoner by the Fourth Army in the Battle of Amiens.

RIGHT *A Mark V Tank Going Into Action*, by Bernard Adeney. The successful combination of armour, infantry and artillery defined the final campaigns of the British Army in the First World War.

THE BATTLE OF MEGIDDO

In early 1918, General Sir Edmund Allenby had been compelled to send large numbers of his troops to the Western Front to help stem the tide of the German spring offensive, though he retained the Desert Mounted Corps that had served him so well in the battle for Gaza. By the start of September 1918 Allenby's forces had been reinforced, largely by troops of the Indian Army and he could now field the Desert Mounted Corps with three divisions, XX Corps with two infantry divisions and XXI Corps with five infantry divisions. In additions he was supported by a mobile corps-sized force of cavalry and infantry known as Chaytor Force and Arab irregulars that had been fighting in the Hejaz. Against this the Turks had three armies in the Yilderim Army Group under the command of the German general Liman von Sanders, with the Eighth Army holding the coast, the Seventh the territory up to the Jordan Valley, and the Fourth the Transjordan and the desert flank. Allenby planned to destroy the Turks by pushing his main force through by the coast and then encircling the Turkish troops with his cavalry. Having deceived the Turks into believing that his main effort was coming in the Jordan Valley, Allenby launched his coastal attack with XXI Corps on 19 September and immediately broke the Turkish lines, pushing them back in headlong retreat. With the aircraft of the RAF destroying the Turkish rear area communications, Allenby's cavalry crossed the River Jordan on 20 September and the Turkish position collapsed. Damascus fell on 1 October to Allenby and the Arab irregulars with Lawrence, followed by Beirut on the 7th. The Turks sought an armistice, which was agreed on 30 October taking Turkey out of the war.

The fall of Turkey

Private J. Wilson of the 179th Company Machine Gun Corps (part of the 60th Division) took part in the advance through Palestine and the climactic battle of Megiddo, and recorded his thoughts in his diary:

Thursday, September 26th.
"So rapidly has the situation developed, and so completely has the appearance of the campaign changed, that it seems impossible

ABOVE Men of the 2nd Battalion The Black Watch, in a trench on Brown Ridge after the action at Arsuf on 8 June 1918.

LEFT Australian members of the Imperial Camel Corps near Jaffa in Palestine prepare to mount.

even now that only a week has passed since our first attack. A week ago we were still marking time on the line we had held throughout the summer; and now, by one swift and sure blow, the Land of Christ is ours for the trouble of walking over; and the enemies' forces have probably ceased to exist, though the gladdest stories we hear are not official.

"By the time it was light [on Friday 27 September 1918] we reached Tul Keram, the Turk's chief railway centre in this district and an Army Headquarters. Here we first heard news of our operations: that the Australian cavalry had captured Tul Keram the previous morning, that twelve thousand prisoners and thirty guns had been taken, and that the victory bade fair to be the greatest yet achieved out here."

BELOW *Charge of the Second Lancers at El Afuli in the Valley of Armageddon,* by Thomas Cantrell Dugdale.

THE CAVALRY

Although the Battle of Megiddo proved to a be an ideal hunting ground for the mounted formations of the Egyptian Expeditionary Force, in general the First World War as a whole proved a frustrating experience for the cavalry units of the British Army.

At the beginning of the war three types of mounted unit existed in the British Army: Regular cavalry regiments, Territorial Yeomanry regiments and Special Reserve horse regiments. The mounted unit that accompanied the original BEF was the 1st Cavalry Division, which was later joined by the independent 5th Cavalry Brigade, which became the 2nd Cavalry Division. These units took part in the early mobile battles of the BEF and carried out their true cavalry role in actions such as the charge of the 12th Lancers at Cérizy on 28 August 1914. There, the German infantry were caught in the open and cut down. Following the onset of trench warfare the newly formed mounted divisions were either shipped overseas or used in the infantry role as dismounted cavalry. In fact, at the end of 1915, the General Headquarters of the Expeditionary Force created the largest force of dismounted cavalry yet to be seen on the Western Front by temporarily converting a very large portion of the Cavalry Corps into the Dismounted Cavalry Division. In order to make this new formation possible, the three component divisions of the Cavalry Corps – the 1st, 2nd and 3rd Cavalry Divisions – each formed a dismounted cavalry brigade.

BELOW The Pattern 1908 cavalry sword was the last sword design accepted for service in the British Army. The design had its origins in complaints received about the effectiveness of existing swords during the Boer War. A committee was set up to select an improved pattern. The outcome was revolutionary in concept, as it featured a thin, tapering blade, intended entirely for thrusting. The sword was superbly designed, having perfect balance in the hand and an unusual "pistol" type grip, which automatically brought the sword into thrusting position when correctly gripped. The sword proved successful in the mounted actions in which it was employed during the First World War.

LEFT *Shoeing under Difficulties, the Jordan Valley*, by Thomas Cantrell Dugdale.

Trooper William Clarke of 2nd Dragoon Guards (The Queen's Bays) served in the cavalry throughout the war, and remembered his experiences as a dismounted cavalryman:

"There was never a chance to use cavalry as it was intended – and for a couple of times when the chance was there, the advantage was never taken so for most of the war we were used as infantry – in the trenches, the horses being looked after well back from the front line. We only used them on long marches, mostly at night, passing through devastated villages unknown to us by name ... We were often hungry, and so were the mules and horses and how those poor creatures suffered. I think they must have been more tired

and out of condition than we were. Innocent victims of man-made madness. They broke your heart, especially when you passed the injured ones, left to die, in agony and screaming with pain and terror."

The cavalry divisions of the BEF spent most of the middle years of the war waiting in reserve in order to exploit the elusive breakthrough. It was only with the resumption of mobile warfare following the summer of 1918 that British cavalry could resume its traditional role.

Private V. E. Fagence, of the 11th Battalion The Queen's Royal Regiment (West Surrey), witnessed cavalry being used offensively in the open during the latter stages of the war:

ABOVE When the stalemate on the Western Front finally ended in 1918, the Allied cavalry resumed the offensive, pursuing and attacking the retreating German forces. Canadian cavalry are shown here passing through newly captured country near Cherisy.

"Whilst we were there, I saw for the first and only time in my life, British cavalry going into action. They were on our left, between us and the village. They had come from somewhere at the rear, and were cantering towards the village of Bertry, some distance ahead. It was a fine sight to see them, squadron after squadron and regiment after regiment. There must have been at least two to three thousand horsemen."

THE WAR IN ITALY

Italy entered the war on the side of the Allies on 24 May 1915 and immediately advanced into Austrian territory on the Trentino, Alpine and Isonzo fronts. On 23 June the First Battle of the Isonzo started, which became an attritional affair characteristic of the 11 battles of the same name that were to follow throughout 1915, 1916 and 1917. British reinforcements to the Italians initially came in the form of heavy artillery batteries, which proved influential in reducing Austrian positions and, by August 1917 it appeared that the Italians were on the point of a decisive breakthrough. However, the Germans reinforced the Austrians with significant quantities of troops and artillery and the 12th Battle of the Isonzo,

otherwise known as Caporetto, proved to be a disaster for the Italians who were pushed right back by the German offensive on 20 October 1917. By the time the rout stopped on the line of the River Piave on 7 November, the Italians had lost 10,000 killed, 30,000 wounded and 265,000 captured.

The two immediate results of this colossal defeat were the decision to create a unified command for the Allied forces and the dispatch of British and French forces to bolster the Italian Front. XIV Corps, consisting of the 23rd and 41st Divisions under the Earl of Cavan, arrived on 11 November 1917 and the 5th, 7th and 48th Divisions followed later, along with General Sir Hebert Plumer who assumed command.

Fighting in the mountains

Gunner Heraty served in an 18-pounder battery, part of the 241st Brigade RFA, 48th Division, which was transferred to the Italian front following the disastrous defeat at Caporetto in October 1917. The division moved in November and, as Gunner Heraty describes:

"All the way from Genoa they gave us V.I.P. receptions at every stop, and if it happened to be a station they were lowering baskets of fruit and foods of all descriptions on pieces of rope and string from the bridges above, even bottles of 'Vino' galore."

After a period of acclimatization, the division moved up to Montecchio Maggiore on Monte Grappa.

"We were in this little place for about three weeks, trying to mix up a bit with Italian people, and trying to say 'Bon Juorno' and 'Bon A Sarah' as it sounded to us, learning to say 'Uno' 'Due' and 'Tre', etc., until the time came for Action Stations. The Italian lorries, which were 'Fiats', and specially built for mountain climbing, with five or six forward gears, and they were to take us right to the top of the Grappa Mountain which was 7,000 or 8,000 feet above sea level, and it took the best part of a day to get to a place where we could look across the valley into Austria.

RIGHT The Battle of Vittorio Veneto, Italian troops in Val d'Assa.

These British forces remained in Italy until the end of the war. They played a major role in the Vittorio Veneto offensive launched on 24 October 1918, which finally broke the Austrian will to fight.

OSTERIA del TERMINE
09.35 hours   Nov 3 1918.

1. In response to the Austrian Parlementaires the General Commdg 48th British Division states that the British forces have received no order to suspend hostilities and that, in accordance with orders he has given orders for his troops to occupy LEVICO, PERGINE and TRENTO. He demands the unconditional surrender of both troops in the above area and an assurance that no action will be taken against the troops of the Entente.

2. He will hold General ROMER as hostage whilst the occupation of the above area is carried out

3. He demands that food be provided for all British troops in the above area

4. He sends his Chief of Staff with this demand to H.Q. 11th Austrian Army LEVICO.

5. He reserves to himself the right to take such steps as will ensure the control of the troops and civilians in the above area, and the prevention of the removal of enemy troops from the Austrian front.

O. F. Morshead
Major Gen Stf
for 48. 48th Brit. Divn.

"We had left the plain where it was scorching hot and up to the top of the mountain where the snow was above knee deep ... if you slipped off the beaten track you could be swallowed up; the 'Hairpin bends' on the way up were breathtaking, and at times they could not get round in one lock and had to reverse, and when we got near the edge you could look down 2,000 to 3,000 feet below, one little mistake on the driver's part and you had had your 'chips'. The Italians reckoned they averaged one lorry a day lost over the course of the war."

LEFT Major Owen Morshead (bottom row, second from left) served as the GSO 2 of the 48th Division and, following the Battle of Vittorio Veneto, it fell to him to take the official surrender of the Austrians:
"At 5.30 next morning (Nov. 3rd) the advance was continued against what proved henceforward an unresisting enemy; thousands of Austrians surrendered freely under the impression that an armistice had been signed with effect from 3 a.m. that morning: it was like hunting penguins. Many Parliamentaires came in under white flags, some of whom we sent down to Army Headquarters and some of whom we detained. Eventually the General decided to send off Iscariot Howard with one lot to treat with the Austrian Command and take their surrender. It fell to me to draft his terms and write out his authorization."

103

THE END OF THE WAR

Following the success of the Battle of Amiens, the commander-in-chief of the Allied forces, Marshal Ferdinand Foch, devised a strategy that would finish the war in the west. It was to consist of a series of offensives on different sectors of the front, interconnected hammer blows that would leave the Germans with little chance of moving reserves to reinforce threatened sectors. The first of these blows fell in the Meuse–Argonne region on 26 September with an assault by French and American forces; the second assault started on the 27th and involved the British First and Third Armies around Cambrai. On the 28th the Flanders Army Group started its advance between the Lys and the sea and on the 29th the British Fourth Army under Rawlinson began its assault of the Hindenburg Line.

Ludendorff realized straight away that his forces were unequal to dealing with these combined assaults and told Hindenburg that Germany must seek an armistice. While the political and diplomatic wrangling continued the Allies maintained their pressure on the German front lines. In October, the BEF advanced 20 miles, though at a cost of some 120,000 casualties. By the beginning of November the situation for Germany was beginning to unravel. Turkey signed an armistice on 30 October, as did Austria-Hungary on 3 November. On 9 November the Kaiser abdicated and fled to Holland. At 0500hrs on 11 November 1918 the Armistice was signed, to come into effect at 1100hrs that morning. The First World War was finally over.

Armistice

The news of the Armistice travelled rapidly around the various fronts. On the Western Front Captain Westmacott was the Deputy Assistant Provost Marshal of the 24th Division:

"I was woken up with a wire that hostilities would cease at 11am. There were no great demonstrations by the troops, I think because it was hard to realize that the war was really over. Very lights were let off after dark, but that was all. Shortly before 11am our Divisional Artillery let the Hun have it with every available gun, I never heard such a row. A great contrast to the deathly silence that followed at 11am. The next time I heard British guns fire was a year later, when the guns fired a salute across the Rhine in Cologne to celebrate the peace."

Far to the east, Private Wilson of the Machine Gun Corps was stationed in Palestine:

"Tonight for the first time for many a long day, the moon shines down upon a world at peace. About four in the afternoon the news came that Germany had accepted our terms of armistice, and that hostilities had ceased at 11 o'clock this morning. At first everyone received the news quietly, but after dark rockets and Very lights began to go up in all directions, and the boys began to catch something of the excitement of the great hour. Even up at distant Ramallah in the hills we could see the lights going up. At Ludd [now Lod] station every engine turned its whistle on for half an hour. Artillery fired, as well as smaller arms; bonfires were lit; and the singing, cheering and other hilarious noises lasted till past the accustomed hour of retirement. We may well rejoice, for we shall never live to see such a great day again."

LEFT *The Menin Road*, by Paul Nash. He received the commission for this work, which was originally to have been called *A Flanders Battlefield*, from the Ministry of Information in April 1918. It was to feature in a Hall of Remembrance devoted to "fighting subjects, home subjects and the war at sea and in the air". However, the Hall of Remembrance was never built and the work was given to the Imperial War Museum.

RIGHT Unveiling of the permanent Cenotaph at Whitehall, by King George V on 11 November 1920, the second anniversary of the Armistice.

INSET Crowds waving and smiling around the Victoria Memorial outside Buckingham Palace in London on Armistice Day.

SHOT AT DAWN

One of the most controversial aspects of the British Army's behaviour during the First World War is the fact that 346 British and Commonwealth soldiers were executed by firing squad during the years 1914 to 1918, out of 3,080 who were sentenced to death. The vast majority of those executed were shot for desertion in the face of the enemy. Even in a society that was well accustomed to capital punishment, the execution of fellow soldiers proved highly controversial:

The Reverend T. Guy Rogers prepared a deserter prior to his execution:

"It has just fallen to my lot to prepare a deserter for his death – that meant breaking the news to him, helping him with his last letters, passing the night with him on the straw in his cell, and trying to prepare his soul for meeting God, the execution and

burying him immediately ... Monday night I was with him, Tuesday morning at 3.30 he was shot. He lay beside me for hours with his hand in mine. Poor fellow, it was a bad case, but he met his end bravely, and drank in all I could teach him about God, his Father, Jesus his Saviour, and the reality of the forgiveness of sins. I feel a little shaken by it all, but my nerves, thank God, have not troubled me."

Captain M. S. Esler of the RAMC was attached to the Middlesex Regiment and attended an execution in 1918:

"The Colonel sent for me and said that he knew that I should hate it as much as he did. One of the men had been punished on several occasions for desertion in battle. The fifth time he did it he was sent up to Brigade Headquarters for a court martial, and that, being the most serious of offences, and a demoralizing example to other men, he was sentenced to be

RIGHT Methods used by Americans to mark stragglers and deserters at Florent on 5 November 1918. In contrast to the British, no American soldiers were shot for desertion in the First World War.

LEFT A photograph purporting to show an English firing squad about to execute a blindfolded prisoner. This "mock" execution was staged in England possibly in 1915 and is certainly not on the Western Front.

shot, and I was to attend the execution the following morning. Nobody enjoyed the thought of one of our own men being shot by our own troops, and a silence and melancholy pervaded the camp all day. The execution took place at dawn. I was to see him in his hut before he was taken out and tied to a post. I had to pin a piece of red paper over his heart area. Only two of the six members of the firing squad had a loaded rifle, the others had blanks so that nobody firing should actually know who had killed him. I thought that I would make it as easy for him as possible, so I took half a pint of brandy in a glass and told him that if he drank that off he would know very little about it. He said 'what is it?' I replied 'brandy'. 'No' he said, 'I have never drunk spirits in my life, there is no point in starting it now.' So, there it was, he who had run away from battle showed a spurious sort of courage in the end. I had seen many men shot, but never one of our own men by our own men and it made me feel very sick, I who thought that I had grown hardened to death."

Following years of campaigning by various pressure groups, the British government announced on 7 November 2006 that those executed for military offences during the First World War would receive a posthumous conditional pardon.

1918–1939

Mounting displays at the Imperial War Museum before it opens to the public at Crystal Palace, London, in June 1920. Soldiers of the Royal Army Ordnance Corps are moving a newly acquired First World War gun into position. In the background is a large photograph of a scene on the Western Front by the Australian official photographer, Frank Hurley.

THE ARMY BETWEEN THE WARS

The post-war period was a time of dramatic change for the British Army. Its wartime strength was drastically reduced to previous peacetime levels (falling from over 3 million personnel to just under 400,000), and its annual budget fell accordingly. It once again became an all-volunteer army. From 1922 the cavalry was subject to a gradual process of amalgamation and increasing mechanization, following the lessons learned towards the end of the First World War and the rapid technological developments in armoured vehicle design. Numerous new corps were formed, among which the Royal Corps of Signals (1920, raised for the specialist task of wireless communications), the Royal Army Pay Corps (1920), the Army Educational Corps (1920), the Army Dental Corps (1921), the Corps of Military Police (1926), the Small Arms School Corps (1929), the Pioneer Corps (1939) and the Royal Armoured Corps (1939). Several inter-war regimental amalgamations also took place between 1920 and 1935. However, the lasting legacy of the period comprised political inertia in defence planning and a serious lack of investment in training, weapons and munitions. This meant that the British Army would find itself ill prepared and poorly equipped when war broke out again with Germany in 1939.

The occupation of Germany

William John Collins was a Staff Sergeant with 37th Casualty Clearing Station, Royal Army Medical Corps, in Germany, 1919:

"We crossed the German frontier on 1 December [1918], and the first thing I saw there was a German in uniform who went up to a door in a village, and knocked on it. No reply. He knocked again, and a woman came out with an axe! It caused some amusement to us. We thought 'Thank god the English women aren't like that!' All the way through to Bonn, the German civilians put up an enormous display of welcome for their own troops. They had placards, displays at every railway station and every town. As for us, they just accepted us. They thought that we were going to do much more plundering. As a matter of fact, there was no plundering, as we brought our own rations with us, and they had none to spare. They were very short of food the Germans ... They were quite indifferent ... We crossed the Rhine at Bonn ... In England at the time, there was a popular song called 'When we wind up the watch on the Rhine', and there were all these troops winding up their watches as they were crossing over the bridge. I had no watch, but it made me laugh, they were all simple fellas ... We stayed in Heppendorf (about 15 miles from Cologne) from December to the following September ... We were just doing nothing, routine parades, any drills necessary ... Most of the personnel had been turned over, and most of my time was spent training these 18 and 19 year olds in the work of the RAMC ... We were billeted on the local population, in their homes ... After 4½ years of sleeping on the ground, it was a luxury. I was billeted on a small farm. The eldest daughter even washed all my smalls for me! But the young men

OCCUPATION DUTIES

From 1918 the British Army oversaw the occupation of defeated Germany in the northern Rhine area, based around the key river-crossing city of Cologne; it would remain in Germany until 1929. The Army was also stationed in the territories of the partitioned Ottoman Empire from 1918, including Iraq and Palestine (both mandated territories, which would remain more or less under British control until the late 1940s), and Constantinople (together with French troops, until 1923).

in Heppendorf didn't take too kindly to us going there. One morning on the village pump was written the following message in German; 'It took four and a half years for the brave British troops to conquer the German army, but they conquered the girls of Heppendorf in one night.' I think it was a bit of an exaggeration, but there was no doubt about it, the attitude of the ladies in Heppendorf was a very friendly one. A few bars of chocolate changed hands. … There was one incident when, one night, the oldest man in our unit was roughed up by a few youngsters on his way back home … that was the only incident antagonistic to us I can remember in the whole of my time there."

LEFT Two British official war correspondents and Royal Navy photographers with cameras on the bank of the Rhine, Cologne, Germany, in 1919. The British were generally well received by the Germans. One brigade commander wrote to his mother: "The Bosch people don't in the least seem to resent our being here. In fact they are undoubtedly glad, as we are at any rate preferable to their own Bolshevists, or the Belgians, or the French. They are very respectful; all the men take off their hats to an English officer."

LEFT AND ABOVE A selection of post-war Army recruitment posters. Manpower levels were dramatically reduced in the Army in the five years following the end of the war, and its status as a volunteer army returned. New recruits were always required to fill the ranks, as well as to relieve those men who had served in the war and were anxiously awaiting demobilization. One private in the Royal Engineer Signals wrote to his wife from Germany in 1919: "I don't suppose I shall be out for some time yet, as there are such a lot here with much more service in, and they don't seem to be getting off yet … I was out for a walk last night, and saw a lorry with this chalked on the back in big letters 'Speed not to exceed Demobilization'. If they keep to that I shouldn't think they will send it on many long journeys."

THE RUSSIAN CIVIL WAR INTERVENTION, 1918–1920

In July 1918 the British government began to give limited military support to Russia as part of the international North Russian Relief Force. The Force's aim was to prevent stockpiles of Allied *matériel* stored in Archangel from falling into the hands of the "Red" Bolsheviks, and to give support to the anti-Communist "Whites" during the Russian Civil War. Further reinforcements in the shape of British expeditionary forces were sent to the northern front (based at Murmansk and Archangel) and the southern front (based at Novorossiysk on the Black Sea, and in the Crimea) in early 1919; many of the troops sent were volunteers. The White Army was initially successful in its offensives against the Red forces in the increasingly bloody civil war, but Bolshevik counter-offensives caused a collapse among the Whites in November 1919 across all the fronts, leading to the retreat and withdrawal of British troops before the onset of winter, together with the evacuation of many White Russian refugees and troops – a process that continued with British help into 1920.

ABOVE An RASC recruitment poster for the North Russian Relief Force, dated 1919.

From north to south: service in Russia

Major John Frederick Ford served with 155th Field Ambulance, Royal Army Medical Corps in the North Russian Relief Force, 1919:

"I was detailed to go on the North Russian Relief Force. At that time I knew nothing about it, but I made some effort to find out. Apparently the force was to go to North Russia to relieve the troops who were due for demobilization, but which had to remain in Russia due to the ice. The force was originally to be a volunteer force ... The infantry consisted of men from all sorts of regiments. Many were ex-officers who found no work to do in England, or were ex-prisoners of war ... While we were waiting in Murmansk, we were all issued with the medal ribbon of the British War Medal of the First World War, with the instruction that we were all to wear it ... My brigade went on to Archangel, and we all marched through it ... When we read about our arrival in the papers afterwards, they said 'Everyone was a bemedalled hero'! A lot of us already had one ribbon, but even the new recruits had got one on ... We were billeted there in a convent in tents, and were bitten to death by mosquitoes, despite the cold – there was one man had to go into hospital ... The people I was sent out with didn't grumble about being in Russia, they knew they were going back. The troops who we replaced didn't like it there; everyone in France had been demobbed, and they were still there ... We had no contact with the troops in the south of Russia."

ABOVE The British War Medal (1914–1920). The medal was issued to those who had entered a theatre of war on duty or rendered approved service overseas between 5 August 1914 and 11 November 1918. It also covered service in Russia between 1919 and 1920.

RIGHT Men of the North Russian Expeditionary Force pose for the camera in the snow at their British Lewis gun post at Lumbuski Bridge, 1919.

Sergeant Horace Ashley of 19th Battalion, Machine Gun Corps, volunteered for service in south Russia on 23 March 1919:

"We crossed the Black Sea, arriving at Novorossiysk, South Russia on 21 June 1919 and joined the British Military Mission of Maj Gen Holm ... I then received orders to report to the Machine Gun School at Novocherkask. There was also another Sergeant who came with me for the Lewis gun ... Gen Holm happened to be traveling on the

same train to Novocherkask, and he had a special coach, so we went to see him, and he took us ... Arriving there on the 29th, the General disappeared leaving us two on the station. We could not speak a word of Russian, and there was nobody to meet us ... For the next few months we travelled about the line, to different battalions, instructing them. The British issued thousands of khaki suits, but I never saw any at the front ... The troops were dressed very bad, some did not

even have boots. Their clothes were sack cloth. Only a few had rifles ... In December the crash came. Denikin's army could not hold the Bolshies, and they advanced very quickly. We had to leave Novocherkask in a great hurry. During the night of 2 January 1920 Rostov was in a terrible state, as the people in the towns had turned Bolshevik and had started murdering the remainder. After a lot of trouble we got to Ekaterinodar. It was only by threatening the Kubans that the

British would send an army out if anyone touched us that we got through to Novorossiysk. The work was in full swing of evacuating Russian refugees, of which there were thousands ... I stayed at Novorossiysk doing defence work until 12 March, when I was sent to Theodosia in the Crimea to another MG school. Shortly after the whole mission had to evacuate Novorossiysk."

THE FAR EAST

The Army's colonial duties remained a key part of its activities in the inter-war period, and the Far East saw several major incidents. The Third Anglo-Afghan War erupted in 1919, following a declaration of independence by the Afghan king Amanullah Khan. Up to that point, Britain had controlled Afghanistan's foreign policy dealings and significant amounts of its territory (partly as a barrier to Russian interest in India), but Amanullah Khan wished to exert more control, and attacked the British in May, proclaiming a holy war. Amanullah's initial attack across the border into India was followed by an expedition into Afghanistan of British troops, at which point Amanullah sued for peace. The British Army would maintain its presence in the border region throughout the 1920s and 1930s, with garrisons (such as the large base at Razmak) protecting against continued uprisings and raiding in Waziristan (bordering Afghanistan and modern-day Pakistan), and in the independent tribal territories of the North-West Frontier. British soldiers also formed part of the Shanghai Defence Force (1927–1940), with two brigades protecting commercial interests in Shanghai from the effects of the Chinese warlords' infighting and from Communist forces.

Service on the North-West Frontier

Private William Daly was born in London in 1899. Having begun his service in the Royal Marines, in November 1922 he enlisted in the Oxford and Buckinghamshire Light Infantry, and was drafted to the 2nd Battalion in India. He contracted typhoid soon after his arrival there, and was sent to convalesce in the foothills of the Himalayas, a process that took some nine months in total, after which he rejoined his regiment at Rawalpindi:

"Soon after my return, we were told that the next move of the Regiment would be to Razmak (Waziristan) in Afghanistan. I think it was about five days' march, perhaps more ... We did so many marches, all of them under the same conditions, long dusty tracks and trails, sometimes marching two abreast owing to the narrow tracks, hairpin bends, precipices with a thousand foot drop ...

five companies, each with four platoons, and between each platoon four or five or more camels and a medical section, and a Regiment of Sikhs, a battery of Royal Artillery, mules ... Each man carried a service water carrier, but no man was allowed to drink: when you got to camp, you were marched to the cookhouse (where trenches would be dug for trench cooking) and all the water from the

LEFT Men (possibly the signals section) from a battalion of the Durham Light Infantry during a break in a march on the North-West Frontier in the 1930s.

bottles was emptied into doxies for cooking and making tea ... After six or eight hours of marching through four to six inches of fine, almost white sand, it gets down your back, in the corner of your eyes, between your toes, and your eyelashes turn white, and the further back in the column you are the more sand you collect ... At Razmak, once a week, companies took it in turn to conduct 'road opening', advancing section after section to occupy the hills on either side of the road ... Each section covered the other until all were in position, and the sections returned by the same method when the convoy was safely through ... There was no entertainment in the camp at all; two football teams from the off-duty regiment played a match on two occasions in the two years we were at Razmak, and they were under cover of the machine guns. We had to watch the progress of the match from the perimeter, and the pitch was outside the barbed wire. All you had was a pack of cards, or a three-week-old newspaper to read, or if you were one of the lucky ones you had a letter from a girlfriend, wife or mother, just a letter from someone ... If you had a close friend, perhaps he would let you read his letters, or would read them out to you."

ABOVE A marching column on the North-West Frontier in the early 1930s, consisting of British infantry and pack mule transport.

RIGHT The India General Service Medal (1908–1935). The medal was the penultimate in a long line of campaign medals awarded for service in the Sub-continent.

THE ANGLO-IRISH WAR

In 1919 the "Troubles" broke out in Ireland, which was at the time part of the United Kingdom of Great Britain and Ireland. Tension had been simmering between the Catholic and Protestant communities since before the First World War, and paramilitary pro- and anti-home rule groups had appeared. There were over 30 British Army infantry battalions stationed in Ireland at the outbreak of the war, which is often taken to be 21 January 1919 when the IRA ambushed and killed two Royal Irish Constabulary constables. From March 1920, the Black and Tans – Royal Irish Constabulary auxiliary recruits from Britain, who were mostly ex-Army officers – began to arrive in the country. There were no pitched battles during the conflict; instead, British soldiers carried out patrols and police protection duties, and enforced martial law as required. Such duties were no less hazardous to the common soldier, and casualties escalated as the conflict dragged on inconclusively, reaching over 500 fatalities by the end of the war. In December 1921, the Anglo-Irish Treaty was signed, which paved the way for the partition of the country into north and south, and ended the war. The seeds of a much later conflict had been sown for the British soldier. Following the British withdrawal in 1922, civil war broke out, lasting until 1923.

ABOVE The cap badge of The Devonshire Regiment, worn from 1901 until 1956. In 1958 the regiment was amalgamated with the Dorset Regiment to form the Devonshire and Dorset Regiment. The badge features as its motif a star and Exeter Castle, adopted by the regiment in 1883 from the Devon Militia.

The Anglo-Irish War

Gerald Frederick Stone was a platoon commander with the Devonshire Regiment in Ireland during the Troubles, arriving in March 1921:

"Before I went to Ireland, we heard from the battalion and from officers out there what it was like. We gathered from them what the situation was. You had the IRA, which you were up against, and there were ambushes chiefly. The IRA used to try to prevent us getting along in our Crossley cars, which we always moved three cars at a time, 150 yards between each, so that if any were ambushed only the outside two would be in the ambush. You had the IRA blocking the roads in three different ways; they would cut a trench nearly across the road, just allowing a cart to go around. To deal with this we would carry planks to put across the trench. Then they would cut down trees across the road, and they were too difficult to deal with. So you would look for a gate on the field side to get around the tree – if you couldn't you would have to take another road. The third way was to destroy the back axle of the Crossley; they used to put potholes for 100 yards down the road, which would possibly break the back axle. Another nasty thing they used to do was, about dusk, they would put a piece of

BELOW British soldiers search civilians at Fermoy Station, Northern Ireland, in February 1921. A lieutenant from the Suffolk Regiment summed up the Army's difficulties in Ireland: "It was a confusing and frustrating experience. We were on 'Active Service' for discipline, crime and punishment, but not for pay, privileges, allowances and compensations. No medals were awarded and the role of the military was difficult to define."

barbed wire across the road, about neck high, to catch people sitting in the front of the cars in the neck ... A friend of mine I knew could only whisper for the rest of his life because he was caught in the wire ... One always had to see that there were no ambushes when the road was blocked. It was the first thing one did ... A friend of mine was stationed at Waterford and the Tremore Police Barracks had shots fired at it. He was in mufti; the young subaltern in charge of the party tasked with investigating was new from Sandhurst, and so my friend thought he had better go out with the party in a separate vehicle. The subaltern's party was ambushed by the IRA in their Crossley. But this officer in mufti found out where the firing was coming from. It was coming from a hedge overlooking the road; he left his vehicle and went along that hedge using his revolver as a humane killer, and killed about a dozen of them. They were so

ABOVE British soldiers involved in clearing a road at Carrignavar, Cork, 10 June 1921. A ditch has been cut across the middle of the road, which a Rolls-Royce armoured car is attempting to outflank.

busy firing on to the road they didn't realize what was happening ... Morale was very high in Ireland in my battalion, we knew we were getting the better of the IRA."

THE MIDDLE EAST

British and Arab irregular forces had captured Palestine in 1917 from the Turks, and the territory was placed under British military administration. Although Britain had given assurances of self-government to the Arabs, it also recognized the Jewish desire for a homeland in Palestine, something it had made clear in the Balfour Declaration of 1917. In 1922, the League of Nations tasked Britain with the implementation of the Palestine Mandate, and tensions soon arose among the Arab population over the allocation of Palestinian lands to Jewish settlers. This was exacerbated by the increasing number of Jewish settlers arriving in the region. The British Army was involved in keeping order throughout the 1920s, when several major disturbances took place. Sporadic trouble continued into the 1930s between Arabs and Jews, and a major rebellion occurred in the wake of the increasing influx of Jews fleeing Hitler's Germany. Jewish extremists began attacks against British authorities in 1936 following an imposition of immigration quotas by the British and restrictions on land purchase, and at the same time an Arab rebellion broke out, which would last until 1939. Urban areas were bombed, and Jews and Jewish property were attacked, as were British military personnel.

Policing Palestine

RIGHT A British Army convoy returns fire during an ambush on the Jenin Road, Palestine, in 1936.

LEFT Palestine police with riot shields and batons charge massed Arab demonstrators in an attempt to disperse the crowd in Clock House Square, Jaffa, during the Jaffa riot of 27 October 1933.

Ivor George Thomas was a clerk with the Royal Army Service Corps, Force HQ, Palestine, between 1936 and 1938:

"It was pretty difficult for the British Tommy to realize who he was up against … The British soldier was suddenly very friendly with the Arab, the chap he was supposed to destroy eventually … There we were supposedly to prevent an Arab strike, and everywhere around us the Arab population was very friendly … There were a tremendous number of troops there, finally, for what was in effect a small upset in the end. The 'cowboy stories' about chasing the leader of the Arab band backwards and forwards into Iraq was absolute nonsense, I don't think they wanted to get him, and they could have got him hundreds of times … The intelligence was very, very good, and when we set up chase on him, he was able to get a warning about it. But I don't want to denigrate the infantiers and the fighting soldiers who were there. They had plenty of trouble in these awful spots like Jenin and Nablas, pretty bad places. They had plenty to do and in the end they were stretched well over the country. There were plenty of side shows going on … It was a pretty fearful charter we first had, it was to take over the government of the country … The whole concept of setting up military government is a tremendous task when one goes into it. There was resentment, open resentment, at all levels … I think the British troops got on better with the Arabs than the Jews. There was no going in for a cup of tea, the Jews completely ostracized the British Army, certainly in Jerusalem where I was. Tel Aviv and Haifa were exactly the same. There was a great barrier set up. Whether this was by design or not, I wouldn't know. Certainly it didn't help their cause with the British troops. The Tommy has this characteristic of going for the underdog."

RIGHT An Army recruiting poster from the early 1920s, extolling the virtues of travel to exotic destinations such as the Middle East.

1939–1945

British troops line up on the beach
at Dunkirk to await evacuation,
26–29 May 1940.

1939–1940

THE NORWEGIAN CAMPAIGN

On 9 April 1940 Germany invaded Denmark and Norway, in an effort to secure Scandinavia's mineral resources as well as bases for the U-Boat fleet. The British North-West Expeditionary Force was soon dispatched to Norway, comprising men from the regular army, volunteers and the Territorials. French, Polish and Norwegian troops also fought alongside the British in the campaign. The 24th Guards Brigade landed at Harstad near Narvik on 14 April, while the 146th Territorial Brigade landed at Namsos on the 16th, and the 148th Brigade landed at Andalsnes on the 18th.

The Battle of Lillehammer took place on 22–23 April – the first significant engagement between British and German land forces of the war, where men of the Royal Leicestershire Regiment and the Sherwood Foresters (148th Territorial Brigade) were badly mauled, and many men were captured. Meanwhile, on 23–24 April the 146th Brigade was driven back towards Namsos following the Battle of Visit. On 23 April the British 15th Brigade landed at Andalsnes, having been transferred from 5th Division in France; the brigade consisted almost entirely of infantry, having lost the ship carrying its artillery and transport en route. The Norwegian Army's resistance gradually crumbled, and soon the position for the poorly equipped, inexperienced and exposed British expeditionary force became untenable. Between 2 and 3 May British forces were evacuated from Andalsnes and Namsos. In the north, 24th Guards Brigade, supported by French and Polish units, had assisted in the lengthy operation to recapture Narvik, but the defeats further south meant that they too would be evacuated by 7 June, leaving the whole of Norway in German hands.

122

The formation badge for the British V Corps. The Corps formed part of the Norwegian expedition in April 1940 and the badge was chosen subsequently to commemorate this. It incorporates in part the traditional Corps colours of red and white. V Corps fought in French North-West Africa in 1942, Sicily and Italy, ending the war in the Po Valley.

Norway 1940

Donald Creighton-Williamson was a British officer serving with 1st Battalion The York and Lancaster Regiment, 15th Infantry Brigade, in Norway 1940:

"We were told that there was a plan for the invasion of Norway, or at least that the Germans were likely to invade Norway. To pre-empt the German invasion, the Norwegian ports were going to be mined and/or occupied. We had heard that there had been naval engagements, serious encounters at sea, and one didn't quite know what the Norwegian government was going to do because it was then early days ... We were told that we were going to go in at Trondheim supported by naval bombardment, and that the capture of Trondheim (the port and the airfield) would be supported by pincer movements from Andalsnes on the right or south side, and Namsos on the north or left. Then, at the last moment, we were told that the Navy thought it too risky to put their big ships in the fjord and the frontal attack wouldn't take place ... There was a small flotilla, the cruiser HMS Sheffield and three destroyers, taking the companies that

BELOW Troops on board a troop ship watching the sunset off the Norwegian coast, shortly after the first Allied contingents began landing in Norway to counter the German invasion, 20 April 1940.

were going in to follow up the King's Own
Yorkshire Light Infantry, who were ahead of
us going to the rescue of 148th Brigade.
The battalion HQ and the main body went
across on the Sheffield. I was with them,
and going across the Navy decided it was
too risky to run a big ship up the fjord, as
Andalsnes was already getting a
hammering by this point. So, she put us
down at a place called Molde just opposite
the mouth of the fjord, and there we
transferred into trawlers to chug across
very slowly to Andalsnes on the other side.
The first sighting of the enemy I got was
the strafing of the town as we waited in the
woods outside of Andalsnes to get in the
train to follow up ... The whole thing was
dominated by the Germans and we were
concerned with stemming their flow and
our survival ... The Germans had planned
this operation and executed it with great
skill, and, of course with the connivance of
Quisling, which helped them infiltrate three
divisions with air support ... We all felt that
if we had only brought some sort of
artillery, if only we had an aeroplane or two
to counter them for however short a time,
we could have held them. Whether we
could or not, one will never know."

RIGHT British troops
queue for a meal after
coming ashore in
Norway in April 1940.

THE PHONEY WAR TO THE FALL OF FRANCE

In September 1939, the British Expeditionary Force (BEF) had been dispatched to France under the command of Lord Gort. Britain had declared war on Germany on 3 September 1939, but no offensive action took place during the "Phoney War". The British prepared the "Gort" defensive line in the meantime.

The German drive to the west began with Army Group B attacking the Low Countries on 10 May in a deliberate attempt to convince the Allies that the main attack would be in this area, while von Rundstedt's Army Group A pushed through the Ardennes, crossing the River Meuse on 13 May 1940. The BEF advanced into Belgium taking up positions on the River Dyle, while German Army Group A began an arc movement to cut the BEF off at the Channel, breaking through the French lines at Sedan. Gort realized on 19 May that he was about to be encircled, and so Matilda tanks of the BEF counter-attacked the advancing forces of Army Group A at Arras on 21 May, pushing southwards to stem their advance to the coast. Although the attack was unsuccessful, it allowed time for the main body of the BEF to fall back on Dunkirk. The evacuation of British troops came under the name Operation *Dynamo*. By 4 June over 338,000 Allied troops had been evacuated, although much vital heavy equipment was left behind. Dunkirk was not the only evacuation site. For the next six weeks troops continued to be withdrawn from France from other ports, adding a further 200,000 to the total safely escorted across the Channel.

LEFT Troops show the strain of the retreat, on their way to the port at Brest during the evacuation of British forces from France, June 1940.

Dunkirk

Victor George Gilbey was an NCO serving with the 1st Battalion The Oxfordshire and Buckinghamshire Light Infantry in France and Belgium 1939–1940. He was evacuated from Dunkirk on 1 June:

"What did I think of the Germans? I though they were very good soldiers, and their equipment was good. For an advancing army, they had mobility that we never did. Their motorcycle machine-gun battalions were used very, very cleverly and they were used a lot for covering fire. They would come forward in their BMWs very quick, machine gun mounted on the sidecar. Then they would take up a defensive position while the ordinary infantryman with his mortar would come up and take up position, and he would be covered with the machine-gun motorcyclist ... Dunkirk would have been a beautiful place for a holiday, wonderful sand, but at that time it was packed with troops trying to move forward, and at the same time being shelled and machine-gunned ... During the move along the beach we lost about a dozen men, which we considered, after we had time to think, to be very lucky ... There was very strict control by the Royal Military Police. If a person was seen to come out of his column and tried to get forward he was immediately grabbed by the scruff of his neck and pushed back ... We just waited our turn to be moved onto the mole for the best part of the night. In the very early hours of the morning we moved onto the mole where we stood for about four or five hours, under bomb and machine-gun fire. There was nothing you could do except get down and pray you would be able to get back up again. I left on HMS Worcester, some of the battalion went over on the Maid of Orleans, a pre-war Channel ferry. When we eventually arrived home we finished up with nine officers and about 350 men in the battalion."

ABOVE *Dunkirk Beaches, 1940*, by Richard Eurich, RA (oil on panel cardboard). Lines of soldiers are preparing for evacuation and walking through the surf to small boats waiting offshore.

ABOVE The first-pattern formation badge for 1st Armoured Division (and 2nd Armoured Brigade). 1st Armoured Division was neither fully equipped nor trained at the outbreak of war. Although significantly deficient in many of its tanks and supporting services, the Division was sent to France, arriving through Cherbourg in mid May 1940. The Division fought, alongside 51st Highland Division, under French command. Most of the personnel were able to return to the UK but all equipment was lost.

RIGHT A Bible associated with the Second World War experiences of Gunner C. Hedley (G Battery, Royal Artillery), who served as a long-term prisoner of war of the Germans in Stalag VIIIB (Lamsdorf, Poland). Gunner Hedley was captured during the defence of Calais on 26 May 1940 in the attempt to hold up the German advance. The frontispiece bears the inscription: "Stalag VIIIB Gepruft Nr 26/W Heffer & Sons Ltd/Sidney Street, Cambridge/Gnr C. Hedley Captured May 26th 1940 Calais France/To my Dear Daughter Ann 'She is more precious than rubies and all things thou canst desire are not to be compared unto her.' Proverbs III. 7-XX/Sgt. Ord. T/Feb 3rd 1943 Lamsdorf Germany".

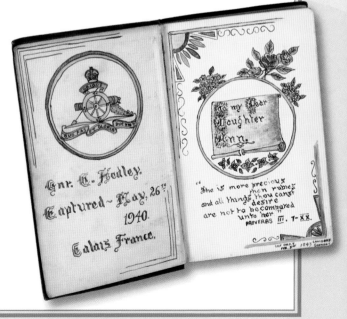

1940–1941

OPERATION *COMPASS* AND BEDA FOMM

In June 1940 Mussolini declared war on Britain and France. On 12 June British forces stationed in Egypt began small-scale raids across the frontier into Italian Libya, but the Italians were already planning an invasion of Egypt. The British ground forces available to confront the invasion comprised Western Desert Force, under the command of Lieutenant-General Richard O'Connor. Its main elements were 7th Armoured Division (including the famous 7th Armoured Brigade), 4th Indian Division and later 6th Australian Division.

The Italian invasion of Egypt began on 13 September 1940. A slow advance saw the Italians reach Sidi Barrani, where they built defensive positions and camps while awaiting reinforcements; they were still some 60 miles from the main British defences positions around Mersa Matruh. The Commander-in-Chief of Middle East Command, General Sir Archibald Wavell, planned an attack on the Italians from the rear and a deep push into Libya – Operation *Compass*. After weeks of secret training, the ground offensive began on 8 December 1940, with assaults against the Italian positions at Tummar, Nibeiwa, Sidi Barrani and Buq Buq. After brief but

Operation *Compass*

Frank Proctor was an NCO serving with D Company of the 1st Battalion The Argyll and Sutherland Highlanders in North Africa in 1940–1941. He describes his part in the battle for Sidi Barrani:

"Around about 7 December 1940 we had orders to move forward. Now that was some sight. When we got up on the escarpment and looked along our lines one could see trucks, troops for miles. General Wavell was the officer commanding forces; he came down the line talking to each regiment in turn of what was going to happen, and as young soldiers we were keen – 'let's get up there and get them' was our attitude. For a couple of days we went forward. The actual battle for Sidi Barrani was the morning of 10 December ... As we moved up we could hear heavy guns rumbling away in the distance, which suddenly sobered us all up insomuch as 'Aye aye, this is the real thing' ... Then came the signal, 'Forward, fix bayonets'. We ran forward and the obstacle in our way was an anti-tank trap, which was a deep dug-out position, and in we went ... Over the top we went up the hill and took it down. There were three main ridges there, they were the stumbling blocks to the taking of Sidi Barrani. When we cleared it out there were no prisoners, they were dead or had run away – scarpered back down the hillside – and we rested on our laurels and thanked ourselves that we hadn't been killed ... Dawn broke quietly, there were no heavy guns, no noise, but what I did hear was A Company on our flank, and their piper playing 'Flowers of the Forest' ... and it was just on the wind you could hear him playing the lament for the dead. This was taken up by two other pipers in the distance, I presume on the CO's instructions."

LEFT A column of Italian prisoners captured during the assault on Bardia, Libya, march to a British Army base on 6 January 1941.

fierce fighting, the positions fell. The Italians regrouped around Bardia and Tobruk, which were heavily fortified. Bardia was attacked on 3 January 1941 by the 6th Australian Division and 7th Royal Tank Regiment. It fell on the 5th. Tobruk, with its precious and sizeable harbour and water distilleries, was the next priority for O'Connor. The 1st Battalion, The Royal Northumberland Fusiliers, attached to 6th Australian Division, played a key role in the assault on the outer fortifications on 21 January. All Italian resistance ended by the 22nd, and 25,000 Italians were captured. Benghazi was the next objective, a potentially important naval and air base. The Commonwealth forces continued their push westwards, reaching Derna on 30 January 1941. The Italians were by now in full retreat from Cyrenaica towards Tripoli, but O'Connor

planned to trap them by sending 7th Armoured Division on a difficult "short cut" across the desert to meet them at Beda Fomm, while 6th Australian Division pressed them from the rear. The plan worked. The trapped Italians attempted to break out on 6 February, but their tanks and artillery were destroyed piecemeal. By 7 February, the Italians had nothing more with which to fight their way out, and the remnants of the Italian Tenth Army surrendered. Over 115,000 Italians had been captured since the outbreak of war.

RIGHT The Beretta M1934 was the most successful of a series of pistols produced by Beretta for the Italian Army. It was designed by Beretta's chief designer, Tullio Marengoni, in response to a decision to replace all existing service pistols with a single new model. The Army selected the 9mm Short (.380) cartridge which, while not as powerful as the 9mm Parabellum round used in some other countries, allowed the new pistol to employ an unlocked breech mechanism. Consequently the Beretta M1934 was a compact, simple and reliable weapon. It entered service in 1935 and variants continued to be produced on a commercial basis well into the 1950s. This particular pistol was taken from General Annibale Bergonzoli, commander of the Italian XXIII Corps, after his surrender at Beda Fomm in February 1941. A British ambulance driver, V. F. G. Hudson, dispossessed the general (popularly known as "Electric Whiskers") of it, before driving him off into captivity.

RIGHT Port installations burn in Tobruk harbour, Libya, on 24 January 1941. It had been captured by British and Australian troops two days earlier. M11/40 (on the left) and M11/39 (on the right) Italian tanks can be seen in the foreground. White kangaroo symbols can be seen on the tanks, indicating these are now the possessions of the 6th Australian Division.

THE EAST AFRICAN CAMPAIGN

On 4 August 1940 Italian troops under the Duke of Aosta invaded British Somaliland from Ethiopia (Abyssinia), threatening British access to the Red Sea and the Suez Canal. British forces in the country numbered only the 2nd Battalion The Black Watch and Indian and African troops, who put up a brief defence before being evacuated by sea. By early 1941, Wavell had built up sufficient troop numbers (including the 4th Indian Division transferred from North Africa) to attempt to retake the lost territory. In January 1941 British forces invaded Italian-held Eritrea, with the 4th Indian Division heavily involved in the fighting at Keru in February and the capture of Keren in March. The invasion of Italian Somaliland from Kenya in late January met little resistance, and British forces pushed up through Ethiopia to the border with British Somaliland. By May 1941 the main body of Italian resistance had been crushed, leading the Duke of Aosta to surrender. Pockets of Italian resistance would continue to hold out until 1943 though.

The battle for Ethiopia

Peter Gerald Upcher was a British officer in the Sudan Camel Corps, Sudan Defence Force, 1937–1943. He served in Ethiopia 1940–1941 and fought at the Battle of Keren:

"We got blasé ... We got held up at Keru and we came from rather broken ground into an open plain ... and at the other side we were held up by mountains that absolutely blocked our passage completely. It looked like we were going to be held up for quite a long time. The 4th/11th went into action, and our gunners went into action, and we were sitting there saying 'Oh well, I expect we shall be able to get on soon enough.' Suddenly from our left flank (we were more or less nose to tail miles down this road) there was a sound, noises and a certain amount of dust, and then there was the sound of hooves, and then it suddenly appeared that there was a

ABOVE The formation badge of the 4th Indian Infantry Division. The Division was nicknamed the "Red Eagles" after the bird of prey on its badge. The first badges worn in North Africa were given by the women of the Punjab, at the instigation of the then Prime Minister, Sir Sikander Hyat Khan, who visited the Division in the Middle East. Elements of the 4th Indian Division left India for Egypt in 1939. The formation fought with the Western Desert Force at Sidi Barrani. It was then withdrawn to East Africa, where, together with 5th Indian Division, it was instrumental in the defeat of the Italians at Keren. The Division then returned to North Africa.

LEFT Indian troops clearing a village in Eritrea, 11 March 1941.

cavalry charge ... It wasn't the Duke of Aosta's Special Cavalry but it was something like that, and it was commanded by a baron on a white horse. Of course, we were taken completely by surprise, and actually we did (though we didn't mean to do it) exactly what we were supposed to do – we held our fire – but actually because we couldn't get the flipping guns to work! ... Eventually we got them to work and the gunners turned their guns around and fired over our heads at them and it was terrible because there was so much carnage, especially of the horses. I think we felt more sorry for the horses than we did for the men. But they very nearly succeeded, and it was a very brave thing to do and rather typical of the sort of thing that we always heard the Italians would do, but as far as I know they never did it before and they never did it again."

BELOW British soldiers await their turn for food at a meal parade in Eritrea, 11 March 1941.

129

THE GREEK DISASTER

The Greek mainland

On 28 October 1940 Mussolini began a botched invasion of Greece, with the Italian Ninth and Eleventh armies crossing the border from Albania. The invasion quickly stalled and a Greek counter-offensive drove the Italians back to the border. British reinforcements were sent to aid the Greek resistance, further stretching the British Army's commitments at a time of great need globally. RAF squadrons were sent from November 1940, and an infantry battalion was sent to Suda Bay in Crete. British forces in Greece came under Wavell's Middle East Command. In March 1941 "W Force", led by General Henry "Jumbo" Wilson, was sent to Greece. It comprised an armoured brigade from 2nd Armoured Division, and the 6th Australian and the New Zealand Infantry Divisions. However, on 6 April 1941 German forces invaded Yugoslavia (Operation *Strafe*) and Greece (Operation *Marita*, launched from Bulgaria and Yugoslavia), a move that forced the outnumbered British and Commonwealth troops to withdraw southwards. On 26 April British troops fought a delaying action at the Corinth Canal, which was attacked by German paratroopers. The bridge across the canal was damaged in the action, cutting off numerous British troops on the north side, who were subsequently captured. The Allies also lost large amounts of equipment during the retreat, and Athens fell on 27 April. By 30 April all remaining Commonwealth forces (some 20,000 men) had been evacuated to Crete.

130

ABOVE A British anti-aircraft gun site in Greece, late 1940.

The retreat through Greece

Walter Frederick Dale was a trooper serving with A Squadron, 3rd Battalion The Royal Tank Regiment in Greece and Crete, 1941. He arrived in the port of Piraeus in early 1941, and moved into the mountains in the Florina area, before moving to Monastir after the German invasion of Greece in April 1941. He describes the retreat southwards, leading up to his evacuation to Crete:

"We moved to a valley, where we were to stop the German armoured vehicles coming through. There were only six

BELOW A British Army 15-cwt truck heads south through Greece, 21 April 1941.

tanks left and one of them we had to tow up to the top of the hill. When they did come through, my job, as a gunner, was to take out the first part of the convoy, and so on right the way down the line until it was blocked. Well, I took the first two motorized infantry trucks out, full of infantry, and also the carrier, and then I think they were really stopped then because we had them all right down in front of us. But then we had to evacuate; it was no good bringing the tanks in, as

we'd fired all our ammunition. I remember taking all the breech blocks out and then setting fire to the tanks ... We had to make our own way right back to Athens. We walked for the first two or three days until we got to a valley where a Greek infantry brigade must have been caught in the bombing in their trucks and coaches. They were just sitting there, concussion must have killed them. Because a lot of our drivers were mechanics as well (that was their training), they got a vehicle going and

they sucked the fuel tanks from the other ones, and we eventually got to Larissa. There we came across a NAAFI depot; the MPs were just going to blow it up, and so they let us go in and help ourselves to what we wanted because we didn't have anything. Then we made our way back to our unit. We were bombed and machine-gunned all the way down."

The fall of Crete

Crete had been occupied by the British in late 1940 as a possible base for future operations in the Mediterranean. From early May, the island was subjected to German air raids, and on 16 May men from the Leicestershire Regiment arrived to bolster the 30,000-strong defending forces, followed by men from the 1st Battalion The Argyll and Sutherland Highlanders on 18 May, both part of 14th Infantry Brigade defending Heraklion. Men from the Royal Welch Fusiliers, the Ranger Battalion and the Northumberland Hussars were stationed around Haina, while the 19th Australian Brigade defended Rethmynon and the New Zealand Division covered the area west of Haina. A full-scale German invasion of the island (Operation *Merkur*) was launched on 20 May, spearheaded by Fallschirmjäger (airborne) troops landing around Heraklion, Maleme, Haina and Rethmynon. In the fighting around Haina, the Royal Welch Fusiliers put up a stubborn defence, as did the Australians against the 2nd Fallschirmjäger Regiment at Rethymnon. Around Heraklion, men of the Leicestershire Regiment and the Black Watch, reinforced by men from the 1st Battalion The Argyll and Sutherland Highlanders, who arrived from their landing at Tymbaki, fought off the attacks of the 1st Fallschirmjäger Regiment.

However, the various Fallschirmjäger units gradually managed to link up and German reinforcements began to arrive on the island; retreat once again became inevitable for the Commonwealth defenders. The New Zealanders attempted a counter-attack at Maleme, but were forced to withdraw to a

The Cretan campaign

Frank Proctor was a private serving with 1st Battalion The Argyll and Sutherland Highlanders in Crete in May 1941, having been transferred from North Africa. He was captured by German paratroopers during the fighting and spent the rest of the war in captivity:

"We came off the main road and rested in the vineyards and olive groves, only to be visited by the Stukas. There were three runs from the Stukas but we lost no men, though the village was clouted about and various people were killed I understand – but we were OK. Rumours were flying about of paratroopers already established on the island and of the Cretans committing atrocities against the paratroopers – of them having shot them, not always honourably, removing their private parts and stuffing them in their mouths and leaving them in the village for everyone to see. We found out about this because the Germans dropped pamphlets ... The message was to the effect that British troops would be shot on capture. I understand this order was countermanded a couple of days later when they established that it wasn't British soldiers who committed these atrocities but the Cretans and civilian population ... We pushed on up through the groves, over walls, until we were met by gunfire. Being the leading section, I received an order from a sergeant to shut them down. They were on our extreme right-hand flank, a little nest of them. We engaged them, things went silent, and then they came down out of the heavens. It was a killing field ... and I engaged them with a Bren gun, firing as they were landing, giving them a burst, firing on them as they were coming down. I used my magazines up, called for more magazines and got no reply. Suddenly I was alone ... I thought 'Christ, what do I do now?' Things went quiet and then there came three German aircraft, troop carriers, and they piled out. By this time I had used the rest of

LEFT A pall of smoke hangs over the harbour in Suda Bay where two ships, hit by German bombers, burn themselves out during the battle for Crete in May 1941.

defensive line near Galatos on 23 May. The German attacks persisted, and from 26 to 30 May the Commonwealth forces withdrew first to Suda Bay and then over the mountains southwards to the port of Sphakion, while those defending Heraklion retreated to the port there (being evacuated on 28 May). Many men of the Royal Welch Fusiliers, the Ranger Battalion and the Northumberland Hussars were cut off and captured during the retreat from Hania. By 1 June thousands of Commonwealth troops had been evacuated by sea from Crete, but the Royal Navy was forced to abandon the evacuation process due to the risk to shipping. Over 12,000 Commonwealth troops entered captivity.

my ammunition. I thought, 'I'm going to move out now.' I called out and got no reply in English and I started to worm my way back between the groves there. Coming towards me were two paratroopers doing the same as I was doing, lying face down wriggling forward. The only thing I had was a Fanny – a knife with a knuckleduster on. I unclipped it and slipped it onto my hand, still going forward. I do vividly remember looking at their faces, I'm sure they were looking at mine ... one of them leaped and I took him on the Fanny. Suddenly I was hit on the back of the head and I passed out. When I came round and rolled onto my back all I could see was feet surrounding me and I let my eyes run up their bodies and I realized they were German paratroopers ... They took me forward to a German officer who was propped up by the wall and bleeding rather badly, he was probably the one I hit on the way down ... He spoke very good English, and explained to me that the war was over for me ... He asked me to remove my equipment, which I did ... He spoke to two paratroopers and ordered them to take me out of the line as a prisoner of war."

RIGHT A group of British soldiers with fixed bayonets in a trench on Crete, May 1941.

RIGHT Lieutenant-General Bernard Freyberg, VC, the New Zealand commanding officer on Crete, gazes over the parapet of his dug-out in the direction of the German advance.

ROMMEL'S ARRIVAL IN NORTH AFRICA AND THE BATTLES FOR CYRENAICA

On 12 February 1941, Generalleutnant Erwin Rommel and the Deutsches Afrika Korps (DAK) arrived in Tripoli, days after the surrender of the Italian Tenth Army at Beda Fomm. The British and Commonwealth forces had advanced as far as El Agheila following their rout of the Italians, but their lines of supply and communication were now stretched, and the demands for troops for service in Greece and East Africa in particular had drawn off vital manpower and equipment. Brigades from 7th Australian Division were added to Western Desert Force's order of battle. The Italians had also sent fresh troops to North Africa, nominally under independent command. Rommel quickly moved to the offensive, and in March began his drive into Cyrenaica, with the aim of pushing the Commonwealth forces back to Egypt and the Suez Canal. Western Desert Force chose to withdraw from its forward positions rather than attempting to defend worthless terrain.

The opening moves of the battle for Cyrenaica saw the British 2nd Armoured Division withdrawing from its blocking position along the main line of Axis advance at Mersa Brega on 31 March 1941; Rommel soon organized the harassment of its retreat, pushing deep inland. Meanwhile, the Italian 27th "Brescia" Division advanced along the coast road towards Benghazi. The British 3rd Armoured Brigade was caught between the strands of the Axis advance, and withdrew in disarray, devoid of fuel. As the Brescia Division advanced, the Australian 9th Division withdrew to Tobruk. The stand by the 3rd Indian Motor Brigade at Mechili between 6 and 8 April was vital in delaying Rommel's forces, allowing the Commonwealth forces to retreat into the Tobruk garrison without being destroyed.

The siege of Tobruk

Rommel's lightning advance in early April 1941 had achieved its initial objectives well ahead of schedule, but the vital port of Tobruk (through which the sole metalled road called the Via Balbia passed) remained in Allied hands. The Australian Major-General Leslie Morshead organized its defence. In addition to the Australian troops in the port, there were men from the Indian 18th Cavalry, Royal Northumberland Fusiliers, Royal Horse Artillery, Essex Yeomanry and South Nottinghamshire Hussars, plus tanks from the Royal Tank Regiment. Other troops were quickly brought in by sea to bolster the garrison to over 30,000 Commonwealth troops. Tobruk's defensive perimeter consisted of minefields, anti-tank ditches, barbed and concertina wire, and trenches.

134

The siege of Tobruk, April–December 1941

Harold Atkins was a British NCO serving with the 2nd Battalion The Queen's Royal Regiment (West Surrey). He was posted to Tobruk to relieve the Australian troops in September 1941. He describes his arrival:

"We got on the destroyers and we sailed in the hours of late evening. After we cleared the Alexandria Harbour and into the open sea it was announced over the tannoy that we were heading for Tobruk. The reason for us being sent to Tobruk was to relieve the Australians so that they could be sent home ... We negotiated that voyage very successfully, except for one minor dropping of some bombs ... and then towards the hours of darkness on the second day we approached the Tobruk Harbour. Now, Tobruk under those conditions was suffering air raids nearly every night from the German air force, which was very near by, and it was our very good fortune to have arrived in Tobruk on one of the very few nights when there was no air raid, which was a blessing as far as we were concerned. The Royal Navy were absolutely slick, they knew that the lives of their ships depended on getting in and out and

BELOW British gunners, manning German 149mm guns captured from the Italians, play a game of darts at Tobruk, 1 September 1941.

as far away under cover of darkness as it could be safe to do so, so there was no 'hanky panky'. The destroyer pulled up along some sort of hulk in the harbour which was connected to the shore by some kind of plank, and we were told 'Right, pick up your kit, away you go.' All done quietly, and with great efficiency on the Navy's part. We found ourselves ashore in Tobruk where, within the space of half an hour or so, we were gathered together, mustered and marched out to the outer fringes of the Tobruk area in open desert, straight into the perimeter."

ABOVE A soldier on guard duty at Tobruk, 12 September 1941. In the distance a derelict Italian lorry, loaded with ammunition, has been hit.

LEFT A cigarette case associated with the Tobruk service of Trooper Harold Lee, C Squadron, 1st King's Dragoon Guards (2nd Armoured Division). The incised and ink inscriptions inside read: TOBRUK MAY 9TH – NOV. 21ST 1941 / EL-GUBI. JUNE–SEPT. / 7905322 TPR LEE 1ST KDG; and 1941 TOBRUK MAY 9 – NOV 21.

Rommel's initial attempt to capture the port on 13–14 April saw the 5th Panzer Regiment penetrate the outer defences, but Australian anti-tank gun fire forced it to retreat. A further Italian attack on 15 April failed, and a state of prolonged siege ensued. The defenders were subjected to frequent air attack by Stuka dive-bombers, and spent much time improving the defences, particularly trenches, foxholes and shelters. Between 30 April and 5 May, Rommel launched another assault on the Tobruk perimeter, but heavy casualties and tank losses resulted for little territorial gain. Rommel decided to abandon direct assault, and was now forced to attempt the starvation and strangulation of the garrison and the interdiction of supply and evacuation by sea – Tobruk's lifeline.

Operations *Brevity* and *Battleaxe*

The losses inflicted on the DAK at Tobruk suggested to Churchill that the Axis forces could be pushed backwards and the port relieved, and he put pressure on Wavell to move onto the offensive. An Allied counter-attack was planned in two phases, under the names *Brevity* and *Battleaxe*. Operation *Brevity* would see the Axis forces pushed back from Sollum and Capuzzo, before moving as near as possible to Tobruk. The attack began on 15 May, and Matilda tanks of 4th Royal Tank Regiment and men of the 22nd Guards Brigade secured the Halfaya Pass with heavy losses. The 1st Battalion The Durham Light Infantry and surviving tanks of 4th Royal Tank Regiment managed to capture Fort Capuzzo, but were driven back later in the day by a 5th Panzer Regiment counter-attack.

Operation *Battleaxe*

Peter Alfred Lincoln Vaux was a British officer serving with the Reconnaissance Troop, Headquarters Squadron, 4th Battalion The Royal Tank Regiment, during Operations *Brevity* and *Battleaxe*. He recalls his role in Operation *Battleaxe* in June 1941:

"Halfaya Pass was actually a fort in the sense that it had stone sangars, trenches and so forth at the top of the Pass. Down at the bottom of the Pass was the coast road that ran through Sollum and up to Bardia, and we had two troops down there with Indian soldiers who were to attack along the coast road at the same time as C Squadron was at the top. We attacked with B Squadron south of Halfaya, C Squadron at Halfaya, and A Squadron in reserve. It was pretty disastrous. C Squadron were annihilated as they attacked Halfaya. The guns they had there were very big ones, huge guns – naval guns. I suppose they were 6in. guns, the Germans would have called them 150mm. The squadron commander, before he was killed, sent a radio message that I remember well, in which he said 'These bloody guns are tearing my tanks to pieces!' And they were literally doing that, with tanks split apart like a nutshell, like two halves of a walnut. Almost all of those tanks were lost. [The German commander] successfully beat that attack off. Later on in a German magazine we captured there was an

account of that battle and of the courage of him and his men. Down below the two troops ... ran straight into a minefield that they knew nothing about and several tanks were blown up ... A Squadron ran straight into German tanks and anti-guns. The Germans had this trick of massing their tanks and anti-tank guns together, and A Squadron suffered very heavily from them, so much so that they

ceased to be really operational for a while ... Wavell never wanted to do the operation, he was forced to by Churchill. So much stuff had been sent to Greece and we weren't strong enough for it. It wasn't until the following November when the Crusader operation occurred that we had been built up ... Wavell was such a taciturn man that you couldn't judge anything from what he said."

RIGHT The formation badge for XIII Corps, and subsequently that of HQ British Element Trieste Force (BETFOR), showing a leaping gazelle. XIII Corps was formed in the Western Desert and was the first corps to operate in this theatre. As part of the Eighth Army it was involved in the hard fighting of the winter of 1941–1942, including the relief of Tobruk. It participated in the Battle of El Alamein and the advance through Libya and Tunisia. Subsequently XIII Corps landed in Sicily. In September 1943 it landed on the Italian mainland and remained there until the end of the war. It participated in the final campaign in the Po Valley. At the end of hostilities, the corps occupied part of Austria and the north-eastern corner of Italy including Trieste.

RIGHT Soldiers of the 4th Indian Division inscribe the side of their lorry with "Khyber pass to Hellfire Pass" in June 1941. "Hellfire Pass" was the nickname for the strategically important Halfaya Pass, fortified by the Germans, which the British attacked during Operations *Brevity* and *Battleaxe*.

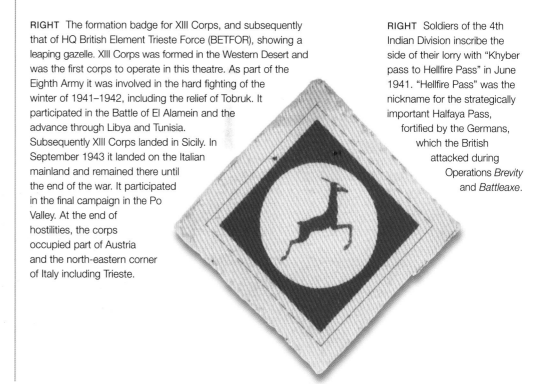

In late May, 7th Armoured Division received a vital injection of tanks and vehicles, including the brand-new Mark VI Crusader tanks. Wavell came under increasing pressure to launch Operation *Battleaxe*, the follow-up to *Brevity* and aimed at destroying Axis forces in the Sollum and Bardia area. The attack began on 15 June, with the Matildas of 4th Royal Tank Regiment once again coming under heavy fire on Halfaya Pass, and losing almost all of the tanks. The 4th Indian Division attempted to secure the foot of the Pass, but was halted by enemy fire. Fort Capuzzo was recaptured by 4th Armoured Brigade and 22nd Guards Brigade, while 7th Armoured Brigade attacked Hafid Ridge, coming under strong counter-attack by 5th Panzer Regiment. By dawn on 17 June, accurate fire from dug-in guns and pressure from the German 5th Light Division began to tell, and the Allied forces retired back to their starting lines. Operation *Battleaxe* had been a humiliating defeat for Wavell, and many of the precious new tanks had been lost. Wavell was replaced as the Commander-in-Chief of British forces in the Middle East by General Claude Auchinleck in July 1941; Wavell then transferred to India, where he swapped jobs with Auchinleck, who was Commander-in-Chief of the Indian Army. Prior to this appointment, Auchinleck had commanded the British North-West Expeditionary Force in the Norwegian campaign. He would oversee the creation of one of the most famous British Army formations to serve during the war – Eighth Army – which would soon be blooded in the Operation *Crusader* fighting in November 1941.

OPERATIONS IN IRAQ AND SYRIA

While preparations for *Brevity* and *Battleaxe* were ongoing, pro-Axis rebels in Iraq rose up in revolt, overthrowing the pro-Allied government and causing further problems for Middle East Command. Britain operated key air bases at Habbaniya and Basra, and feared the pro-Axis leanings of the new government – as well as the country's oil reserves falling into Axis hands. "Habforce" was put together and sent to Iraq from Transjordan to relieve the surrounded air base at Habbaniya in May, and men from the 10th Indian Division moved up from Basra to surround Baghdad. By the end of May, the pro-Allied regent of Iraq had been restored to power. On 8 June 1941 a Commonwealth and Free French force invaded the Vichy mandate of Syria. "Habforce" was sent from Iraq following the end of hostilities there, and Damascus was captured on 17 June. Although the campaign was brief, it was a costly one for the Australian and Indian troops involved.

ABOVE The cap badge (in white metal and brass) of the Essex Regiment. The badge was worn from 1900 until 1958 when the Essex Regiment amalgamated with the Bedfordshire and Hertfordshire Regiment to form the 3rd East Anglian Regiment. The Sphinx was awarded for the Egyptian campaign of 1801 and the "Castle and Key" of Gibraltar for the defence of the island fortress during the long siege of 1779–1783. Men of 1st Battalion The Essex Regiment formed part of "Habforce", which took part in the 1941 invasion of Iraq.

Iraq 1941

David de Crespigny Smiley was a British officer serving with the 1st Household Cavalry Regiment in Iraq and Syria in 1941:

"We heard through the grapevine that my regiment, the Household Cavalry, had lost their horses, had been requipped with trucks, and were going into action in Iraq, against Iraqis ... The regiment drove across the desert from Jordan into Iraq with the object of raising the siege of Habbaniya, where British troops were surrounded by Iraqis. I was in 4th Cavalry brigade, which also included an infantry battalion, and RAF armoured cars – it was a mixed bunch ... I was in charge of a troop, which consisted of four 1,500-weight trucks ... I remember the first battle. I was the advance troop, and there was a station on the railway line from Baghdad up to Mosul, and as we went down the main road parallel to the station we were fired on. I was told by my squadron leader to try to capture the station ... We had four Hotchkiss guns, which were dreadful and kept jamming (I had been trained in Bren guns before the war, but all our Brens were given to the BEF in 1940 and we were issued with Hotchkiss ones instead), and opened up on the station. All the Iraqis upped tools and fled, and the station was ours. They left some weapons behind, including Bren guns! So we took them over and used them ... We surrounded Habbaniya. We had a whole brigade and battalion of the Essex Regiment. Eventually one or two of our aircraft bombed it, and the Iraqis withdrew towards Baghdad, and we followed them up. I think our embassy there was under some sort of siege too. From there we formed a column and shot up to Mosul, where there were quite a lot of German aircraft on the airfield there. Their German markings had been overpainted with Iraqi ones; they had German pilots and German ground crew, but they had buzzed off by the time we got there to Turkey. When we got to Mosul, I was told to go off with my troop and try to cut the road leading into Iraq from Turkey."

INSET The higher formation badge for Persia and Iraq Command (PAIC). The elephant emblem is said to be a reference to the first commander of Persia and Iraq Command, General (later Field Marshal) Sir Henry Maitland Wilson, whose nickname was "Jumbo". The badge was also worn by British Troops Iraq. Although Persia and Iraq were both nominally independent neutral countries they were within the British sphere of interest because of their rich resources of oil. Thus the pro-German rebellion in Iraq in June 1941 and the concern about German influence in Persia in August 1941 both resulted in British military intervention. Persia and Iraq Command (PAIC) under General Wilson was opened on 15 September 1942 in Baghdad. Although the command never saw combat, it was responsible for a massive logistics effort in creating roads, railways and water transport facilities.

RIGHT British troops gaze across the Euphrates at Baghdad, 11 June 1941.

THE RELIEF OF TOBRUK

Many of the troops garrisoning Tobruk were gradually relieved throughout mid 1941. Due to political pressure at home, the Australian 9th Division was relieved (by sea) by the British 70th Division, the Polish Carpathian Brigade and 32nd Army Tank Brigade. Most of the British units in the garrison remained. In September 1941, due to the rapid expansion of Commonwealth forces in North Africa, Eighth Army was formed. It consisted of XIII and XXX Corps and the Tobruk Garrison, and came under the command of General Alan Cunningham.

A new offensive, Operation *Crusader*, was planned to drive the Axis forces out of Cyrenaica and relieve Tobruk. XIII Corps would advance and attack at Sollum and Halfaya, while XXX Corps would swing south before heading for Tobruk. The Tobruk garrison would also break out at the same time to support the massive offensive. The attack began on 18 November 1941, and caught Rommel by surprise. In the course of the prolonged and complex fighting, Eighth Army lost numerous tanks and the 5th South African Brigade was overrun and captured near Sidi Rezegh. However, 4th New Zealand Brigade managed to make contact with the Tobruk garrison on 27 November. On 7 December, his supplies low and his troops exhausted, Rommel ordered a retreat to El Agheila. *Crusader* had succeeded in its objectives, but the Desert War was far from over.

The crew of a Matilda tank take a break during the fighting near Tobruk, 28 November 1941.

Operation *Crusader*

Walter Frederick Dale was an NCO serving with 3rd Battalion The Royal Tank Regiment in North Africa, 1941–1942. His unit was one of those equipped with the new "Honey" and Grant tanks. He describes his unit's role during Operation *Crusader* in the closing months of 1941:

ABOVE Men of the Surrey and Sussex Yeomanry lighting up Italian cigars in Tobruk, 10 November 1941.

"We pushed the Germans back to El Agheila and moved to where the Foreign Legion were in the desert [Bir Hakeim]. It was reported that the Germans were going to attack and they came round the fort, Bir Hakeim, and we moved out to meet them. My squadron was put up to the right, and they didn't realize the big fellows, the Grants, were waiting for them. The battle went on and we knocked out about six or seven tanks – Mk IIIs – because we were hull down. Eventually we had to move back towards Sidi Rezegh, because it got really bad. When we got there we were in leaguer one night, and the Germans did a night march and caught everybody on the hop – it was every man for himself – staff cars and lorries all over the place. We were given a map reference and told to

RIGHT A British Crusader tank passes a burning German PzKpfw IV tank during Operation *Crusader*, 27 November 1941.

meet up. When we got there, there were only 13 of us. We got ourselves organized and formed a composite squadron, and got a call to help the South African Infantry Brigade out. When we got there they were overrun. It was a terrible thing, I never saw anything like it, and eventually we went into the attack with them and they pulled back, fortunately. The infantry got back over the hillside and we took up hull down positions and we were all sitting there waiting to see what was happening. There was a bit of shellfire going on, but nothing to worry us – then all of a sudden we heard what to us was like a bugle sound, and when we looked over to the valley we could see one of the Hussar regiments attacking the Germans through the bottom of the valley. It was a fantastic sight to see."

1941–1942

THE WAR IN THE FAR EAST

The Japanese conquest of the Pacific

Throughout the 1930s, Japan had become increasingly involved in the fragmented political turmoil in China, seeking both to protect her interests in Manchuria province and Korea and to dominate all of China. In late 1931 Japanese troops invaded Manchuria, establishing a puppet government. In July 1937 a full-scale invasion of northern and central China took place. The 1940 fall of France meant that French territories in Indochina were now prey to the Japanese, and moves to occupy them began in September 1940. Japan now put plans in place to create an ambitious defensive perimeter around her new possessions, seeking to defend them from British, Dutch and American encroachment or attack. The creation of this perimeter would also allow the seizure of precious resources, such as oil, rubber and tin, for which Japan was dependent on other countries. Japan was particularly dependent on the United States of America for its oil needs.

On 8 December 1941 Japanese forces moved into Siam (forcing it into an alliance with Japan) and began operations against British forces in Malaya. The Japanese 38th Division cleared any British troops from the defensive positions on the

The fall of Hong Kong, 25 December 1941

Harry Sidney George Hale was a British NCO serving with 2nd Battalion The Royal Scots in Hong Kong at the time of its fall. He was captured and was a prisoner of war until 1945:

"I was playing tennis on the Sunday afternoon. We were asked if there were any service personnel playing, and if there were then we should return immediately to our units as they were fearful that some action was going to be taken against the colony ... We never really believed it would happen, there was nothing to say it would. The fact that we were under canvas and training didn't seem to matter – we had been under canvas before. Two Canadian units came over to us – the Winnipeg Grenadiers and the Royal Rifles of Canada – they were untrained and came with no equipment whatsoever. They had to share what equipment we had and some of them had never even fired or handled a rifle ... About seven o'clock in the morning we realized that the Japanese were attacking the Kai Tak Airport. There was no resistance to them that I can remember ... The planes continued to come over several times during the day; we had our Bren guns for anti-aircraft purposes but we never had occasion to use them ... I remember our first encounter with Japanese troops. We pointed our rifles, our Bren gun and our Thompson machine gun at these individuals on the verge and gave out the classic challenge: 'Halt,

who goes there?' We didn't have to wait for very long because they turned and fired at us and we opened fire at the same time. The fire came very quick and heavy at us, my machine gun used its drum up. I yelled out 'Every man for himself!' I saw two of my men and followed them right over the side of a cliff; we spun over and over, and I rolled right down to the bottom, where I could hear the firing still going on ... The surrender took place on Christmas Day. We understood that the Japanese were not going to take any prisoners and we wondered very much what our fate was going to be. I had ended up in hospital, having lost fingers following a mortar hit.

We never saw any Japanese on Christmas Day, but on Boxing Day three Japanese came walking round the beds, heavily camouflaged, one with a machine gun pointing at the various beds, while the other two soldiers had drawn revolvers pointing. They walked round from bed to bed looking at each person but did nothing, and, as far as we could understand, never said anything, at least in English. But we still didn't know what was going to be the outcome. We learned later that all the personnel in the Stanley Hospital had been murdered in their beds and the nurses had been raped and killed."

LEFT Newly trained officers and NCOs of the Chinese Battalion, Hong Kong Volunteer Defence Corps, in December 1941. The Corps was the largest military unit of the Hong Kong Garrison at the time of the Japanese invasion.

RIGHT Japanese troops led by Lieutenant-General Takashi Sakai and Vice-Admiral Miimi Massichi enter Hong Kong on 26 December 1941.

Chinese mainland on 10 December 1941, and soon moved to occupy Hong Kong, the defence of which was considered impossible by this stage. British (including men from the Royal Scots), Canadian and Indian Army forces, aided by the Hong Kong Volunteer Defence Corps, were tasked with its defence. The colony and defending garrison fell on 25 December 1941, with hundreds of British and Commonwealth troops surrendering. In late December, Japanese troops landed on British North Borneo, and Sandakan was finally occupied on 17 January 1942.

ABOVE The cap badge worn by the other ranks of the Royal Scots (The Royal Regiment). The badge was worn until 2006 when the Royal Regiment of Scotland was formed, bar during the brigade system 1958–1969. The 1st Battalion usually wore red cloth behind the voided centre and the 2nd Battalion wore green cloth. The 2nd Battalion The Royal Scots was among the units fighting in Hong Kong at the time of the surrender, together with a battalion from the Middlesex Regiment.

The invasion of Burma

The Japanese considered Burma an important territory to seize, in order to protect its gains in China and to disrupt Allied supply to anti-Japanese forces there. In 1941 there were few British troops stationed in Burma; defensive priorities had been assigned to Malaya and Singapore instead. The garrison consisted principally of Indian Army brigades, the Burma Rifles and the Burma Auxiliary Force (which comprised British, Anglo-Burman and Anglo-Indian troops), and, from February 1942, 7th Armoured Brigade, transferred from Egypt. Chiang Kai Shek's anti-communist Chinese Fifth and Sixth Armies, under Stillwell's command, also moved southwards in an attempt to aid the defence of the Shan States in the north of Burma. The Allies regarded the Chinese contribution as an important one.

The Japanese Fifteenth Army began limited operations on 8 December 1941 at the same time as the advance into Malaya. Following a series of defeats, the Commonwealth forces withdrew to the natural barrier of the Sittang River. On 21 February 1942, the Sittang Bridge was blown and many troops of the 17th Indian Division were left stranded on the wrong side. This spelt disaster for Burma's defence. The capital of Rangoon was evacuated and Japanese troops entered it on 8 March. British and Chinese troops subsequently attempted to make a stand in the north of the country, but were ordered to abandon Burma on 25 April 1942, and to destroy precious oilfields (such as those at Yenangyaung) during their retreat. From May 1942 pro-Japanese Siamese (Thai) forces crossed into the Shan States, harassing the retreating Chinese forces.

The retreat through Burma, February–April 1942

Neville Graham Hogan was a Karen Burmese private who served with an armoured car section of the Burma Auxiliary Force at the time of the Japanese invasion:

"I was at annual camp at the beginning of December 1941 during the Japanese attack at the Mingaldu Aerodrome. I was now in the Armoured Car Section and we were doing perimeter patrols. I think it was Christmas Eve when they bombed us ... I witnessed Rangoon more or less being drained of all its civilian population ... thousands upon thousands of bullock carts and rickshaws carrying whole households on their heads. It became a ghost town ... Shortly after that, at the end of January, the Armoured Car Section was ordered to go down to the south of Burma on the road to Mataban and Bormain. On 19 February we were ambushed by Thai troops 8 or 9 miles north of Mataban. As we came round a bend there was a tree felled on a culvert. I was in the second car, and the leading car just about managed to stop and touch the barrier – the brakes on those armoured cars were very primitive. The Thai soldiers (as we found out later, forced to fight for the Japanese) were literally sitting on

BELOW Electrical equipment at the Yenangyaung oilfields is destroyed as part of the "scorched earth" policy pursued by the British in the face of the Japanese advance into Burma, 16 April 1942.

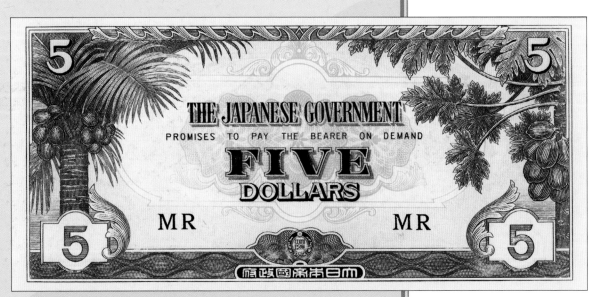

ABOVE This five dollar note, an example of Japanese invasion money, was used in Malaya and North Borneo from 1942 until 1945.

the tree watching us come round, and when the first armoured car came round the bend they stood up – so we shot at them! And they in turn opened up. We backed up and they didn't follow up ... We then fought a rearguard action all the way to Sittang Bridge. We were bombed by the RAF, in spite of us waving at them ... I was on sentry duty in a slit trench at the bridge, wondering whether the Japs would attack us the next morning, when there was a terrific crackle, the tearing of steel – the Sittang Bridge was blown, and we were cut off. If ever one could feel lost, devastated, it was then ...The next three or four days were absolute chaos ... We followed the river, which is a tidal bore, about two miles up river. The local villagers reckoned a good swimmer from there would come out near the bridge – after that you're too near the sea. We started making rafts for the poor Gurkhas with us, who couldn't swim. It's a fast-flowing river, quite terrifying ... I got to the north bank about 300 yards from the bridge, and we made for the railway line ... It was a 42-mile walk to Pegu [50 miles north-east of Rangoon], which we did in two days."

ABOVE The formation badge for General Headquarters India.

145

The capture of Malaya, December 1941–February 1942

Japan's drive to control the Gulf of Siam also involved the capture of Malaya and heavily fortified Singapore. The Japanese Fifteenth Army advanced through Siam (Thailand) into northern Malaya by land, while combined naval and air landings by the Japanese Twenty-fifth Army placed troops on the eastern coast of the peninsula at Singora and Patani in Siam on 8 December 1941. British defensive efforts in Malaya at the time of the invasion were hampered by the nature of the terrain to be defended. The mixture of British, Australian (8th Division), Malay and Indian Army units were widely dispersed, poorly prepared, and ill equipped for jungle warfare. As the Japanese offensive from the north developed,

British troops were forced into retreat southwards towards Singapore. At the Battle of the Slim River near Kuala Lumpur in early January 1942, the Commonwealth forces were heavily defeated, overcome by a Japanese flanking manoeuvre. Among the units involved were the Argyll and Sutherland Highlanders and the 11th Indian Division. Between 29 January and 5 February, the Commonwealth units were reinforced by the arrival of the British 18th (East Anglian) Division. All British forces had evacuated the Malayan mainland by 31 January, withdrawing to the fortress of Singapore. However, with the causeway over the Johore Straits and the water supply between the mainland and the island both destroyed, its fall was only a matter of time. Japanese troops crossed the Straits on 8 February and by the 13th had

The fall of Singapore

James Roland Gregory was a British NCO serving with a mortar battery of 6th Battalion The Royal Norfolk Regiment (part of 18th Division) in Malaya, arriving in Singapore aboard HMS *Dorsetshire* in January 1942. He became a prisoner of war following the fall of Singapore, and worked on the Burma–Thailand railway:

"The day we arrived the Japs bombed the docks. Fortunately they missed completely. There was torrential rain and we went to a camp, arriving about 4 o'clock in the afternoon … It seemed to be chaos, troops were all over the place. There were two commanders, one Australian, one British; Percival was the British commander … The camp we were in was overrun with all sorts of troops from different regiments, nobody knew what was what. We were delighted to be told that night we were going into action the following morning. At first light on the second day we were sent out of that chaos to the comparative peace of the front line. At least we knew what we were doing there, in the camp it was absolute bedlam. It was a case of the left hand not knowing what the right hand was doing … I remember our encounter with the Japanese troops. Through my glasses I could see Japs landing but they were out of range of my guns, so we had to sit and wait until they came into range … The first fire we came under was from their mortars, which outgunned mine. They had the equivalent of a 4-inch mortar, which gave them a range of about 2,500 yards, almost 1,000 yards more than I could do. So it was a matter of counting the seconds and hoping their troops were still coming forward. I just blazed away, I ordered

RIGHT Lieutenant-General Percival and his party carry the Union Jack on their way to surrender Singapore to the Japanese at the Ford Motor Factory, 15 February 1942.

the two guns to open fire – rapid fire – into the jungle. I hoped that my shells were landing among them because we knew they were there somewhere. It was a case of taking pot luck … The following morning we saw them, they came across the road, with screaming and yells and firecrackers, but the attack was beaten off … 24 hours later they came at us from behind, they'd gone around and came up the hill behind us. Their aircraft came over too. The strange thing about that was that the chap used to sit there with the bombs on his lap and just drop them on us, they were anti-personnel bombs … We got down the hill and rejoined our company. There was no Allied air cover … The

Japanese always used psychological tactics. They used firecrackers to distract you, and came at you like a bunch of screaming women. They didn't take prisoners. We saw our troops beheaded – chaps they had caught – others bayonetted to death … Morale started to get low, we were forever withdrawing. There was disorder, we really weren't able to have a good go … We withdrew once more, and three days later I got wounded, two bullets through my ankle. I was taken down to the General Hospital at Singapore, and then to a smaller hospital, and that's where I was when the Japs walked in on 15 February."

secured the north-western part of Singapore, forcing the defenders back to Singapore city. With supplies running out, the island was surrendered by the British commander Lieutenant-General Arthur Percival on the 15th. By the end of the Malayan campaign, over 100,000 Commonwealth troops had been captured. The Japanese occupiers renamed Singapore *Syonan-to* ("South Island"), and the reprisals against the Chinese population were particularly brutal.

RIGHT The formation badge for 18th Division. The "windmill sails" badge denoted the association of the Division with East Anglia, it being a Second Line Territorial Division composed of men from Essex, Norfolk, Suffolk and Cambridgeshire. The 18th Division was sent to India in at the end of 1941 but was diverted to Singapore. It landed at Singapore in late January 1942, and after participating in the defence of the island, surrendered with the rest of the fortress garrison on 15 February.

LEFT A soldier of the 1st Battalion The Manchester Regiment uses a tree for cover while aiming his rifle, 17 October 1941. He is in training in Malaya prior to the outbreak of hostilities.

DECISION IN THE DESERT
The Battle of Gazala

In January 1942, Axis forces in North Africa began a counter-offensive, recapturing Western Cyrenaica before Rommel's advance came to a halt against a string of Commonwealth interconnected defensive "boxes" which stretched from Gazala on the Mediterranean coast to Bir Hakeim in the open desert to the south. Between February and May 1942 both sides rested and re-supplied. The British XIII Corps (consisting mostly of infantry units) defended the front-line defences from Gazala southwards, while the armoured elements of XXX Corps were deployed to the rear of the Commonwealth lines, where key supply dumps were located. Tobruk was held by the 2nd South African Division, with the 1st Free French Brigade stationed at Bir Hakeim some 55 miles to the south.

Rommel renewed the offensive on 26 May 1942, launching a diversionary Italian attack against the centre of the Gazala defensive line, and an outflanking manoeuvre by the Afrika Korps into undefended territory deep to the south of Bir el Hakeim. Eighth Army, now under the command of Lieutenant-General Neil Ritchie, was taken by surprise, and could only launch a series of poorly coordinated and isolated counter-attacks, which were easily defeated. On 28 May, the Axis forces pushed past the Knightsbridge defensive box, but the DAK advance was checked by counter-attacks of 1st Armoured Division. However, Eighth Army's command was plagued by indecision and uncertainty, and opportunities were missed to inflict damage on the overstretched DAK spearheads. On 5 June a major British counter-attack was launched, but this was destroyed piecemeal, and 21st Panzer Division resumed the offensive, overwhelming the Gazala defences. On 12 June the DAK defeated British armoured units at the Knightsbridge box, destroying over 100 tanks. A further counter-attack by 4th Armoured Brigade on 17 June at Sidi Rezegh also failed, and Eighth Army began to withdraw. On 21 June, a lightning German assault captured Tobruk and its large quantities of ammunition and supplies. Over 30,000 Commonwealth troops entered captivity. Following the disaster, Eighth Army began a rapid retreat back to the Egyptian frontier and the defensive positions at Mersa Matruh, with a further withdrawal east to El Alamein completed by 30 June. With outright defeat a distinct possibility, General Auchinleck took command of Eighth Army from Ritchie. Ritchie's career was not over though, and he would go on to command the 52nd Division, and later XII Corps during the 1944 invasion of France..

148

Gazala and the fall of Tobruk

Gerald Brian Fisher was a British officer commanding a troop of Valentine tanks of the 4th Royal Tank Regiment in North Africa, 1942. During the Battle of Gazala he was positioned at the Knightsbridge defensive box before retreating to Tobruk, where he was captured by Italian troops:

"I thought the Valentine tank was very good, very reliable and tough. Of course it was only a three-man tank, which was rather unsatisfactory for a troop commander as you wanted the extra man in the turret. The other fellows were disappointed to lose their Matildas, the Valentines seemed smaller and lighter than them.

BELOW The crew of a Valentine tank have a wash and shave in the Western Desert, 27 March 1942.

We found that Rommel had broken through at Bir Hakeim. We went over a ridge and saw some tanks advancing towards us; we didn't know whether they were ours or theirs, and we turned back. The transporters went as fast as possible back up to the ridge, dropped the ramps out and we were off ... There was chaos, not only in the Knightsbridge box, but in general because of this sudden breakthrough by Rommel south of Bir Hakeim. The Free French were there. Nobody quite knew what was happening; people didn't seem to know what the position really was until eventually it settled down and we had to withdraw into Tobruk, which then became besieged ... We later heard from the commander that Tobruk was going to surrender the next morning and it was every man for himself ... We all expected to hold out just as the Australians had done in November before the breakout, we never thought to surrender. We were rather angry, we all felt we could have held out for longer."

ABOVE A Vest Pocket Kodak Autographic still camera (with autographic pen and case) dating from the Second World War service of L. Jackson, Royal Artillery. He carried this camera during the campaign in the Western Desert.

RIGHT A British Matilda tank passes the "Knightsbridge" road junction on 1 June 1942, shortly after the major tank battle there during the Battle of Gazala.

The First Battle of El Alamein

The first battle that took place at the El Alamein defensive positions following the British retreat and the Axis pursuit was a confused two-week affair that ended in a virtual stalemate, although it did prevent Rommel from driving further into Egypt towards Cairo and the Suez Canal. Between 1 and 3 July 1942, the German 90th Light Division launched a series of infantry attacks against the El Alamein defensive box, while the Afrika Korps also attempted an outflanking manoeuvre to the south. However, neither was successful, with the British artillery playing a telling role in holding them up. A further German attack on 9 July involving 21st Panzer Division was also unsuccessful. A series of attacks by Commonwealth troops followed in the northern sector.

The Australian 9th Division captured the key position of Tel el Eisa near the coast from the decimated Italians between 10 and 14 July. The New Zealand Division unsuccessfully attacked Ruweisat Ridge between the 15th and 17th, and a combined Commonwealth attack on Rommel's centre took place between 21 and 22 July. On 26 July the Australians launched a further attack from Tel el Eisa towards Myteirya Ridge, but this also failed to dislodge the enemy. Both sides realized that further gains were unlikely and reverted to the defensive, taking the opportunity to rest and resupply.

Alam el Halfa

On 12 August 1942 Bernard Law Montgomery was appointed to the command of Eighth Army. The command had

The First Battle of El Alamein

ohn Albert Luxford was a British NCO serving with 1st Battalion The King's Royal Rifle Corps, 1941–1943:

"The 25-pdr was one of the greatest guns of all time and I believe many of us alive today have got a lot of thanks to say to it. It really was the weapon of all weapons. On the day of the battle of El Alamein those guns fired so much they had to take them out of action because the barrels were white hot. I think if you talk to any ex-serviceman and mention the 25-pounder gun, he would really have the greatest of praise for it. Obviously the German 88mm outdistanced it, but in action it was really mobile, inasmuch that it was easy to handle – far more so than the German gun which was a big cumbersome weapon that used to stand on a big four-wheeled trolley – it used to take them quite a while to keep moving it, so the 25-pounder in all did have that big advantage ... During our retreat to El Alamein, our morale was not wonderful. It's like when you have a personal accident, it takes a little while to come round again, and especially being chased as we were. I remember sitting in a truck, driving it night and day, with the Germans behind us all the time for four to five days, where my only meals were a tin of 'M and V' behind the wheel. And the only way you could get a meal was to open a tin and go along at the same time holding a steering wheel with the tin between your knees and a fork or spoon in the other hand ... To get across the depressions in the desert, where there was very soft sand, we had to be escorted by light tanks, so that should we get stuck the tanks would be able to pull us out and we could continue. Otherwise if we were left there we would be written off because there was no way you could get out. This was all a complete nightmare, something you could never forget."

originally been given to Lieutenant-General William Gott, but he had been killed in a plane crash on a return journey to Cairo. Montgomery brought a confident air with him, and exercised a tight grip on the command and control of the army. In the temporary lull that followed the end of the First Battle of El Alamein, Montgomery quickly set about consolidating the defences along the front line. He prepared his forces to work in a concentrated and closely coordinated manner, and to gain numerical superiority for the next Allied offensive. Rommel was aware of this, and resolved to act quickly before the defences became too formidable. He determined on a southern outflanking manoeuvre around El Alamein, before pushing up to occupy the crucial Alam el Halfa Ridge, which commanded the surrounding terrain.

He then intended to head north to the coast – hoping to cut off Eighth Army in the process.

The ridge had been heavily fortified by the British, and was defended by the 44th Division. The German offensive began on 31 August 1942, and it soon encountered elements of the British 7th Armoured Division, which slowed the advance. It also became bogged down in the prepared minefields. The German attack on the Alam el Halfa Ridge began on 1 September, with the odds stacked in the defenders' favour. The Germans particularly suffered heavily from withering British anti-tank and artillery fire. By the next day the attack had been called off and the Germans withdrew, having suffered significant losses that would prove to be telling in the engagements to follow.

LEFT The 25-pounder Quick Firing (QF) gun. The first 25-pounder appeared in 1935 and the final stages of its development were hastened by the outbreak of the Second World War. Initial production was slow, but by 1945, over 12,000 had been manufactured. It became the Army's basic close support artillery weapon, and doubled as an anti-tank gun in the North African campaign. It was also employed in jungle, airborne and mountain roles, and was still in widespread use in the mid 1970s. This example, a Mk II Gun on a Mk I carriage, served with the 11th Field Regiment in North Africa. On 2 July 1942, it helped to halt a major German advance at Ruweisat Ridge, where the regiment suffered nearly 25 per cent casualties.

LEFT An infantry section on patrol near El Alamein, 17 July 1942.

RIGHT *25-Pounder Gun and Team in Action on the El Alamein Front*, by John Berry (oil on panel, 1942).

The Second Battle of El Alamein

Following a further period of recuperation for both sides, Montgomery launched Operation *Lightfoot* on 23 October 1942, heralded by a massive "creeping barrage" artillery bombardment of the German defensive positions. The aim was for four infantry divisions (including the 51st Highland) of XXX Corps to breach the German defences in the north around Tel el Eisa and the Myteirya Ridge, and for the highly mobile armour of X Corps to create two corridors through the German minefields and break through. The infantry divisions would then widen their breaches, "crimping" away at the outer defences. Meanwhile, diversionary attacks would be launched in the south by British XIII Corps.

The Allied attacks failed to make good progress, and on October 27 Rommel counter-attacked 1st Armoured Division around Kidney Ridge, before being checked by heavy anti-tank fire. Montgomery had ordered 8th Australian Division to attack towards the coast in the north.

ABOVE *Sergeant B Montague MM: One of the 'Desert Rats' (7th Armoured Division)*, by Henry Carr (oil on canvas, 1943).

The Second Battle of El Alamein

Bill Partridge was a British officer serving with B Company, 9th Battalion The Durham Light Infantry (part of 50th Northumbrian Division, XIII Corps) during the Second Battle of El Alamein in October 1942:

"Everyone in the battalion knew that we were being moved from the centre of the line to the north for a special purpose ... As quickly as possible we were told why. We were told that the breakthrough had got to be done, and who was going to do it? 50th Division! So off we went, and we trucked our way north. The moment we got to an assembly area the drill for the major attack took place: first of all we had as many rations and as much water as we wanted – we were allowed far more than we had previously. We were allowed the airmail cards, which were always strictly rationed – we could have as many of those as we liked ... Every piece of equipment that had been mislaid or lost was replaced in double-quick time. The medical officer, the doc, seemed to come round and speak to every single man, looking at them. And the RSM organized the zeroing of weapons – all in three or four days. In the meantime, we were briefed. First of all the CO

RIGHT British infantry advance through the dust and smoke, in a posed reconstruction of the Second Battle of El Alamein, 24 October 1942.

ABOVE The formation badge for the 7th Armoured Division ("Desert Rats"). The original badge is said to have been designed by the wife of Sir Michael O'Moore Creagh, who commanded the division from December 1939. The original design was a jerboa, in either red or, according to some reports, "pink", on a white or buff circle on a red square, very similar to the 7th Armoured Brigade sign. The second version, in which the jerboa had a distinct red colour and was embroidered directly onto battledress material, may have been adopted as late as 1943 when the division was in the Tripoli area.

gathered the company commanders and briefed them. Then the company commanders briefed their companies, they briefed by rank – platoon commanders, platoon sergeants – to make sure they knew exactly what it was. They then went to the platoons and each platoon commander or sergeant briefed his platoon. It was at that level that the battle was to be fought ... The day before we were due to set off, our tanks arrived for us; ours were from the Warwickshire Yeomanry ... Every man knew that every possible thing had been done. For taking men into what was going to be not only vital tactically but a very harrowing

experience, it was an example of almost perfect preparation ... I remember our advance during Operation Supercharge. Us soldiers were between 3 and 5 yards apart, varying of course according to what you are walking into, but we knew that we just had to keep going, so we did. The pace was that used for route marches, 3 miles an hour, a steady pace that took account of the equipment you were carrying, the ground you were walking over, and the fact that you were looking for trouble in front of you. We knew that we were walking through probably the most intensive minefield that had ever been laid. That was one of the reasons why there had been no

breach before this. The German's called it the 'Devil's Garden'. Because they had had weeks and weeks to build it up, and they were so good at this, it literally consisted of everything from a little shoe mine to a buried aircraft bomb. As far as we were concerned our job was simply to get to the other end through the minefield, then we were not expected to do any more ... I finished up with only a third of my platoon at the far end. It was bullets, mines, and at the very end were grenades – because the infantry in the firing positions just beyond their minefield did not give up, they had to be fought out."

Due to Operation *Lightfoot*'s stalling, on 1 November Montgomery launched Operation *Supercharge* to the south of the 9th Australian Division's positions at Point 29. This time Montgomery's attack succeeded, and on 2 November the Commonwealth infantry broke through the German defences; with 9th Armoured Brigade holding the gains, the British 1st Armoured Division, equipped with newly arrived Sherman tanks, penetrated the German lines. Over the next two days the German defences were gradually broken down, and by 4 November a German retreat had begun back across the Egyptian border and back into Tripolitania. The Axis forces had lost over 500 tanks, 1,000 artillery pieces and 80,000 troops captured.

154

ABOVE A Sherman tank of C Squadron, 9th Queen's Royal Lancers, 2nd Armoured Brigade, 1st Armoured Division, in the desert, 5 November 1942. Second El Alamein witnessed the first engagement of the Lend-Lease Shermans.

Operation *Supercharge*

John Douglas Semken was a British officer serving with The Nottinghamshire Yeomanry (Sherwood Rangers), Royal Armoured Corps, at the time of the Second El Alamein battles.

"I don't remember whether we did any tactical training. The tactics seemed to be perfectly bloody obvious: you found a ridge, and then you hid behind it, and you fired at the enemy, and then you tried to get a bit closer ... I can remember that on the second morning of the [second] Battle of Alamein I was sitting just behind the crest of a feature, and I could see 200 tanks all lined up. You could tell looking along the line which tanks were occupied by officers, because all the others were about six feet behind them. We were to break though the German minefields and advance to our position along three tracks – the 'boat' track, 'hat' track and another track, marked by lanterns inside petrol cans into which shapes had been punched. We set off at dusk and travelled right through the night and ultimately passed most of the way through the minefields, but found ourselves at dawn still lined head to tail actually in a minefield, and we lost

RIGHT Men of the 1/6th Battalion The Queen's Regiment marching into Tobruk, 18 November 1942.

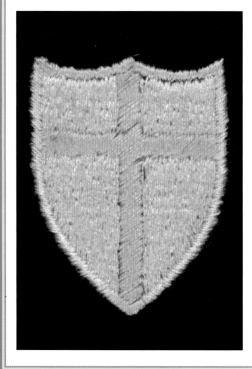

LEFT The formation badge for Eighth Army, and, post-1945, of British Troops Austria. The badge is said to owe its origin to the fact that Eighth Army's first operation was Operation *Crusader*; as the design of a badge was at that time under consideration, a crusader's shield seemed a suitable emblem. The adoption of a yellow cross on a white shield was to avoid confusion with the Red Cross symbol.

one or two tanks ... During Operation Supercharge, we were engaged in three sessions of about three days and three nights each. By this time we had sustained quite a few casualties, but then the thing broke through and the idea was now to gallop on like mad. But the trouble was that the rain came and converted the whole area into a sort of quagmire. We made far slower progress than we had hoped for, but we ultimately got as far as Mersa Matruh where the battle was over and we stopped ... After that we went on and took Tripoli and beyond that to Bengadeni, somewhere in Tunisia. By this time I was feeling pretty damn low. You can only live on adrenalin for so long. By this time I had lost most of my close friends, and it looked as if it was going on and on and on, like a dripping tap. I was greatly startled to discover that I was to be sent back on a course to Cairo, because they had worked it out that I was the only officer in the regiment who hadn't been out of the fighting at all since it began."

The origin of the Combined Operations Headquarters lay in the inter-war years. A closer cooperation between the branches of service (land, sea and air) was desired, particularly with regard to amphibious landings and the seizure or destruction of key military objectives. In the opening phase of the Second World War, and in particular following the Dunkirk disaster and the failed 1940 cross-Channel raids on Boulogne and Guernsey by the "Independent Companies" (Operations *Collar* and *Ambassador*), the momentum increased for the creation of a permanent body overseeing such operations. In July 1940 Roger Keyes was given charge of Combined Operations, with the title of Director from August 1941. He would hold this position until October 1941, when Lord Louis Mountbatten took over. Keyes brought together key staff from all three branches of service in an effort to improve planning and coordination; the key combat arm of the Command comprised the Commandos, ten units of which were first raised (from volunteers) in the UK in June 1940.

The Commandos (renamed Special Service Battalions, part of the Special Service Brigade, between November 1940 and February 1941) were initially tasked with executing limited hit-and-run and harassment missions against enemy forces and installations on the Continent and in Norway, and with gathering intelligence on enemy forces. Such raids provided a much-needed boost to home morale in the dark early war years. Several Commando units were also formed in the Middle East, and Colonel Robert Laycock's "Layforce" also joined Middle East Command's order of battle in March 1941, taking part in the fighting in North Africa, Crete and Syria. Training was a vital part of Commando activity, and this came under a centralized system, based at the Commando Training Depot at Achnacarry from February 1942. This year also saw the formation of the Commander of Combined Operations Pilotage Party (COPP); these teams, each of 10–12 men, operated in small groups in canoes launched from submarines or surface craft. Their main role was the clandestine surveying and sampling of enemy beaches as possible landing sites, and the provision of markers to guide assault fleets. In addition, Royal Marine Commandos were formed for the first time in 1942, and an Inter-Allied Commando (comprising refugees from nations under German occupation) was created. No. 30 Commando (a.k.a. Special Engineering Unit) was also formed for the specialist role of intelligence gathering this year.

Lessons learnt during Operation *Torch* in North Africa in late 1942 (where ill-prepared and inadequately equipped Commandos spent prolonged periods fighting in the front line, in sharp contrast to their envisaged role) brought about a fundamental change in the deployment of Commando forces. Whilst still retaining the capacity and skills to conduct raids

LEFT Admiral Lord Louis Mountbatten, GCVO, KCB, DSO, a portrait by Bernard Hailstone (1945). Mountbatten began his career in the Navy aged 16 during the First World War. In 1939 he was commanding the destroyer HMS *Kelly*. In 1941 he was made head of Combined Operations Command. In late 1943 Mountbatten was appointed as head of the South East Asia Command by Churchill. He worked with General William Slim to direct the liberation of Burma, Malaya and Singapore from the Japanese. Mountbatten's experience in Asia, together with his relationship to the British Royal Family, made him an obvious candidate for the office of Viceroy of India in 1947. As the last viceroy, he presided over the Independence process, including the birth of Pakistan as a separate Muslim state. Afterwards he returned to naval service, rising to become First Sea Lord, and then Chief of the Defence Staff. He was killed by a terrorist bomb on 27 August 1979, while sailing in Donegal Bay near his holiday home.

ABOVE The formation badge for Combined Operations (worn by Army personnel). The emblems featured are an anchor, a Thompson sub-machine gun, and an eagle.

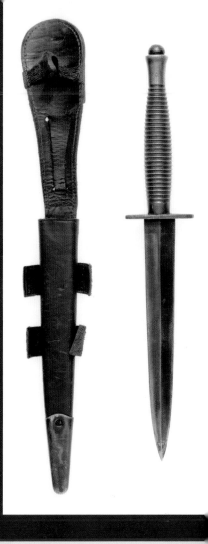

their role would be as lightly equipped assault infantry at the forefront of major landing operations, paving the way for the main body of troops and equipment to follow, whilst retaining the possibility of participating in any extended fighting that followed. This move was accompanied by an expansion and reorganization of the Commandos, overseen by Major-General Robert Laycock. Heavy weapons (mortars and machine guns) and transport were now at the disposition of each unit. The preparations for the invasion of Europe in 1944 added further impetus to this process. The four brigades of the new Special Service Group would see service in North-West Europe, the Far East and the Mediterranean, playing a leading role in the path to final victory.

RIGHT The Fairbairn-Sykes Fighting (or Commando) knife was designed in 1940 by Captain W. E. Fairbairn and Captain E. A. Sykes. These officers were assigned to train British, and later US, special forces personnel in close combat techniques, which they had learnt while serving in the Shanghai Municipal Police Force. The FS knife was issued principally to the Commandos and members of the Special Operations Executive, although many soldiers acquired them.

ABOVE *"Troops To Military Boat Stations". The Commando files on deck for the tensest moment in a raid*, by Brian Mullen (ink, wash on paper, 1944). In a dimly lit ship's hold, a Commando group in full kit waits to disembark via a ladder to

ABOVE Two Commandos of the Royal Engineers with their Yukon packs (containing the gear with which they land on the beaches) practise assault tactics at the Combined Operations School at Dundonald Camp in

RETURN TO THE CONTINENT

Between May 1940 and August 1942, British Commando troops conducted numerous raids against German installations and positions in occupied North-West Europe. The sequence of defeats and setbacks that faced the nation in the opening years of the war were in some part countered by the psychological boosts these raids provided, and numerous important lessons were learnt in the process.

The first raid was Operation *Collar* on the night of 24/25 June 1940. No. 11 Independent Company (one of several prototype Commando units formed in 1940) was tasked with conducting a seaborne raid on Boulogne, France, to capture German prisoners and reconnoitre the situation on the ground. Several vessels failed to make the shore during the landing, and no contact was made with the enemy. No. 11 Independent Company and No. 3 Commando's 14 July 1940 raid codenamed Operation *Ambassador* (an attempt to harass German troops and destroy the airfield on Guernsey in the Channel Islands) also failed to achieve its objectives, and was plagued by poor planning and disorientation.

The 27 February 1942 raid on Bruneval by men of the 2nd Battalion, 1st Parachute Brigade (Operation *Biting*) met with greater success. British scientists were keen to obtain further details of German gun-tracking radar systems, and the men were tasked with taking as many images, and removing as much equipment, as they could. Major John Frost led 120 men in the parachute raid, which succeeded in capturing some enemy equipment and a German technician, before

The Bruneval raid

Macleod Forsyth was a member of C Company, 2nd Parachute Battalion during the Operation *Biting* raid on Bruneval, France, in February 1942:

"We were chosen for special training and we went down to Larkhill on Salisbury Plain. We were issued with live ammunition, and we knew we were going on a special raid ... And then we went to Bruneval. We got on the planes and headed off to France. We knew we were jumping into enemy territory, but it was just another jump, and I never saw any of the boys having any fear. When the red light went on it meant 'get ready to jump', and I was watching the first man on his feet in the hole, who was the corporal; I saw his face turn a different colour. The green light came on and it was 'go, go, go' ... There were two objectives. One was to pinch a radar because our scientists wanted to know if theirs was better than ours and how it worked; we pinched it all right. The other one was as a morale booster, for, by God, we needed it then ... It was a very well planned operation, the best planned operation of the lot ... The papers more or less said 'we can do it', and we could. A lot of people thought 'the Germans could do this and the Germans could do that and they're so bloody clever' – but they weren't so bloody clever then. We caught them with their trousers down, round their ankles, they hadn't a clue."

LEFT A Royal Navy MTB brings men of C Company, 2nd Parachute Battalion into Portsmouth harbour on the morning after the Bruneval raid, 28 February 1942. The Commanding Officer of the assault force, Major J. D. Frost, is on the bridge, second from left.

RIGHT The Wurzburg Radar near Bruneval, a photograph taken by Squadron Leader A. E. Hill on 5 December 1941. Reconnaissance photos such as this one enabled the raiding force to locate, and make off with, the radar's vital components on 27/28 February 1942 for analysis in Britain.

ABOVE *The Raid on the Bruneval Radio-location Station, 27–28 February 1942*, by Richard Eurich, RA (oil on canvas).

withdrawing by sea. Men from No. 3 Commando covered the paratroopers' evacuation. The raid was well received by the British press.

In March 1941, Nos. 3 and 4 Special Service Battalions executed Operation *Claymore*, an attack on the northerly Lofoten Islands in Norway. This was the first large-scale Commando raid of the war. The Commandos departed Gourock, Scotland, on 21 February, arriving in the Lofotens on 4 March. The small German garrison was quickly overwhelmed, and numerous factories and ships were destroyed. A further Commando raid on Norway was carried out on the port of South Vaagso (Operation *Archery*) in December 1941. It met with stiffer resistance and 20 Commandos were killed, with a further 57 wounded. This raid was also highly successful, with much damage inflicted on enemy shipping and the port's industrial infrastructure.

The Commando raids were by now growing in ambition and scale. The St Nazaire raid (Operation *Chariot*) took place in March 1942. The French port was a crucial one for German capital ships with the large Normandie dry dock and U-Boat facilities, and it lay six miles up the River Loire. On the night of 27/28 March the flotilla of small ships with the Commandos aboard reached St Nazaire, with the explosive-laden HMS *Campbeltown* ramming the dry dock; it blew up at 1030hrs the next morning, putting the dock out of action for the rest of the war. A further raid took place against Hardelot on 21/22 April (Operation *Abercrombie*), involving No. 4 Commando and Canadian troops.

The raid on Dieppe, 19 August 1942

William James Spearman was a British NCO serving with No. 4 Commando during the Dieppe raid:

"Our objective at Dieppe, No. 4 Commando, was to destroy one of the two gun batteries guarding the bay ... As my particular landing craft landed on the beach, the front door dropped down and machine-gun fire came right into the boat. Until that moment we'd had no trouble at sea, but No. 6 Commando, who attacked the other gun battery, were unfortunate enough to run into a convoy of E-Boats. They were sitting in assault landing craft and they didn't have a hope in hell of surviving; they were blown out of the water ...Your one inclination was to dig into the shingle and make a hole for yourself – the wrong thing to do,

and when the second front actually happened later on you could see it. The people who went in before us dug a hole and never got off it; they got slaughtered ... The Bangalore torpedoes never went off, something went wrong with them ... One chap was told 'Right, throw yourself on the wire.' ... All of 30 of us funnelled ourselves through the wire and got on with the march up to the battery. But this chap got so entangled in the wire after everyone had run across him that he couldn't disentangle himself, so he got left behind and got taken prisoner ... As soon as the RAF strafing had finished, we assaulted the battery. Pandemonium broke loose then, total confusion. Anyone who wasn't a Commando, you just killed them. People were running out of buildings, some were quite brave, but

they didn't really get a chance ... Nobody escaped, they had nowhere to escape to ... When everything quietened down, the explosives were set to destroy the guns, and we were in haste to get away. We knew the tide had gone out, and there would be 200–300 yards of beach to cross ... By now we had prisoners, we had wounded to carry on made-up stretchers, we were a bit lumbered ... We all got back onto the beach – we never doubted the Navy would be there. As soon as we got there, the Germans started shooting us up ... There were too many people to get back in the boats, so the only thing they could do was shoot some of the prisoners, and they were left on the beach."

ABOVE The Thompson Model 1928A1 sub-machine gun. It fired .45-inch cartridges, and provided a readily available answer to urgent demands by both the US and British and Commonwealth armed forces for sub-machine guns. It was expensive to produce however, and was eventually superseded by simpler designs.

The 19 August 1942 raid on the fortified port of Dieppe, France (Operation *Jubilee*) involved a controversial frontal assault across the town's beaches by Nos. 3 and 4 Commandos, and Canadians from the 4th and 6th Infantry Brigades, with Churchill tanks in support. This was to be the largest raid to date, and involved all three services. The attackers were pinned down on the beaches with heavy losses from enemy fire, and as German reinforcements rushed to the scene the battered survivors were withdrawn by boat later that same day. Although Lord Lovat's No. 4 Commando did manage to destroy the Hesse gun battery five miles west of Dieppe, the raid was a disaster for Allied arms, with over 3,500 men killed, wounded or captured, most of them Canadians. However, key lessons were learned about amphibious landings.

BELOW Churchill tanks, burning landing craft, and Allied dead litter the beach after the controversial raid on Dieppe, 19 August 1942.

RIGHT Tired and dishevelled troops at Newhaven after their return from the Dieppe raid.

1942–1943

THE END IN AFRICA

While the Axis forces in North Africa were in retreat westwards following the defeat at El Alamein, Operation *Torch* took place, with an Anglo-American force landing in Vichy French Morocco and Algeria on 8 November 1942. The British units involved comprised troops from the amphibious-trained British First Army. The 78th Division and two Commando troops were among the first British troops to land unopposed at Algiers on 8 and 9 November. Men from the British 1st Parachute Brigade arrived a few days later. Meanwhile, Hitler dispatched Fifth Panzer Army to Tunisia from Italy to reinforce the Axis forces in the east, which had withdrawn to the Mareth Line defences.

The Allied forces in Algeria began a drive across the border and into Tunisia, with British First Army reaching Tebourba, ten miles short of Tunis, on 27 November, where the offensive ground to a halt following a German counter-attack on 1 December and the onset of winter. The 1st Parachute Brigade was heavily involved in the fighting during the advance. On 12 November the British 3rd Parachute Battalion dropped on and captured the vital airfield at Bone between Algiers and Tunis, and was reinforced later by men from No. 6 Commando. On 29 November the 2nd Parachute Battalion dropped onto the airfield at Oudna, but ended up stranded 50 miles behind enemy lines, and had to conduct an epic fighting retreat. In late February all Allied forces in North Africa were united in Eisenhower's 18th Army Group.

LEFT The cap badge of the Durham Light Infantry, which was worn from 1901, bar change to Queen's crown, until 1968. A smaller version was produced for wearing on the beret after the Second World War. In 1968 the Durham Light Infantry was amalgamated with the remaining light infantry regiments to form The Light Infantry (The Light Division).

The Durham Light Infantry at the Mareth Line

William Watson was a British officer serving with 6th Battalion The Durham Light Infantry (part of 151st Brigade) during the Mareth Line battle. He describes his unit's approach to the battle:

"We could hear the guns now and knew we were pretty close to the front line. On 21 March we did in fact assault the Wadi [Zigzaou]. The Battle of the Mareth Line has been clearly described in all the history books, but I'll try and give you a picture of what the battlefield really looked like. Probably it was the worst battle in which the 6th DLI, 151st Brigade, took part in the whole of the war. Its failure, because it was a failure in my humble opinion, was due to various reasons. The brigade front was much too large, it should have been dealt with by at least two brigades, not one. It was extremely difficult, owing to the nature of the ground, to recce the Wadi itself – its banks and its depth. And also, just beyond the Wadi, the anti-tank ditch – which was 11ft deep. I don't think any proper thought had been given to getting the vehicles, such as the mortars and tanks and carriers and ambulances, across the Wadi. Seemingly there was no bridging equipment in the whole of the Eighth Army. And finally there was the rainstorm in the Matmata Hills that created a flood. The brigade commander was very inexperienced and he had wearying conferences when we were at Diof far into the night. One got nearly fuddled with these long conferences and he was sacked immediately after the battle, within a matter of 12 hours. He came to say farewell immediately afterwards, and he made it very clear to us, as did the corps commander who also came round, Oliver Leese, that we were not to be blamed in any way whatsoever."

RIGHT Sergeant Elms of 16th/5th The Queen's Royal Lancers and his tank crew at El Aroussa, while preparing for the drive on Tunis in 1943. Trooper Bates, Royal Armoured Corps, Signalman Bower, Royal Corps of Signals, and Trooper Goddard, Royal Armoured Corps, are cleaning the 6-pounder gun of their Crusader tank.

LEFT Two wounded soldiers from the Durham Light Infantry show their scars following the Mareth Line battle in March 1943.

163

Meanwhile, to the east, on 23 January 1943 Eighth Army occupied Tripoli in Libya, and on 4 February advance units crossed the border westwards into Tunisia, heading for Tunis. However, Rommel planned one last offensive against what he considered were inexperienced American troops occupying the vital crossing points in mountainous central Tunisia (including Kasserine Pass). This move would protect the vulnerable central sector of the German front line. It would also provide launching points for further attacks against the Allied forces in Tunisia and Algeria, particularly against the British flanks to the north. Despite initial successes, his armoured forces failed to break through. British troops from 6th Armoured Division and 26th Armoured Brigade were heavily involved in the fighting at Kasserine.

In the east, 7th Armoured Division had captured the villages of Tatouine and Medenine, but these lead elements were soon counter-attacked by Rommel's forces on 6 March. The Axis forces were now based at the Mareth Line, a French-built system of blockhouses, gun emplacements, minefields and wire belts, together with formidable natural features such as the deep ditch of the Wadi Zigzaou. Reconnaissance by the Long Range Desert Group indicated that the positions could be outflanked by crossing the sand sea to the south, and Montgomery sent the New Zealand Division and 8th Armoured Brigade to do this. The main attack against the line by 50th (Northumbrian) Division and 4th Indian Division began on the 20 March. The men of the Durham Light Infantry of 151st Brigade, supported by Valentine and

Lance-Corporal John Patrick Kenneally, VC

Lance-Corporal John Patrick Kenneally, 1st Battalion Irish Guards, was awarded the Victoria Cross following his part in the fighting around Tebourba in the final drive on Tunis in 1943. This is the text from his official citation (No. 2722925) in the *London Gazette*:

"The Bou feature dominates all ground east and west between Medjez and Tebourba. It was essential to the final assault on Tunis that this feature should be captured and held.

"A Guards Brigade assaulted and

LEFT Troops from 6th Armoured Division gather round a road sign during the advance on Tunis, 6 May 1943.

captured a portion of the Bou on April 27, 1943. The Irish Guards held on to points 212 and 214 on the western end of the feature, which points the Germans frequently counter-attacked. While a further attack to capture the complete feature was being prepared, it was essential for the Irish Guards to hold on. They did so.

"On April 28 1943, the positions held by one company of the Irish Guards in the ridge between points 212 and 214 were about to be subjected to an attack by the enemy. Approximately one company of the enemy were seen forming up preparatory to attack and L/Cpl Kenneally decided that this was the right moment to attack them himself. Single-handed he charged down the bare forward slope straight at the main enemy body, firing his Bren gun from the hip as he did so. This outstanding act of gallantry and the dash with which it was executed completely unbalanced the enemy company, which broke up in disorder. L/Cpl Kenneally then returned to the crest further to harass their retreat.

"L/Cpl Kenneally repeated this remarkable exploit on the morning of 30 April 1943, when, accompanied by a Sergeant of the Reconnaissance Corps, he again charged the enemy forming up for an assault. This time he so harassed

Scorpion flail tanks, led the advance, attempting to breach the minefields in front of the Wadi Zigzaou ditch. The battle over the defences ebbed and flowed over the next three days, with German counter-attacks pushing the attackers back to their starting positions. Montgomery now switched his effort to the south, where the New Zealanders, reinforced by X Corps, had come up against 21st Panzer Division. Following fierce fighting, the Axis troops were forced to abandon the Mareth Line and retreat to a second defensive line based at Wadi Akarit. On 5–6 April 1943 Eighth Army managed to penetrate the defences and link up with the Americans of II Corps. With attacks pressing from all sides, Tunis fell on 7 May. On 9 May, Fifth Panzer Army surrendered, and on 12 May 1943, the remaining Axis forces in North Africa followed suit.

RIGHT The Africa Star (1940–1943) medal was awarded to the armed forces and Merchant Navy, and to members of the ATS, WRNS and WAAF, and the nursing services, for entry into an operational area in North Africa between 10 June 1940 (the date of Italy's entry into the war) and 12 May 1943 (the end of operations in North Africa). It was also awarded for service in Abyssinia, Somaliland, Eritrea and Malta. A silver Arabic "8" or "1" worn on the ribbon in undress indicates service with the Eighth Army between 23 October 1942 and 12 May 1943, or the First Army between 8 November 1942 and 12 May 1943. The obverse design bears the "GRI VI" cipher in a circular centrepiece surrounded by an edged band bearing the text "THE AFRICA STAR". The design of the ribbon is attributed to HM King George VI. The buff colour represents the desert; the red the armies; the dark blue the naval forces and Merchant Navy; and the light blue the air forces.

the enemy, inflicting many casualties that this projected attack was frustrated. The enemy's strength was again about one company. It was only when he was noticed hopping from one fire position to another further to the left, in order to support another company, carrying his gun in one hand and supporting himself on a Guardsman with the other, that it was discovered that he had been wounded. He refused to give up his Bren gun, claiming that he was the only one who understood that gun, and continued to fight all through the day with great courage, devotion to duty and disregard for his own safety.

"The magnificent gallantry of this Non-Commissioned Officer on these two occasions under heavy fire, his unfailing vigilance, and remarkable accuracy were responsible for saving many valuable lives during days and nights in the forward positions. His actions also played a considerable part in holding these positions and this influenced the whole course of the battle. His rapid appreciation of the situation, his initiative and his extraordinary gallantry in attacking single-handed a massed body of the enemy and breaking up an attack on two occasions, was an achievement that can seldom have been equalled. His courage in fighting all day when wounded was an inspiration to all ranks."

RIGHT *Sergeant J. P. Kenneally, VC: 1st Battalion, Irish Guards*, by Henry Carr (oil on canvas, 1943).

ABOVE A close-up of a heavily armed patrol of L Detachment, Special Air Service in their jeeps, just back from a three-month patrol in January 1943. The crews of the jeeps are all wearing "Arab-style" headdress, as copied from the Long Range Desert Group.

During the First World War, "Light Car Patrols" (consisting of imperial troops travelling in Ford cars) had been briefly used to cross the Western Desert during fighting against the Senussi tribe – terrain that hitherto had been restricted to foot and camel movement. However, it was only in the mid 1920s that attempts to develop motorized movement across the desert were revisited. Ralph Bagnold, who went on to form the Long Range Desert Group in 1940, was with the Royal Engineers in Egypt in 1926, and was one of a team of officers involved in this process:

"The general opinion even then was that the motor car was meant for roads, and as there were no roads out of Egypt and only roads along the Nile Valley, I and a few other people thought it was rather restricting. Why shouldn't one use Ford cars to travel across country and make roads for oneself, or use camel tracks? We were the pioneers of desert motoring; we developed it to a certain extent that we managed to be self-contained in water, food and petrol for as much as 1,500 miles and we were able to penetrate further into the living desert than anyone had penetrated before."

The outbreak of war in 1939, and the threat posed to the British Army's presence in North Africa, allowed Ralph Bagnold to develop and propose his ideas further. In October 1939, he had a meeting with General Sir Archibald Wavell, the Commander-in-Chief of Middle East Command:

"I went to see Wavell, a stocky, short man with one eye. One felt as if there was something about him, that made one think 'Here's a very strong personality.' He said 'Where are you going?' I said, 'I've been posted to East Africa.' He said, 'Wouldn't you rather be here?' I said 'Yes certainly I would'. He said, 'I'll fix it.' Within 48 hours I was reposted to Egypt. When the hot war broke out in June 1940, I saw that we had no real preparations for a war in Egypt at all. In fact the army in Egypt had been there since 1882 merely for internal security purposes and as a force to protect the Suez Canal."

Bagnold's ideas of a desert reconnaissance force remained stillborn for several months, until June 1940 when he again approached Wavell.

"I took my courage in my hands and sent a note and asked a friend of mine to put it on the Commander in Chief's personal desk, and within half an hour I was sent for. Wavell was alone, and he said, 'Tell me about this.' I told him what I thought was wrong. I said that we ought to have some mobile ground scouting force, a very small force that would be able to penetrate the desert to the west of Egypt to see what was going on, because we had no information about what the Italians might be doing. He said, 'What if you find that Italians aren't doing anything in the interior at all?' I said, without thinking, 'How about some piracy on the high desert?' His rather stern face broke into a broad grin and he said 'Can you be ready in six weeks?' And I said, 'Yes, provided …' 'Yes, I know,' he said 'there will be opposition and delay.' And he rang his bell and a lieutenant-general came in, his chief of staff, and Wavell said: 'Arthur – Bagnold seeks a talisman, get this typed out and I'll sign it straight away: "I wish that any request made by Major Bagnold in person should be met instantly and without question.'" It was typed, and Wavell signed it, and I used it as a talisman. I had complete carte blanche to do anything I liked."

Several Long Range Patrol units were authorized that month, and from August 1940 they began deep penetrations into the desert to provide vital tactical reconnaissance on the movement and dispositions of the Italian forces in North Africa – something which foot and air reconnaissance were unable to provide. The patrols also harassed the Italian lines of communication. The benefit of the information provided was immediately recognized during Operation *Compass*.

In December 1940 the Long Range Desert Group was formed under Bagnold's command, with an increase in strength of the fighting patrols, and the addition of new vehicles, such as the Chevrolet 30-cwt truck, Ford V8 scout cars, and captured Italian vehicles. From March 1941 Ford 30-cwt trucks were allocated to the LRDG. Willys jeeps also began to be used by patrols from mid 1942 onwards. The volunteers who made up the patrols of the LRDG (many of whom were from Commonwealth countries) needed to be tough, resilient, multi-skilled (in communications, repairs and weaponry), capable of acting independently, and to demonstrate flexibility. The desert provided considerable challenges, which were eventually overcome by the development of equipment such as the sun compass and water condensers for car radiators, and techniques for movement across sand dunes and extracting vehicles that became stuck in the sand.

Overall, the LRDG conducted hundreds of operations in North Africa, such as pathfinding the route through the desert for the New Zealand Division during the outflanking of the Mareth Line defences in March 1943. From 1943, troops of the LRDG would also see service in Greece, Italy and Yugoslavia.

The LRDG was not the only special forces group to operate in the desert. In the early stages of the war, Middle East Commandos were also active in theatre, raiding Bardia and attempting to capture Rommel in 1941. From November 1941 L Detachment of the Special Air Service Brigade, under the command of David Stirling, began to work closely with the LRDG, who often led them to and provided support for hit-and-run missions against specific objectives, particularly Axis airfields. From 1942 a unit known as Popski's Private Army, under Major Vladimir Peniakoff, also conducted raids against the German and Italian forces in North Africa.

ABOVE Three Long Range Desert Group 30-cwt Chevrolet trucks in the desert, May 1942.

RIGHT The cloth cap badge of the SAS. In an effort to consolidate the identity of his new unit, Colonel Stirling privately arranged for this insignia to be made up by a Cairo tailor. The cap badge was originally designed as a flaming "sword of Damocles" but ended up as a winged dagger. The motto "Who Dares Wins" summed up Stirling's original SAS concept.

BELOW Two men of a Long Range Desert Group patrol make use of available cover while on a road watch, May 1942.

168

THE INVASION OF ITALY
Operation *Husky*: the invasion of Sicily

On the night of 9 July 1943 the Allied invasion of Sicily (Operation *Husky*) began, with the British Eighth Army executing combined airborne and seaborne landings on the east coast of the island. 1st Airborne Division was tasked with the seizure of the vital Ponte Grande (Operation *Fustian*) and Primosole (Operation *Marston*) bridges between Syracuse and Catania in advance of the main seaborne landings. On 9 July the glider troops of 1st Air-Landing Brigade took off, but many failed to reach their objective of the Ponte Grande, landing in the sea instead due to poor visibility. The 2nd Battalion The South Staffordshire Regiment did manage to make it to the bridge, seized it, and then had to endure repeated enemy counter-attacks, before finally withdrawing. The main Allied ground forces arrived the next day and the bridge was retaken.

ABOVE At Milo in the north of Sicily, County of London Yeomanry tank men are accorded a warm reception by the citizens of the town on 15 August 1943. Sicilian children are riding on the tanks as they rumble down the main street.

The Sicily landings

Peter Lawrence de Carteret Martin was a British officer commanding C Company, 2nd Battalion The Cheshire Regiment (a mechanized machine-gun unit) in Sicily in 1943.

"On the 5th of July in the morning the convoy sailed (from Suez), and as soon as it had sailed briefing was allowed to start ... I remember the gasp of amazement when I told them that we were going to Sicily, because I think everyone had been under the impression that we were either going to Crete or Sardinia, another favourite, or more probably Greece. So Sicily was a real surprise ... The plan for my particular company was to support 151st Brigade, which was to be the assault brigade for 50th Division and 151st Brigade was to land with two battalions up – 6th Durham Light Infantry on the left and 9th Durham Light Infantry on the right. They would secure the beaches at Avola and form a tight bridgehead on the high ground. The 8th Durham Light Infantry were then also to secure the high ground overlooking Avola from the west. The initial plan was for the company to send one platoon up to join each of these three battalions as soon as they had landed and we would then take it from there as to what was to happen next, according to the amount of opposition that was to meet us. We had every reason to believe that there were Italian troops in the coastal defences, and from past experience we didn't expect them to put up a great deal of resistance, but we did expect to meet German troops as we pushed in from the beaches. I went up on deck in the early hours. We had been woken at midnight and H-hour was supposed to be at 0245 hours ... We went up for breakfast, and it all seemed extremely unreal to think that we were about to land on a foreign coast. When breakfast was over I went down to see the rest of the company, and rum ration was issued. Everybody was in very good form. I went up on deck and one could just see the faint outline of the coast ahead and particularly an enormous lowering black mass which was obviously Mount Etna. The ships were

RIGHT *The Black Watch landing in Sicily at Red Beach*, by Ian Eadie (watercolour on paper).

moving very slowly by now and we could see a fire burning away to the west, and bombers and aircraft towing gliders came overhead with their lights on ... The ship then stopped and the first flight of landing craft was lowered away. There was then a very long period of waiting. A searchlight from the shore swept the water, hesitated, then went out. We thought for a moment that the assault craft going in had been spotted, but nothing happened. We were due to be landed at 0420, the assault flight having gone in at 0245, but nothing happened. Dawn came, and we were still waiting. Daylight brought a fantastic sight, the morning sun shining on all the white houses, towns and villages while out to sea were ships of all sizes steadily closing in towards the beaches."

ABOVE British troops wade ashore from landing ships during the Sicily landings, 10 July 1943.

In Operation *Marston*, launched on 13 July, the paratroopers of 1st Parachute Brigade fared little better, with its units scattered across a wide landing area; a mere few hundred made it to the Primosole Bridge objective. A counter-drop by the German 4th Parachute Brigade brought about a fierce firefight between the opposing airborne troops, and the British paratroopers were forced to temporarily withdraw until the arrival of the Durham Light Infantry of 151st Brigade finally helped capture the bridge.

Despite pessimistic predictions, the British seaborne landings, which took place between Pachino (on Sicily's southernmost tip, XXX Corps) and Avola (south of Syracuse, XIII Corps), met with little opposition from the poorly equipped Italian defenders. The Black Watch landed at Pachino on 10 July, and as they pushed inland men from the 5th Battalion encountered stiff German resistance at Vizzini, which was captured on the 12th. The town of Augusta to the east fell on 13 July. Montgomery now began a drive north to capture Messina, the Allies' prime objective on the island and the port closest to the Italian mainland – but the drive became bogged down at the Gerbini airfields south of Catania when it came up against the Hermann Göring Division. By early August the Germans had retired to the Etna Line defensive positions, south of the mountain, and their dogged defence of the rugged terrain here allowed their forces to withdraw across to the Italian mainland. The British 78th and 51st Divisions eventually closed the net around the town of Adrano on 6 August, making the German position untenable.

The invasion of mainland Italy

John Winthrop Hackett was a British officer commanding 4th Parachute Brigade during the Sicilian landings and the invasion of the Italian mainland:

"My brigade was the one chosen to do the landing at Taranto in southern Italy, so I went up to Algiers to get my instructions for this – but there weren't any aircraft, so we were going by sea. We were going in one British and one US cruiser, HMS Penelope and USS Boise. They were going to take us in and we were going to land in the harbour just like that. I went up to Algiers, to Allied Forces HQ, the planners and I said – 'Well, I know what the idea is, but can you tell me is this going to be an opposed landing?' And the reply I got roughly added up to 'You'll find out when you get there.' 'Oh, come now,' I said, 'if it's going to be an opposed landing we'll need air support, gun support, naval gunfire, we'll need landing craft'. They said, 'Don't waste our time. There aren't any landing craft anyway, they've all gone to the Far East. So you just get off up there and do the best you can.' ... We went ashore on the quay. Early that morning from the bridge of HMS Penelope I had watched the Italian battlefleet steaming out from Taranto under the guard of HMS Howe and HMS King George V, so we tied up at the quayside. We didn't get in unscathed as we had a fast minelayer called Abdiel, which was bringing the division's anti-tank complement in, and it blew up on a mine in the harbour. We lost all our anti-tank guns and a couple of hundred invaluable personnel. So we tied up at the quay and bundled ashore. I believe German parachutists were guarding that place and I don't think they expected anything that idiotic to happen, so we managed to get ashore and over into the customs house and establish ourselves before they came to. That was a bit of good luck. I was in the customs house trying to handle this battle as it rolled on, when a stentorian voice started coming out of the mast of USS Boise saying 'Will General "Haddock" kindly step up.' ... So I strolled back to USS Boise by the quay and went aboard, very untidy but whole, and I went down to the wardroom. It appeared that the Italian general had turned up and the general wanted to surrender, and he would only do this to the senior officer present, so I had to be called out of my battle and be the senior officer present, which I was. I was a brigadier aged 32, commanding a parachute brigade. Here was this Italian general who was as old as God and as thin as a pipe cleaner with beautiful,

ABOVE The British No. 4 rifle was a development of the Short, Magazine Lee-Enfield. It featured a heavier, flat-sided body, a heavier barrel and an aperture rear sight. The No. 4 was approved for service in November 1939 but, due to the difficulties of setting up production in new factories, did not see large-scale issue until 1942. From then on it became the principal British and Canadian infantry weapon.

The US Seventh Army entered Messina on 17 August, leaving Sicily entirely in Allied hands. Its fall led to Mussolini's overthrow and Italy's withdrawal from the Axis alliance.

Operations *Baytown* and *Slapstick*

On 3 September 1943 two divisions (1st Canadian and 5th British) of Eighth Army crossed the three miles of the Straits of Messina in landing craft to Reggio in Calabria on the Italian mainland (Operation *Baytown*). Montgomery considered the landings a waste of time, since these troops would be landed far to the south of the main Allied landings at Salerno. Indeed, following the landings, British troops encountered little resistance from the withdrawing LXXVI Corps and were subsequently forced to make their way some

300 miles north across slower overland routes before linking up with the main body.

On 8 September, the Italian government surrendered, and Italian forces were instructed to lay down their arms. The next day British 1st Airborne Division landed by sea at the port of Taranto in Puglia (Operation *Slapstick*). Although the landing was unopposed, HMS *Abdiel* struck a mine in the harbour; many lives were lost, including men from the 6th Parachute Battalion. The 1st Airborne Division was soon involved in the push northwards following the landings, capturing Castellanata and Gioia from dogged German defenders. Most of the division was subsequently withdrawn to prepare for the D-Day landings. Only 2nd Parachute Brigade remained in Italy, to fight as line infantry.

immaculately polished black boots and a little drawing-room sword, which he wanted to hand over to somebody. So there he was and he was saying 'Dov'è il generale? Dov'è il generale?' ('Where is the general?') and this rather scruffy youthful figure was propelled in his direction and somebody said 'Ecco il generale' ('Here's the general'). And he looked at me with a mixture of surprise and contempt and said, 'Ma è giovane!' ('But he's a kid!') He handed over his sword and I went back to the battle."

ABOVE The view from a landing craft bringing British reinforcements for Operation *Slapstick* as it approaches Taranto harbour on 9 September.

RIGHT During Operation *Baytown*, 3 September 1943, two soldiers pass a sign meaning "Long Live Mussolini" painted on a wall at Reggio.

Operation *Avalanche*: the Salerno landings

On 9 September British X Corps (comprising 46th and 56th Infantry Divisions, 7th Armoured Division and Commando troops) – under the command of US Fifth Army – landed at Salerno (Operation *Avalanche*), aiming to push up the Italian peninsula and capture Naples 40 miles to the north. The 46th and 56th Infantry Divisions would land at Red, White and Green beaches south of the River Picento and attack Salerno five miles to the north before linking up with 7th Armoured Division to capture Battipaglia and the Ponte Sele Bridge inland. Meanwhile, British Commandos would land together with US Rangers and secure the left flank of the infantry landings. The main US landings would take place ten miles further south.

The landings were not preceded by air or sea bombardment, in the hope of achieving surprise. Although the beaches themselves were lightly defended, the landings soon got into difficulty. The interior was heavily defended by German machine-gun nests, tanks and artillery positions, and there followed ten days of hard fighting as the Allies tried to hold on to their slender beachheads against attacks from the 16th Panzer, 15th and 29th Panzer-Grenadier, and later the Hermann Göring divisions. The British 167th and 201st Guards Brigades were involved in the fighting around the "Tobacco Factory" between Battipaglia and Bellizzi. The Germans almost succeeded in pushing the Allies back to the sea on several occasions. By 15 September, having covered the retreat of their forces in the south, and with the main body of Eighth Army arriving from the south, the Germans had withdrawn northwards to a new defensive line on the River Volturno. More than 5,000 Allied soldiers died at Salerno.

On 16 September 1943, 190 British troops of the 50th and 51st Divisions mutinied at Salerno. These troops had all been separated from their units in North Africa due to wounds or sickness, and were subsequently sent (by error) as reinforcements to Salerno. The men thought they were heading for Sicily, but en route they were informed that they were going to Salerno. They also discovered they would not be assigned to their original units – an order that brought about the mutiny. Many of the men had seen hard fighting in North Africa, and were proud of the units they belonged to; the separation was considered an intolerable act of bureaucratic insensitivity. The leading mutineers were tried and condemned. Eventually, most were persuaded to follow orders and join new units, and the sentences passed against them (including the death penalty for the leaders) were subsequently not carried out.

The landings at Salerno

Douglas Waller was a British NCO serving with 9th Battalion The Rifle Brigade in Italy:
"Off we went down to the docks and boarded landing ships (LSTs), and away we went. It was quite pleasant – nothing happened until we got near to Salerno. We were then told we would be under command of the American Fifth Army, who had already landed. They hadn't moved too far inland, as things were still at a stalemate from the landing having gone wrong. It was then what is known as the Salerno Mutiny took place. They were going round the rest camps, convalescence camps, dragging personnel out to send out to fight because they badly needed infantry ... They were obviously held up fairly near, as when our ship pulled in there were shells coming over. It was long-range shelling, but we were getting shelled. They were obviously aware that reinforcements were coming in and they were shelling the ships. Some of them

BELOW A little Italian girl feeds a British soldier with pasta, in September 1943.

were a bit near and went off, and everybody hit the deck. Our dear new colonel was standing there and he said 'Oh my God, what do we do now?' And somebody said, 'Get down before they blow your bloody head off!' And then we landed. I don't think there were any real casualties, it was further inland they were held up and we just drove off and made for Averso. It came as a bit of a shock to us. In the desert there were no civilians involved, just the odd goat herd or Arab, and the towns were not much to talk about anyway. But when we got to Italy suddenly there were villages with bombs and civilians and refugees, and this came as a bit of a culture shock to us ... Before it had been a bit like knights on a battlefield in the desert; you didn't see any civilians involved."

ABOVE British soldiers man a machine-gun post on the beach at Salerno on 9 September 1943, while a column of smoke rises from a transport ship in the background.

LEFT Men of the 2nd/6th Queen's Royal Regiment (West Surrey) advance past a burning German PzKpfw IV tank in the Salerno area, 22 September 1943.

1943–1944

STEMMING THE JAPANESE TIDE

The First Arakan offensive and the First Chindit Expedition

In December 1942 a British offensive led by 14th Indian Division began from Assam in India into the Arakan region of Burma, advancing down the Mayu peninsula towards the port of Akyab. The Japanese defence was solid though, notably at Rathedaung and Donbaik where clashes took place in February. At Donbaik, the Japanese showed the benefits of jungle experience, using clever camouflage and positioning, and proven tactics, when defending a system of bunkers and caves against a sizeable Commonwealth assault. On 17 March a major Japanese counter-attack was launched. In May 1943 the First Arakan offensive was halted. The ill-prepared Commonwealth troops were exhausted, and the replacement system had been shown to be both inadequate and inefficient. Poor leadership, inexperience and one-dimensional tactics (such as infantry advances preceded by artillery bombardments) also contributed to its failure. It seemed to reinforce the idea that the Japanese were unbeatable in the jungle, and that the British and Commonwealth forces

Orde Wingate and the First Chindit Expedition

ominic Fitzgerald Neill was a British officer serving as animal transport officer with 8 Column during the First Chindit Expedition in Burma from February to May 1943. He recalls his first impressions on meeting Orde Wingate:

ABOVE The second-pattern cap badge of The King's Regiment (Liverpool), which was worn from 1926 until 1958, when the regiment was amalgamated with the Manchester Regiment to form the King's Regiment (Manchester and Liverpool). The emblem of the White Horse of Hanover was awarded to the regiment by King George I in 1716 in recognition of its loyal service. The regiment formed part of 77th Indian Infantry Brigade, which took part in the First Chindit Expedition in 1943.

"The first time I met him, he arrived with his soon-to-become famous solar topee and he was dressed in a khaki bush jacket and slacks. When he came to the 8 Column mules and was wandering down the lines with me, he suddenly stopped, pointed to one mule and said to me: 'Neill, what's that mule's number?' Knowing of course they had been recently branded, I explained to him 'I'm sorry sir, I don't really know, they've only just been branded and I haven't memorized the numbers yet.' He looked at me and said, 'Boy, you should know the numbers by now' and passed on. I thought this was very weird. Anyway, he displayed that sort of interest in the mules and looked at them closely, but he never laid eyes on or spoke to any of my Gurkha muleteers. He ignored them completely and that did not impress me ... During the First Chindit offensive, when our Burma Riflemen were collecting the boats from the village of Tongche, we had a signal from Wingate and this I think was in code. What he said, so I was told, was that once we had crossed the Chindwin and we were in enemy territory any man who was wounded and was unable to move would be left in a friendly village to his fate. I thought that, on the eve of battle, to give an order like that was guaranteed to cause men's morale to dip extremely. I know the British soldiers were not best pleased to hear what their fate might be, and for my part I never passed the

message onto my Gurkhas. In those days none of them spoke English and I thought that if I didn't tell them at least they wouldn't know what might happen to them under adverse circumstances ... Following the order to 'disperse, get back to India', we met an ambush ... I don't think we had gone very far from the village when, totally out of the blue, an ambush exploded from my immediate left. I can remember roaring out to my men 'Take cover, right!' before diving into the bushes to the right of the track. Things happened very quickly in an ambush, hundreds of thoughts flashed through the minds of men caught in this way and all in the briefest of seconds. I remember that I wasn't actually frightened, which surprised me, but I was totally and utterly shocked ... A Jap gunner was firing his light machine gun immediately opposite me from the jungle on the far side of the track. He was so close that I could clearly see the smoke rising from his gun's muzzle. His bursts of fire were hitting the trees and bushes above my head; the bullets were cutting the branches and bits of leaf and wood were falling on my pack, on my neck and down my shirt collar ... Never ever during any of my previous training had I been taught any of the approved contact drills – certainly the approved counter-ambush drill was unknown to me. I was utterly appalled to realize that I simply did not know what to do to extract my men and myself from our present predicament."

would be unable to launch a successful offensive against them in the difficult terrain of northern Burma.

The Chindits were a special force of irregular infantry operating deep behind the Japanese lines and resupplied by frequent air drops. The concept was masterminded by Brigadier Orde Wingate. It was felt that any success such groups might have would greatly benefit morale, and could also provide valuable intelligence on enemy dispositions. The First Chindit Expedition in support of operations in the First Arakan campaign, codenamed Operation *Longcloth*, took place between February and May 1943.

RIGHT Orde Wingate pictured after his return from the First Chindit Expedition into Burma, February–May 1943.

RIGHT Chindits with their mules carrying supplies make their way through the jungle.

176

The Chindits' official title was 77th Indian Infantry Brigade, and was made up of battalions from the Burma Rifles, Gurkhas, and the King's Liverpool Regiment who had been on internal security duties in India, together with a Commando contingent. The standard unit was the column, of which there were eight in the expedition, equipped with crew-served weapons and mules for transports. During the operation, the Japanese-held railway lines were cut a number of times between Mandalay and Myitkyina. However, the Japanese soon began to note and target the sites of the British air drops. As a result, the Chindits were ordered to withdraw to India on 24 March, with a further order from Wingate (following an ambush of his men at the River Irrawaddy) to his men to disperse in order to hamper the Japanese pursuit. The troops who emerged from the jungle, together with their inspirational leader, were lionized by the British press. The Chindits were acclaimed as the first British and Commonwealth forces to get the better of the Japanese in the realm of jungle fighting, thus helping to dispel the myth of Japanese invincibility. The operation undoubtedly bolstered morale in both Britain and India. However, only two-thirds of the force made it back to India and, of those, only half were fit for duty afterwards.

ABOVE The formation badge for Fourteenth Army. The sign was designed by Lieutenant-General Sir William Slim, red and black being the colours of the British and Indian Armies. The sword points downwards, in defiance of heraldic convention, because Slim knew he would have to reconquer Burma from the north. The hilt forms the "S", for his own name. On the grip, in Morse code, is the army's title. Formed in November 1943, Fourteenth Army was reponsible for the successful defence of India and the defeat of Japanese forces in Burma; its greatest victories were in the Arakan, at Imphal, Kohima, Kennedy Peak, Mandalay and Meiktila.

The Arakan fighting

Alastair William Mitchell Gauld was a British officer serving with 5th Battalion The Gold Coast Regiment, 81st West African Division, in Burma during the Second Arakan campaign of 1944:

"We arrived at Chittagong in the northernmost part of the Arakan. From there we went by transport to our base camp and in due course we started off down the eastern part of the Arakan Peninsula, basically the valley of the River Kaladan. To do this we had to go over hill ranges, and our African troops had to construct a roadway known as the West African Way. This went on for 75 miles until we got down into the valley of the River Calodan near the village of Calodan itself. We then made our way down the side of the river, and then received information that the Japs were mounting what turned out to be one of their big offensives at this time. Their main thrust came to the west of us towards the coast, and this culminated in one of the more famous incidents of the first campaign, the battle of the Admin Box. We didn't have any direct contact with that, although geographically we were only about 30 miles to the east, but the Japs were coming up in force on our side of the mountain ranges also. My battalion was involved in one really sticky incident at that time, which came to be known afterwards as the battle of Cox's Corner, Cox being the colonel in charge of our battalion. This was on 6 and 7 March 1944. I was, through no particular reason, in the forefront of this because one of our rifle companies, C Company, had been asked to move out eastward to test the Japanese dispositions, and my mortar section was attached to that company. We hadn't gone very far from the Battalion HQ (about a mile and a half) when C Company, which was slightly ahead of my mortar section, was engaged by crippling machine-gun fire from both sides of the point of its advance. The company commander and second in command were both killed instantly. Having mounted my mortars and found the

RIGHT *Arakan Campaign: the Battle of Rathedaung, 1943; 6 Rajputana Rifles attacking Hill North 75,* by Anthony Gross, CBE RA. On arrival in Calcutta in early 1943, Gross had a long journey to find Brigade HQ in the Arakan mountains. He visited the regiments stationed at "Twin Nobs" and was invited by some Indian officers of the Rajput Regiment to visit their forward positions. He finally reached them on a hill overlooking the Mayu River near Rathedaung. From there he was able to observe the Battle of Rathedaung, which took place in February 1943.

range of at least one side of the Japanese attacking position, disposing of quite a number of them by the sound of things, I was somewhat perturbed to find all the visible members of C Company retreating past me back to the battalion at quite a considerable rate of knots. So I thought the only thing to do was to join them, which I did, and got all my mortar section back. We found that the company had been completely taken by surprise. The battalion then regrouped and held its position until it could withdraw and resume the campaign later on in a slightly different direction."

LEFT Lord Louis Mountbatten, Supreme Allied Commander South-East Asia, inspecting British officers near the Arakan front in December 1943, in preparation for the start of the Second Arakan campaign.

Second Arakan and the Second Chindit Expedition

On 18 September 1943 a new Chindit unit was formed designated the 3rd Indian Infantry Division, which included the original Chindit troops of 77th Indian Infantry Brigade. It was in this month that British operations resumed in the Arakan. A major offensive (Second Arakan) involving the British Fourteenth Army began in December 1943, with 7th Indian Division advancing down the west of the Mayu ridge, the 5th Indian Division down the east side of the ridge, and the 81st West African Division heading down the Kaladan Valley to prevent any Japanese counter-attacks from developing.

In early 1944, Orde Wingate gained approval for a Second Chindit Expedition deep behind Japanese lines, aimed in part at supporting the Second Arakan operations by diverting Japanese troops northwards. This formed part of Operation *Thursday*, which also involved the American "Merrill's Marauders". The operation principally aimed to support the Chinese forces in the north of Burma (under the overall command of US general "Vinegar Joe" Stilwell) in their forthcoming offensive into the country. The 20,000-strong Chindit "Special Force", comprising six brigades, would attempt to seize vital airfields, and once again disrupt the lines of communication to the rear of the Japanese 18th Division. The force would be partly flown in, while the rest of the troops marched on foot. Once in country, they would establish and operate from defended bases (labelled "Aberdeen", "Broadway", "White City" and "Blackpool"), while roving columns would be sent out from these to attack the enemy.

The Second Chindit Expedition

Cecil Edgar James Perry was a British private serving with 1st Battalion The Bedfordshire and Hertfordshire Regiment during the Second Chindit Expedition:

"We knew we were an expendable force for long-range penetration for General Wingate's expedition, and we were trained to look after each other ... It was survival, ambush away from the line regiment, hit and run tactics ...

We followed the experiences of General Wingate's first expedition in Burma, that was the basis of our training ... We were a demoralized army when the Japanese threw the British Army out of India, we thought they were invincible. But General Wingate, I remember reading about his first expedition, it raised the morale of the troops up. They weren't invincible; we could fight back on their terms and win ...

Morale was great on the march into Burma towards 'Aberdeen' – we were going back, as Wingate said. Even when we heard of his death, morale continued to be great ... We marched towards Indawgyi where we blew up the railway lines. I brought up the PIAT gun, but due to the dampness of the jungle it didn't fire. We brought up the second gun, that didn't fire. We opened up with machine guns on the railway station and the trucks. It was a surprise attack ... After about 20 minutes it was all over ... What was the overall character of the mission? It was a question of endless marches, attacking, breaking up installations. Mostly we marched a hell of a lot of miles – sometimes 15 miles in a day. That was pretty good going – some days you had to cut your way straight through virgin forest ... [attacking] bridges, railways, trying to throttle out the supplies. Sometimes we would wait a whole week to find out which was the best train to blow up."

LEFT British, West African and Gurkha soldiers waiting at an airfield in India before the start of Operation *Thursday* in March 1944.

RIGHT Orde Wingate (1903–1944) briefing men of 77th Indian Infantry Brigade at an airfield at Sylhet in Assam before an operation. With him is Colonel Philip Cochrane USAAF, who was responsible for the air transport for the brigade's operations.

The first Chindits of 16th Brigade entered Burma on foot in February 1944, on their way to establish the "Aberdeen" stronghold, with 77th Indian Brigade following by plane in early March heading for "Broadway".

On 6 February 1944 the Japanese 15th Army launched a diversionary attack by 55th Infantry Division into the Arakan (the "Ha Go" offensive). The attack halted the Commonwealth offensive by 5th and 7th Indian Divisions, and fierce fighting took place at Sinzweya in the Battle of the Admin Box. However, the Commonwealth defenders held out, thanks in no small part to the supplies dropped by the Royal Air Force. After three weeks the Japanese forces withdrew.

Orde Wingate died in a plane crash on 24 March, and was replaced by Brigadier W. D. A. Lentaigne of 111th Brigade.

Lentaigne did not really share Wingate's vision and the Chindits were now mostly used as infantry. Under Stilwell's command they supported the Chinese offensive in the north-east which began in May 1944. It took three months for the Chindits to capture the airfield at Myitkyina and another three months before the Japanese evacuated the town itself. The Chindits were involved in some of the hardest fighting, holding their strongholds against repeated Japanese attacks and suffering from disease, malnutrition and heat exhaustion. By August 1944 all the Chindit units had been withdrawn from Burma.

ABOVE The formation badge of the 3rd Indian Infantry Division (The Chindits), formed at Jhansi as a special force of long-range penetration troops on 18 September 1943. It was made up of 77th and 111th Indian Brigades, three British brigades (14th, 16th and 23rd) and the 3rd West African Brigade. These were formed into groups of eight columns each, two HQs, and a Force HQ. The Force was designated as 3rd Indian Division on 1 February 1944. The Burmese dragon on the badge is a "Chinthe", whose purpose it was to guard pagodas. The resulting nickname, Chindits, stemmed from the dragon image of the formation badge; it is also claimed that the name of the "Chindwin River" in some way influenced the naming of the force. The 3rd Indian Division was disbanded on 31 March 1945.

Imphal and Kohima

The Japanese "Ha Go" offensive of early February 1944 was intended to divert attention away from the main "U Go" offensive across the River Chindwin and into Assam in India, to capture Imphal (guarding the main potential route of a British advance from Assam into Burma) and Kohima. "U Go" was launched in early March, and by the 29th, the Japanese 15th Division had cut the Kohima–Imphal road. Imphal was now surrounded. The 4th Battalion The Royal West Kent Regiment and the 161st Indian Brigade were quickly rushed to Kohima to reinforce the small garrison of the Assam and Burma regimental troops there.

The Japanese began a series of unrelenting attacks on both Kohima and Imphal, but once again the Commonwealth troops were solid in their defence, with RAF supply playing a key role. The West Kents at Kohima endured two weeks of Japanese attacks before they were finally reinforced by the British 2nd Division and 33rd Indian Brigade. The Commonwealth forces now moved to the offensive, recapturing each hill and feature that had been lost to the Japanese. The victory in the Second Arakan allowed the 5th and 7th Indian Divisions to be sent to Assam, and they now joined the slow and difficult fighting. By 22 June, the siege of Imphal had finally been lifted and the road to Kohima reopened, and Japanese troops began to withdraw back into Burma. "U Go" was a disaster for the Japanese, causing the loss of 60,000 troops and much weaponry, tanks and equipment. Lieutenant-General Slim now had a clear opportunity to defeat the Japanese in Burma.

The Royal West Kents at Kohima

Harry Crispin Smith was a British officer serving with 4th Battalion The Queen's Own Royal West Kent Regiment during the siege of Kohima in April 1944:

ABOVE A view of Kohima Ridge after the battle in 1944.

"As we wound our way in trucks up the earthen road that had been hacked out of the hillside by Coolie labour to Kohima, we were entirely ignorant of what was in store for us. We were glad to get up to 5,000 feet above the stifling heat of the plain. We established ourselves in Kohima with the battalion in the middle and the two Indian battalions either side. We were only expecting very light Japanese forces. Then the next day it was all change, and orders came up from the general commanding the Dimapur district that the battalion was to return back down the hill, 1400hrs. Our brigadier was furious about this, but he had to obey and we left the meagre garrison at Kohima, which

LEFT Cap badge of the Queen's Own Royal West Kent Regiment of the type that was worn pre 1914 up until 1958. The white horse rampant with the motto "Invicta" (Unconquered) derived from the ancient Arms of Kent. The regiment amalgamated with The Buffs (Royal East Kent Regiment) in 1961 to form the Queen's Own Buffs, Royal Kent Regiment, and in 1966 became the 2nd Battalion The Queen's Regiment (Queen's Own Buffs) – losing its county identity.

consisted of an Indian State Regiment, really rather an unreliable body, and various odd bodies from the convalescent depot, Kohima being a hospital area. One can imagine how dismayed they must have felt to see us pulling off downhill again. However, no sooner were we down at the bottom again, at Dimapur, than orders came through for the brigade to move up once more, but by this time the leading Japanese spearheads were on the outskirts of the little town. They had been delayed by some good Indian troops in the Assam Rifles and the Assam Regiment who had been fighting rearguard engagements through the Sambre Hill tracks. As we wound up the road again we met crowds of frightened non-combatants fleeing down the road. The battalion was leading the brigade column and as it approached the actual town itself it came under heavy fire from machine guns and artillery. Evacuating the trucks as quickly as possible, the battalion sprinted up the hill overlooking the crossroads at the bottom and established itself in positions already allotted to it ... Our immediate task was picking off Japanese who had penetrated the company in front and for me this remained the pattern of the rest of the siege. I had under my command the pioneer platoon, about 25 men, odd bodies from the carrier platoon which was on its way up from the Arakan, and some of whose members came up with us. There were also one or two men from the convalescent depot who came to join my company, but otherwise most of my men were out on detachment with one of the rifle companies ... Day after day our hopes were dashed when we expected some form of relief. We began to walk about like zombies because we had no chance of sleep, or very little. The rifle companies on the perimeter were steadily pushed back by the superior numbers of the enemy and as their casualties mounted they were forced to give ground. The 2nd British Division was arriving down at Dimapur at the bottom of the hill and beginning to push up the road and clear roadblocks, but it seemed to take an awful long time to us before any effects were felt ... The situation got graver and graver as our numbers diminished and it was not until 19 April (we had gone in on 4 April) that the two Indian battalions in our brigade were able to fight their way into our perimeter – their positions down the road having been relieved by the leading elements of the 2nd British Division. It was touch and go then. The Japanese were only about 200 yards from the command post at the top, coming round from the other side."

BREAKTHROUGH IN ITALY

Following the Salerno breakout, the German forces in Italy had begun a retreat northwards across successive defensive lines. As autumn set in, British Eighth Army advanced up the east coast of Italy in a sequence of hard-fought river crossings. The Fifth US Army pushed up the west coast; the objective for both armies was the capture of Rome. Following an amphibious landing to capture the port of Termoli on the Adriatic in early October, the British 78th Division and Commandos clashed with the 26th Panzer Division. 56th Division (X Corps), having broken out from Salerno, was involved in fierce fighting at Monte Camino on the River Volturno in mid October during US Fifth Army's drive north. However, the Allied advances on both sides of the Apennines soon stalled as they reached the German defences of the Gustav Line, which stretched from Ortona on the Adriatic to the mouth of the River Garigliano on the Tyrennhian Sea. The town of Cassino, with its ancient Benedictine monastery perched on a commanding hill behind it, lay across this defensive line there. The town was key to the Allied advance, providing access to the main route towards Rome via the Liri Valley, and the area around it had been heavily fortified.

In November 1943, the Allied high command began to plan for an amphibious landing at Anzio (Operation *Shingle*) in Lazio Province to by-pass the formidable Gustav Line

ABOVE Royal Engineers in assault boats embark for the opposite bank of the River Garigliano to repair the last two sections of the pontoon bridge knocked out by enemy fire, 19 January 1944.

Cassino

Horace Roach was a British NCO serving with the 26th Field Ambulance, Royal Army Medical Corps, attached to the 4th Indian Division at Cassino in 1944:

"It was one of those situations where any moves had to be done at night, because of the planes … We were losing heavily. This was the same old poor infantry who had been fighting in the desert. They were getting massacred. As field ambulance, you were attached to the divisions and you went in with them. It was absolutely frightening … I remember our attitude to the monastery – it was something sinister, its eyes were looking at us … I saw the famous bombing of the monastery. The Free French got a few bombs dropped on them too, they lost about 30 or 40 men … Eventually the monastery was just a shell. The situation became that everything had to be hand carried or by mule – ammunition, the wounded, etc. … The German paratroopers would die fighting to

ABOVE Troops clean their weapons among the ruins of Sant'Angelo Church in Cassino, 13 May 1944.

RIGHT A view of Cassino on 18 May 1944 after heavy bombardment. It shows a knocked-out Sherman tank by a Bailey bridge in the foreground with Castle Hill and Monastery Ridge in the background.

the last bullet … They had the Nebelwerfers, they were never accurate, but the sound was frightening, and they were more a psychological weapon … The 2nd/9th Gurkhas got cut off at a place called Hangman's Hill, as well as part of the Essex Regiment. They'd put in an attack early on.

We got through to them and brought some of the wounded back at night. Some of the infantry brought theirs back. A lot of people got killed doing this … I was taken prisoner for a while by the Germans. These blokes came out from nowhere and took me down to a dugout. A German

lieutenant spoke English to me, and eventually he let me go with a note to pass to my colonel saying 'You will not be allowed to come through again if we catch you'. I did go back a second time though and brought some Gurkhas back."

defences. However, the slower than expected pace of the Allied advance north caused delay in its execution until January 1944. A few days ahead of the Anzio landings, British X Corps and elements of US Fifth Army launched an assault against the Gustav Line, attempting to outflank the defences at Cassino. The Anzio landings followed on 21 January 1944. They were preceded by a heavy artillery bombardment. The landings were initially unopposed, and British 1st Infantry Division and Commandos from 2nd Special Service Brigade came ashore on 22 January, to the north of the town, and advanced some ten miles inland. However, the Allied commander, Major-General John P. Lucas, chose not to advance further, electing instead to consolidate the beachhead before the inevitable German counter-attacks.

Meanwhile, the three-pronged Allied land offensive around Cassino (which involved British X Corps' crossing of the River Garigliano on 17 January) had ground to a halt. Winter had set in, and the German defences were being constantly reinforced and improved. Commonwealth troops would be involved in several coordinated (and failed) attempts to take the town and monastery of Cassino between January and May 1944, and the tenacity of the defenders (many of them paratroopers) and the difficult nature of the terrain would make this a brutal and bloody episode that cost many lives.

On the night of 30/31 January, Lucas's forces finally began an attempt to break out of the Anzio beachhead, with British troops securing Campoleone as they headed north into the foothills of the Colli Albani. However, the first of the

The 7th Cheshires at Anzio

Stanley White was a British private serving with B Company, 7th Battalion The Cheshire Regiment, 5th Infantry Division, during the Anzio landings:

"When the time came for us to move we were on landing craft and somebody started talking about Anzio – and consequently in the early hours of the morning we landed there. B Company was in the second wave again. When we landed, at that particular time in the morning, it was pretty quiet. But it would be quiet for half an hour and then the Germans would open up and shell us all over the place. We took up our positions on the coast road from Anzio leading direct to Rome and we were at the perimeter edge. We were in dugouts, sand ones, but thank God we had them with roofs on ... It was hell. The Germans were bombarding us and shelling us. Then they were shelling Anzio, which was behind us (we were a couple of miles up the line) and then they would come back and shell us again. We were losing people, and supplies getting through to us was pretty bad. I remember one occasion; we had two sergeant-majors, both brothers, Charlie and Billy Slater, and they were great men. You would have followed them through hell ... I remember one morning when stand to was on, and we were in the dugouts with the guns. Someone started whispering 'Charlie Slater's been killed

during the night.' And we asked, 'How's Billy taking it?' And the whisper came round, 'He's in a right state, he's in a bad way.' Every now and then we relieved each other on the guns, and this time it was my turn; I went back just a few yards to company HQ and there was a few more of us, and we said 'Sorry about this, Bill.' And he said to us, 'Don't worry Chalky, I'll be up there tonight – and I'll get them.'"

ABOVE British troops from Anzio link up with Americans who have advanced north from the Gustav Line, 25 May 1944.

RIGHT Men of 7th Battalion The Cheshire Regiment (5th Infantry Division's machine-gun battalion) in a captured German communications trench during the breakout offensive at Anzio, 22 May 1944.

expected German counter-attacks was launched on the night of 3/4 February by Fourteenth Army, forcing Lucas onto the defensive and driving the Allies back almost to the sea. The fighting involving 24th Guards Brigade was particularly hard around the industrial town of Aprilia (which subsequently became known as "The Factory"), with the town changing hands several times; the Sherwood Foresters in particular took heavy casualties. A second German offensive was launched on 16 February aimed at cutting the beachhead into two, but this failed. A third attack on 29 February met a similar fate. However, the Allied troops had been tied down, and would remain in a virtual state of siege until June 1944. Both sides now adopted a policy of containment, conducting minor skirmishing and limited engagements.

On 11 May 1944, Operation *Diadem* was launched, a combined assault by US Fifth and British Eighth Armies against the Gustav Line defences aimed at taking pressure off the Allied forces at Anzio – which staged a simultaneous breakout. British 4th, 78th and 6th Armoured Divisions pushed into the Liri Valley south of the town of Cassino and secured the town. On 18 May the monastery at Monte Cassino, which commanded the surrounding countryside, was finally taken by Polish troops of Eighth Army. German troops began a retreat northwards to a new defensive line, the Hitler Line, which fell within days. On 4 June 1944, Rome was liberated, with US general Mark Clark leading Allied troops into the city, but two days later the headlines would be focussed on a new front – the Allied landings in France.

RIGHT The Italy Star (1943–1945). The medal was awarded for operational service on land in Italy, Sicily, Greece, Yugoslavia, the Aegean, the Dodecanese, Corsica, Sardinia and Elba. It was granted to those on service at any time during the campaign from the capture of Pantelleria on 11 June 1943 until VE Day, 8 May 1945. The obverse design bears the "GRI VI" cypher. The design of the ribbon is attributed to HM King George VI, and the colours are those of the Italian national flag.

AIRBORNE WARFARE

The genesis of Britain's airborne forces dates from mid 1940, with the foundation of the Airborne Forces Training School. As well as training soldiers (initially Commando troops, and then later volunteers) for parachute drops, a glider-borne infantry arm was also developed. The parachute unit was initially called 11 Special Air Service Battalion, and its first mission was to destroy an aqueduct in southern Italy in 1941. Unfortunately, all the members of raiding party were captured on their withdrawal – but they had accomplished their mission, and their success spurred an expansion of the service.

In September 1941 the 1st Parachute Brigade was formed under the command of the then Lieutenant-Colonel Richard "Windy" Gale, and 11 Special Air Service Battalion was renamed 1st Parachute Battalion, one of three such battalions in the brigade. The 1st Air-Landing Brigade Group and the Glider Pilot Regiment were also formed, thus expanding the glider-borne capabilities of British forces. In October 1941, 1st Airborne Division was formed, under Brigadier Frederick "Boy" Browning, comprising the 1st and 2nd Parachute Brigades and 4th, 5th, 6th and 7th Parachute Battalions. The battalions were later brought under the parent unit of The Parachute Regiment, part of the Army Air Corps. In the Far East, the Indian Army also began to organize airborne units, which were later to become the 44th Indian Airborne Division, comprising mostly Indian and Gurkha troops.

It was not long before British airborne troops were in action again, conducting the February 1942 raid against the Bruneval radar station (Operation *Biting*), and the disastrous November

ABOVE A paratroop drop over Netheravon during airborne training in October 1942. The paratroopers are exiting an Armstrong Whitworth Whitley of No. 295 Squadron Royal Air Force.

1942 glider-borne assault on the heavy water plant west of Oslo, Norway (Operation *Freshman*). 1st Parachute Brigade took part in the North Africa landings in November 1942, and conducted an assault on the airfield at Bone on the North African coast, before fighting on as ground infantry.

The expansion of airborne forces continued, and on 2 May 1943 the British 6th Airborne Division was raised under the command of Major-General Richard "Windy" Gale; it was only Britain's second airborne division, but the higher number was chosen in order to deceive enemy intelligence into believing that Britain had a greater number of airborne troops. It was a completely new formation, and it had just one year to train and ready itself for its role in support of a major invasion of North-West Europe. Both the divisions would be brought under 1st Airborne Corps, which was established in 1943.

Meanwhile, the 1st Airborne Division fought in the invasion of Sicily in July 1943, under British Eighth Army. Glider and parachute landings were conducted, both of which went badly wrong, but valuable lessons were learnt. During the 6 June 1944 D-Day operations, 6th Airborne Division's role in the opening engagements was vital, in particular providing the "coup de main" force that secured Pegasus Bridge and capturing the Merville Battery.

On 17 September 1944, 1st Airborne Division was heavily involved in the over-ambitious Operation *Market-Garden*

LEFT The formation badge for 1st Airborne Division, 6th Airborne Division, and, post-1945, 16th Airborne Division TA, depicting Bellerophon riding Pegasus, the winged horse. The badge was designed by Edward Seago in 1942, and was worn by all airborne troops, in conjunction with a further patch with the word "Airborne" worn below the badge.

attempting to capture the bridges across the Rhine at Arnhem in advance of an armoured push to the Westwall on Germany's frontier. Later that year, 4th Parachute Battalion landed at Megara in Greece, and fought its way from Athens to Salonika against both German forces, and then various armed Greek factions in the rapidly deteriorating political situation which would lead to civil war.

The last airborne operation of the European war came in March 1945, when 6th Airborne Division crossed the Rhine river during Operation *Varsity*, as part of US XVIII Airborne Corps. The division was tasked with securing vital road objectives on the far side of the river, to prevent German reinforcements from counter-attacking the main force crossing the river. Both parachute and glider landings were

Brigade conducted a drop on Japanese positions at the mouth of the Rangoon River – the only major combat jump in this theatre during the war.

Despite its battle honours, 1st Airborne Division did no survive long after the end of the Second World War. It was disbanded in November 1946. 6th Airborne Division went or to serve in Palestine, but was disbanded in 1948. Parachute forces would remain on the Army's order of battle in the form of 16th Independent Parachute Brigade, though, and the

THE INVASION OF FRANCE
D-Day: 6 June 1944

The invasion of Nazi-occupied western Europe was a major turning point in the war. The British Army's part in the Allied operations comprised an airborne assault by Major-General Richard Gale's 6th Airborne Division on key objectives inland from the coast of Normandy, and separate landings by ground forces on Sword and Gold beaches west of Ouistreham. The two forces would link up around the bridges across the River Orne and the Caen Canal, the capture of which would allow an assault on the key city of Caen, which commanded the road network in the area. The invasion was originally planned for 5 June, but bad weather in the Channel forced its postponement until the next day.

The assault on Pegasus Bridge was one of the first engagements of D-Day. Shortly after midnight, a glider-borne advance party of British 6th Airborne Division landed next to the bridges over the River Orne ("Horsa Bridge") and the Caen Canal ("Pegasus Bridge') near Bénouville. These were the sole crossing points between Caen and the Channel, and crucial for allowing forces from

ABOVE The Denison smock worn by British airborne troops. It was named after its designer, Major Denison. The smock was introduced for service in 1941, and comprised a camouflaged, heavy-duty, windproof, jacket-like garment, to be worn over battledress. Late-war versions of the smock were fitted with windproof woollen cuffs

Pegasus Bridge and the airborne landings

At around 2300hrs on 5 June, a "coup de main" force of six towed gliders set off from England. Within these gliders were D Company and two platoons from the 2nd Battalion The Oxfordshire and Buckinghamshire Light Infantry, led by Major John Howard; also aboard were 30 engineers. These elite troops had been specially selected and trained for the capture of Pegasus and Horsa bridges.

At 16 minutes past midnight the first of three gliders containing the advance party landed with perfect precision in the designated zone between the two bridges. Within minutes, the two other gliders had landed in the same area, while two more gliders landed slightly further north adjacent to the Orne, again with great precision. However, the sixth glider lost its bearings and landed several miles away.

The assault eastwards across Pegasus Bridge was led by Lieutenant Den Brotheridge of 1st Platoon, but he was soon cut down by enemy fire. Meanwhile another platoon cleared the eastern end of the bridge. The men from the second and third gliders joined in the attack as they arrived at the scene from their landing zone. The bridge was soon taken, and the British occupied the German positions, and the accompanying British engineers made sure there were no explosives present. Meanwhile, the men from the first of the two gliders that had landed

ABOVE Four "stick" commanders of 22nd Independent Parachute Company, British 6th Airborne Division, synchronize their watches in front of an Armstrong Whitworth Albemarle of No. 38 Group, Royal Air Force, at about 2300hrs on 5 June 1944, just prior to take off from RAF Harwell, Oxfordshire. This pathfinder unit parachuted into Normandy in advance of the rest of the division to mark out the landing zones.

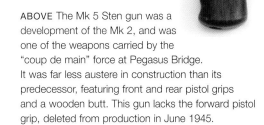

further north, led by Lieutenant Dennis Fox, attacked the Orne (Horsa) Bridge, clearing the machine-gun posts and pillboxes. Both bridges had now been secured, and Howard waited for 7th Parachute Battalion to relieve him.

From 0050hrs onwards, advance elements from the 5th Parachute Brigade started to land east of the River Orne in Drop Zone "N", with a mission to secure the area. At the same time, 12th and 13th Parachute Battalions landed east of Ranville, with orders to secure the area to the south of Horsa Bridge, taking up positions in Le Bas de Ranville and Ranville.

Having gathered at the allocated rendezvous, Lieutenant-Colonel Geoffrey Pine-Coffin, commanding officer of 7th Parachute Battalion, set off with an initial attack force (companies A, B and C) and the advance Battalion HQ for the two bridges, to reinforce the "coup de main" force. The paratroopers quickly crossed the intact bridges and set up hasty defensive positions in and around Bénouville and the town of Le Port. Pine-Coffin then ordered Howard to withdraw his men over Pegasus Bridge, and secure Horsa Bridge and the area between the two bridges. By about 0300hrs, the paratroopers were in position, and would spend the rest of the night, and much of the morning, fighting off German counter-attacks from elements of 1st Panzerjäger Company and troops from 716th Infantry Division. As the day progressed, the situation improved for the Allies, with the arrival of Lord Lovat's 1st Special Service Brigade, which had landed on Sword Beach. During the evening of 6 June, around 2115hrs, the 2nd Battalion The Royal Warwickshire Regiment arrived with armoured support to relieve 7th Parachute Battalion. Their job done, the battalion withdrew from its positions. At around the same time, the British 6th Air-landing Brigade arrived in gliders in Landing Zone "W", just to the north of Pegasus Bridge, completing the assembly of 6th Airborne Division. Major John Howard would later receive the Distinguished Service Order in recognition of his role at Pegasus Bridge.

RIGHT Transport moves across the Caen Canal Bridge at Bénouville, 9 June 1944. The bridge was later renamed Pegasus Bridge, after the mythical winged horse on the formation sign of British airborne forces.

ABOVE The Mk 5 Sten gun was a development of the Mk 2, and was one of the weapons carried by the "coup de main" force at Pegasus Bridge. It was far less austere in construction than its predecessor, featuring front and rear pistol grips and a wooden butt. This gun lacks the forward pistol grip, deleted from production in June 1945.

the landing beaches and the soon-to-arrive main airborne forces to link up. After a brief fire fight, the bridges were captured and held for the next 12 hours against strengthening counter-attacks.

Just before 0730 hrs on 6 June, the first British troops of 8th Brigade, 3rd Infantry Division, came ashore on Sword Beach. The lead elements comprised men from the 1st South Lancashires, 2nd East Yorkshires and 1st Suffolks; self-propelled artillery guns; and specialist vehicles (such as Sherman "floating" Duplex Drive tanks) from 79th Armoured Division. It took an hour for the lead elements of the landing to clear the shore and begin moving inland. Men from the 5th Assault Regiment of the Royal Engineers played a key role in destroying the German beach defences. The tanks of 27th

Armoured Brigade, followed by men from Nos. 3, 4 and 6 Commandos of the 1st Special Service Brigade, under the command of Lord Lovat, then reinforced 3rd Division's toehold. Once ashore, Lovat's Commandos attacked the German gun batteries near the mouth of the River Orne and the strongpoint of the Riva Bella "Casino" in Ouistreham, before fighting their way to Pegasus Bridge to relieve the "coup de main" force. The final elements of 3rd Infantry Division to land were the men of 185th Brigade and 9th Brigade, charged with the drive to capture Caen.

At Gold Beach, the lead assault elements of 50th (Northumbrian) Division, comprising men of the Green Howards and East Yorkshire Regiment, began to land at 0730hrs on 6 June. The men of the 1st Hampshires and 1st

The D-Day beach landings

William Haskill Millin was a British trooper serving with Lord Lovat's 1st Special Service Brigade, part of the Assault Brigade that spearheaded the landing on Sword Beach on 6 June:

"When we landed it was under heavy fire, and lots of people were being killed. I jumped off into the water and started to play the pipes. Lovat looked round when he heard the pipes and smiled, then walked on, and I piped from when the water was about waist high right up until the beach. Then I stopped and I dashed off to see if I could find an exit. When I got to the exit there was a load of wounded all lying about; of course, they saw me with the tartan and they said 'Where are the medics, Jock?' They had been shot when they tried to go up the road

by a German machine gun at the top, about 12 or 14 of them all lying in the sand at the entrance to this road. I said, 'They're coming.' Well, I didn't know if they were coming or not. Just at that moment a burst of machine-gun fire came down the road ... and I tried to pull one or two of them away out of the way of the firing line ... I looked round and heard a clanking and saw a flail tank with the chains to set off the mines coming off the beach and heading for the road ... A bit later on, we came under shellfire ... Lovat looked round and saw me standing there and said 'Give us a tune.' Well, the whole idea was ridiculous – people under shellfire and all sorts of things going on at the time. It was mad enough the three of us standing there. We shouldn't have been standing, we should have been lying

down. He said 'Give us a tune, piper.' And I thought I may as well be ridiculous too, and said, 'What tune would you like, sir?' He said, 'Play "The road to the Isles".' I said, 'Would you like me to march up and down? He said, 'Yes, yes, march up and down. That would be lovely.' The whole thing was ridiculous – bodies lying at the water's edge going back and forward with the tide, and I started off piping. I had gone about a few paces along there and the next thing I felt was a hand on my shoulder. I looked round and it was a sergeant I recognized. He said, 'What are you flaming playing at, attracting all this attention? Every German in France knows we're here now, you silly bastard!'"

Dorsets followed, but became pinned down by enemy fire at Le Hamel soon after landing. The assault elements were able to move off the beach by 0930hrs, with 50th Division (supported by tanks of 8th Armoured Brigade and Royal Marine Commandos) now focussing on capturing Bayeux. On Juno Beach, the Canadian 3rd Infantry Division supported by Canadian 2nd Armoured Brigade, 48 Royal Marine Commando, and elements from 79th Armoured Division, began to land from 0750hrs on 6 June. Once clear of the beaches, the Canadians could join the attack on Caen.

By mid afternoon on 6 June, the British advance inland from Sword Beach had become bogged down clearing inland German strongpoints. The 21st Panzer Division launched a rapid counter-attack, clashing with the King's Shropshire Light Infantry and the tanks of the Staffordshire Yeomanry, before driving for the sea and temporarily cutting the Sword and Juno beachheads off from each other. However, 21st Panzer Division withdrew back towards Caen late on 6 June as more Allied troops arrived by sea and air. The British and Canadians now set about consolidating their bridgeheads.

191

RIGHT British troops crouch down on Sword Beach as they await the signal to advance, 6 June 1944.

BELOW Sections of the "Overlord" tapestry designed by Sandra Lawrence and made by the Royal School of Needlework to commemorate D-Day and the Normandy landings in 1944. Inspired by the Bayeux Tapestry, it traces the progress of Operation *Overlord* and the events preceding it. The tapestry is 272 feet long and took five years to produce. The scenes it depicts are based on photographs held at the Imperial War Museum.

Operations *Epsom*, *Jupiter*, *Charnwood* and *Goodwood*

In the days that followed the Allied landings, the Canadians and British resumed their drive for Caen, with the battle-hardened 51st Highland and 7th Armoured Divisions, who were ambushed by Tigers from 1st SS Panzer Division at Villers-Bocage, both attempting to encircle the city on 11/12 June. However, the stubborn German defence and counter-attacks by 21st Panzer Division and the recently arrived 1st, 2nd and 12th Hitlerjügend SS Panzer Divisions ensured that little progress was made.

On 26 June Operation *Epsom* was launched, a concentrated attempt by the newly arrived British VIII Corps (comprising 11th Armoured, 15th Scottish, and 43rd Wessex Divisions, and later the 53rd Welsh) to cross the River Orne and encircle Caen from the south-west. The operation had been delayed by the destruction of one of the two Mulberry harbours during a Channel storm. Although gains were made, such as the Argyll and Sutherland Highlanders' seizure of a bridgehead over the River Odon at Tourmauville, progress was slow and the offensive ground to a halt with the arrival of German reinforcements. The 11th Armoured Division was involved in fierce fighting around Hill 112 beyond Tourmauville in an attempt to capture the high ground dominating the road network to the south of Caen. The dominating hill would change hands several times in the course of the following weeks, particularly during Operation *Jupiter* executed by the 43rd Wessex Division and their bruising clashes with the 9th and 10th SS Panzer Divisions.

A further British attempt to capture Caen came with Operation *Charnwood*, a massive frontal attack on Caen by the infantry of British I Corps on 8–9 July, preceded by an aerial bombardment of the city's northern areas. The British 3rd and 59th Divisions attacked on the 9th and took the north of the city in house-to-house fighting among the rubble, but the bridges across the River Orne in the centre remained in German hands.

Operation *Goodwood*, launched on 18 July with another heavy aerial bombardment, finally achieved what Montgomery had sought for some five weeks. The 7th, 11th and Guards Armoured Divisions, supported by 3rd Infantry Division, attacked south out of the bridgehead created by 6th Airborne Division and encircled Caen from the east, while Canadian troops launched an attack on the centre. The armoured advance to the east attempted to capture the high ground on the Caen–Falaise road, but stiff German resistance soon halted it. However, the 2nd Canadian Division managed to capture the bridges across the Orne in the city centre, and

The battle for Hill 112

Thomas Henry Peace was the adjutant of the 5th Battalion The Wiltshire Regiment in Normandy 1944:

"We were given an axis of advance to the forward slopes of the famous Hill 112 ... we had our first experience of these Nebelwerfers. I remember seeing a salvo coming over and landing in the middle of one platoon. But they got up afterwards – it was a very frightening weapon but it didn't fragment, it was mostly blast. We made our way to 112 without too much difficulty but a lot of chaos ... There was this great fear of snipers; there were stories that the Hitler Youth were painting their faces yellow and draping themselves over fences pretending to be dead, and then would shoot you in the back as you went past. It was self-defeating, as anyone pretending to be dead soon was anyway. On the forward slopes of

BELOW British troops pick their way through the rubble of the northern district of Caen, 9 July 1944.

112, the company positions were laid out and the CO went off to the brigade for orders. That night, all hell broke loose. Our soldiers, despite all their training, had been prancing about on the skyline, had dug slit trenches only about a foot deep thinking that was enough – and we were under observation from 112 and other hills ... The shelling was intense all night. One of our FOOs [Forward Observation Officers] spotted German troops forming up for an attack and called for artillery fire. In the end the whole Corps' artillery was firing. To be honest, if they'd have come straight at us, I don't think we were in any sort of position to resist a night attack. It was that FOO and the guns that saved us. I think we suffered about 200 casualties that night, the 10th July. The CO was killed, and the second-in-command came to take over ... Keeping up the morale of the troops wasn't easy. Then the time came for the first major battle to clear the hill. The superiority of the German 88mm gun, their accurate mortar fire, and the fact it was a very well constructed defensive position basically meant it got nowhere. The poor Dorsets took Maltot but had to withdraw; the Cornwalls got to the top of the hill, but were wiped out – their CO was last seen at the top of a tree calling down artillery fire on his own position; it was a desperate desolate day, with lots of casualties, and getting absolutely nowhere ... I had an observation post in a sort of mill or house overlooking the battlefield. I hadn't been there long when the next minute the place was round our ears. In hindsight, it was a darn silly place to be ... The 15th Scottish Division were next to make their attack. All that night they were shot up, they took a lot of hammering. They were brave but they got nowhere ... Nobody would learn from the experiences of others, I don't know why ... We were extremely pleased to be told at long last that were were being relieved from our position. We were pretty battle hardened by then."

193

ABOVE Men of 12 Platoon, B Company, 6th Battalion The Royal Scots Fusiliers advance into St Manvieu during Operation *Epsom*, 26 June 1944.

RIGHT A soldier armed with a Sten gun takes cover beneath a jeep during Operation *Epsom*, 26 June 1944.

linked up with the 3rd Armoured Division on 19 July. The city was now in Allied hands, and with US Army pressure in the west exposing their left flank and a further attack towards Falaise by British VIII Corps (Operation *Bluecoat*) in late July, German forces withdrew south.

The Falaise pocket

The American breakthrough of the German lines following the start of Operation *Cobra* in late July drew German forces away from the British lines to the east, allowing British XII Corps to push south of Caen in early August. Between 7 and 14 August, Canadian forces launched two operations (*Totalise* and *Tractable*), aimed at securing the Caen–Falaise road. With increasing US pressure to the west and south, the German 5th Panzer and 7th Armies became hemmed into a pocket of terrain between Falaise and Argentan, with an ever-narrowing escape route to the east. On 15 August 1944 Operation *Dragoon*, the Allied invasion of southern France, was launched; the British contribution to this US-led effort comprised troops from 2nd Independent Parachute Brigade and 1st Special Service Force. In Normandy, the Falaise pocket was finally cut off on 19 August by troops from the 1st Polish Armoured Division, although a mass German breakout was attempted the next day. With the arrival of Canadian and American troops on 21 August, the pocket was well and truly sealed. The Germans lost thousands of guns, tanks, vehicles, horses and troops, mostly from Allied air attacks, and some 50,000 German prisoners were taken. The battle for Normandy was now over. British troops made their first crossing of the River Seine on 25 August at Vernon, and Paris was liberated the same day by Free French forces.

ABOVE Men of the Hampshire Regiment cross the River Seine at Vernon, 28 August 1944.

The Falaise pocket

Raymond Ashton was a British private serving with 15 Platoon, D Company, 1st Battalion The Middlesex Regiment in Normandy 1944:

"After the breakout we were left behind. We weren't directly involved in the fighting at Falaise, but we had to drive through it, and I shall never forget it. Absolutely appalling. If you can imagine how on earth this must have been – whole roads jammed with vehicles and dead horses that the Germans used. This surprised us, as we always imagined the Germans as a mechanized army like our own – but in fact they employed a lot of horses on their guns and so forth ... I can remember we were forced to stay one night there. We were halted and told to bivvy for the night, and there was literally nowhere to lie down. We cleared an area, and buried a couple

ABOVE British troops wend their way through the ruins of Lisieux, Normandy, 22 August 1944.

RIGHT *Normandy: July 1944*, by Edward Raymond Payne (watercolour, 1944). Four British soldiers sit in a ditch at the side of a field near their truck.

of Germans who simply fell apart when we tried to put them in a slit trench. We were violently sick the pair of us, and the meal that night was bully and rice – the rice just looked like a load of maggots, we couldn't eat the meal. But we had a mug of tea, and that was about all we could stomach. The next day we moved on, but we were forced to drive over bodies, and appalling stench, with flies everywhere. I've often wondered how long, and with what horror, it must have been to clear up that mess."

Edward Ronald Douglas Palmer was a British officer serving with the Bedfordshire Yeomanry in Normandy:

"Because we had these long-range guns and radios we were chosen to go with the leading pursuit force. We had some wonderful shooting in the Falaise Gap, largely from spotter aircraft. At one stage there was a frightfully excited air OP (as we called them) who said, 'There are thousands of them down there!' And we had to fire 45 rounds in 35 minutes, which doesn't sound an awful lot for ordinary guns, but for these heavy guns it was a tremendous thing. They got so hot that the paint all the way down the long barrels blistered off. Of course it would never have been allowed in any peacetime thing, but the targets were so tempting that we fired off everything we could as fast as we could. When one drove through the Falaise Gap shortly afterwards it was horrifying, absolutely amazing – the amount of litter, of vehicles, of horses."

195

VISCOUNT MONTGOMERY OF ALAMEIN

LEFT *Field-Marshal The Viscount Montgomery of Alamein, KG, GCB, DSO, by Sir Oswald Birley (oil on canvas, 1948).*

and reticence of recent months, as Stephen Anthony Kennedy, who served with the 6th Royal Tank Regiment in North Africa and was one of the crew of Montgomery's command tank:

"Each day [Montgomery] would visit his corps headquarters from his HQ. He didn't want his generals to go back to him, he would go forward to them. We would go off earlier on and wait for him just near Tel el Eisa, which was in the Australian sector. We would wait by the side of the road and he would come along in his staff car, get into the tank, and go off into the desert to meet up with Corps HQ, which was within artillery range of the enemy ... We would have a cup of tea and the general would come back and have a cup of tea too."

His character was often described as abrasive by his detractors, who also considered him to be vain and arrogant. However, there is no denying Montgomery's capacity for showmanship, particularly in his choice of headwear, which made him both distinct from and recognizable by the troops under his command. One of his most distinctive hats was his tank beret. Stephen Anthony Kennedy recalls the occasion of the beret's presentation to Montgomery:

"We heard that the general was wearing an Australian cap and it kept blowing off. Now, I don't know the real facts about this, but they say that Corporal Fraser (the driver) said 'You could have my beret.' They

Bernard Law Montgomery was born in 1887, the son of the Bishop of Tasmania. He attended St Paul's School in London before going up to Sandhurst. In 1908 he was commissioned into the Royal Warwickshire Regiment, and fought with the regiment in the First World War, receiving a near-mortal wound in 1914 near the Belgian border. He returned to active service as a staff officer and spent time under Herbert Plumer's command, learning about infantry and artillery cooperation. By war's end he had risen to the rank of lieutenant-colonel, and had been awarded the DSO.

Between the wars, Montgomery was with the British Army of the Rhine in Germany, attended the Army's Staff College in Camberley, and served as a brigade commander in Cork during the Anglo-Irish War. In 1925 he returned to the Royal Warwickshire Regiment in command of a company, and by 1931 had risen to lieutenant-colonel. In 1937, his wife of ten years, by whom he had had one son, died.

In 1938 Montgomery was given command of 8th Infantry Division, based in Palestine, and was involved in keeping the peace during the 1936–1938 Arab rebellion. In 1939 he moved to command the 3rd Infantry Division, which saw action in France as part of the BEF. A succession of corps commands quickly followed after the fall of France, together with promotion to lieutenant-general in 1940.

In 1942 Montgomery was appointed to command Eighth Army in North Africa, where his confident and high-profile style of leadership inspired his troops following the confusion

PERSONAL MESSAGE
from the
ARMY COMMANDER

TO BE READ OUT TO ALL TROOPS.

1. When I assumed command of the Eighth Army I said that the mandate was to destroy ROMMEL and his Army, and that it would be done as soon as we were ready.

2. We are ready NOW.
   The battle which is now about to begin will be one of the decisive battles of history. It will be the turning point of the war. The eyes of the whole world will be on us, watching anxiously which way the battle will swing.
   We can give them their answer at once, «It will swing our way».

3. We have first-class equipment; good tanks; good anti-tank guns; plenty of artillery and plenty of ammunition; and we are backed up by the finest air striking force in the world.
   All that is necessary is that each one of us, every officer and man, should enter this battle with the determination to see it through — to fight and to kill — and finally, to win.
   If we all do this there can be only one result — together we will hit the enemy for «six», right out of North Africa.

4. The sooner we win this battle, which will be the turning point of the war, the sooner we shall all get back home to our families.

5. Therefore, let every officer and man enter the battle with a stout heart, and the determination to do his duty so long as he has breath in his body.
   AND LET NO MAN SURRENDER SO LONG AS HE IS UNWOUNDED AND CAN FIGHT.
   Let us all pray that «the Lord mighty in battle» will give us the victory.

B. L. Montgomery.

23-10-42.
Middle East Forces.   Lieutenant-General, G.O.C.-in-C., Eighth Army.

LEFT Montgomery's message to the Eighth Army before the Second Battle of El Alamein, 23 October 1942. A significant factor in Montgomery's leadership was his ability to communicate with and inspire his troops. Stephen Anthony Kennedy, a trooper with the 6th Royal Tank Regiment in North Africa, commented: "He was aloof from us, of course, because we were very junior ranks, but he had the appearance of a real gentleman."

asked his ADC (Captain Poston, 11th Hussar) 'Would the general wear a beret?' He said, 'I'll ask him.' They also asked him if would he wear the badge of the regiment, and he said he would. So we got back to HQ and they were able to order a brand new beret with the badge in. Corporal Fraser, who was the one Montgomery thanked for driving him, stepped forward and said: 'General, would you wear our beret?' He had already been tuned in and knew the form, and said 'Of course I will.' And he wore the beret that day, and the next day he appeared in the beret and he had the general's badge beside it. He's probably the only general in the whole army who had two badges."

The North African, Italian, Normandy and North-West European campaigns (where Montgomery commanded 21st Army Group) were highly successful for Montgomery, with the exception of the over-ambitious Arnhem operation. Montgomery was promoted to Field Marshal on 1 September 1944. In 1946 he was invested with the title of Viscount Montgomery of Alamein. He went on to serve as Chief of the Imperial General Staff and Deputy Supreme Allied Commander Europe before retiring in 1958. He died in 1976.

BELOW The Deputy Supreme Commander-in-Chief of the Red Army, Marshal G. Zhukov, the Commander of the 21st Army Group, Field Marshal Sir Bernard Montgomery, Marshal Sokolovsky, and General K. Rokossovsky at the Brandenburg Gate in Berlin on 12 July 1945. Montgomery had just decorated the Soviet generals.

ABOVE Lieutenant-General Montgomery as General Officer Commanding Eighth Army, watching the beginning of the German retreat from El Alamein from the turret of his Grant tank in November 1942. He is wearing his famous double-badged tank beret.

ABOVE A formal portrait of Lieutenant-Colonel Bernard Montgomery, taken in the early 1930s. Between 1931 and 1934 he commanded the 1st Battalion The Royal Warwickshire Regiment. Following his retirement from active service in 1958, he continued to hold the position of Colonel of the Royal Warwickshire Regiment, for which he held a particular affection.

1944–1945

OPERATION *MARKET-GARDEN*

The Netherlands had been under German occupation since May 1940, with over 102,000 Dutch Jews and Gypsies being deported and murdered, and the country suffering privations and food shortages. With Allied forces gathering on the Netherlands' western borders, Montgomery proposed an ambitious operation to end the war before Christmas, with a thrust by 21st Army Group through the Netherlands and on into Germany. This would outflank the formidable West Wall defences, which lay further south, and gain access to the German industrial heartland of the Ruhr. Troops of the recently created First Allied Airborne Army (comprising two British and three American airborne divisions) would land deep within the Netherlands and capture key roads and bridges (Operation *Market*); this, in turn, would allow the British Second Army (led by the Guards Armoured Division) to link up with these crossing points and advance rapidly across the country, before heading east into Germany's industrial heartland (Operation *Garden*). The airborne landings would involve three divisions, with the US 101st Airborne landing north of Eindhoven, the US 82nd Airborne landing between Grave and Nijmegen, and the British 1st

The liberation of the Low Countries

The rapid drive of Montgomery's 21st Army Group across northern France in pursuit of the remnants of Army Group B quickly led to the liberation of Belgium in September 1944, with troops of the Guards Armoured Division entering Brussels on the evening of the 3rd. The key deep-water port of Antwerp was secured by 11th Armoured Division on 4 September. However, German forces still controlled the banks of the Scheldt Estuary downstream towards the coast, and the port would not be operational until November, following the Canadian First Army's lengthy operations (involving the British 49th and 52nd Divisions) to clear the area of enemy troops.

Peter Carrington was a British officer serving with 2nd Armoured Battalion Grenadier Guards in Belgium and the Netherlands in 1944. He went on to become Foreign Secretary in 1979 in Mrs Thatcher's government:

"There weren't any Germans in Brussels, so it wasn't like Paris, where people were still keeping their heads down. Also, I think the Belgians were rather more pleased to see us, if the truth be told. And we went in there at the beginning of September, the leading troops – we came in one way and the Welsh Guards came in another – and I've never seen anything like the welcome. Everyone jumped onto our tanks. There were 30 or 40 people climbing over our tanks and giving us champagne, and they were really pleased and delighted to see us. Unfortunately, my squadron was immediately sent off to

guard the palace at Laaken where Queen Elisabeth of the Belgians was living at the time, so we spent the night quite some distance from the centre of Brussels. Some people had a rather more amusing time than we did … I remember Queen Elisabeth coming out and looking through the gate of Laaken and waving at us and shaking hands, it was a great occasion … When we got a bit more static after Operation Market-Garden one saw a good deal of the privations and horrors that the Dutch people suffered. I think that the Dutch really had the worst of it all. They were enormously brave in their resistance and they had had a very, very rough time. They were eating tulip bulbs and that sort of thing. The Belgians ran a black market at the expense of the Germans, and managed to survive – they were a remarkable people. But I don't think they had quite the rough time the Dutch did."

RIGHT The formation badge for 11th Armoured Division, derived from the coat of arms of its first commander, Major-General Sir Percy Hobart. 11th Armoured Division was formed in the UK on 9 March 1941. It remained in Home Forces until assigned to 21st Army Group for the invasion of North-West Europe. It formed part of VIII Corps in Normandy. It took part in the bridgehead battles and was in the forefront of the sweep across France and Belgium into Holland in autumn 1944. Following the invasion of Germany it ended the war on the Elbe. The division was disbanded in 1946–1947 but re-formed in January 1951. It was finally disbanded as an armoured formation and re-designated 4 Infantry Division (BAOR) on 1 April 1956.

Airborne Division landing around Arnhem – the furthest north of the three at 64 miles from the operation start line. The British 1st Airborne Division's main objectives were the capture of the road and rail bridges over the lower River Rhine in the city centre, and the securing of the high ground to the north of the town.

The first transports left England on the morning of 17 September, with the pathfinders of 21st Independent Parachute Company leading the way to the Arnhem paratroop and glider landing zones. The zones themselves were scattered several miles away from the primary bridge objectives, meaning that a long approach march was required through the suburb of Oosterbeek. By 1400hrs all the units had landed, and contact was made with the enemy. Meanwhile, British XXX Corps began its drive into Holland towards Eindhoven.

As 1st Airborne's troops approached Oosterbeek, the railway bridge was blown by the Germans, but Major Frost's 2nd Parachute Battalion managed to secure the northern end of the road bridge over the Lower Rhine by early evening on the 17th. The next day both sides began their attacks, with 3rd Parachute Battalion attempting to fight its way to the road

LEFT A tank crew of the 4th Battalion The Royal Tank Regiment, 4th Armoured Division, unpack a parcel near Weert in Holland in November 1944. The crew, who are shown with their camouflaged tank looking like a "travelling Christmas tree", had been together for three years, and had seen action in Libya and Italy before coming to Holland. From left to right, they are Trooper R. Buckley, Trooper J. Round and Sergeant H. Kirk.

RIGHT Dutch civilians hitch a ride on the bonnet of a jeep in Eindhoven, as crowds cheer the British XXX Corps as it passes through the city on 20 September 1944 on the advance into the Netherlands.

bridge, and German attacks against the British landing zones to the west and the northern end of the bridge. The second wave of British landings arrived in the afternoon to the west of the town, including 4th Parachute Brigade.

On 19 September 1st Parachute Brigade began its delayed attack towards the road bridge at Arnhem, but was soon stalled. The fighting reached a stalemate: casualties were mounting, the airborne troops were exhausted, supplies were low, and German reinforcements were arriving all the time. The German attacks continued throughout the 20th. Meanwhile XXX Corps' progress had been slower than hoped and it was delayed at the crossing at Nijmegen. On the 21st the survivors of Frost's 2nd Parachute Battalion on the Arnhem road bridge were overwhelmed, and concerted attacks began on the British positions to the west. Over the following days, the German attacks continued, as XXX Corps slowly neared the Arnhem area. However, a change in strategy by the Allied high command meant that an advance past Arnhem was no longer desired for Second British Army. The airborne troops in Arnhem were given permission to withdraw on the evening of 22 September. A full British withdrawal by boat began on the 25th southwards across the Lower Rhine River.

British losses during the Arnhem operation were heavy, and barely 2,000 of the 10,000 men involved were evacuated. A key criticism of the operation afterwards was that the drop zones were too far away from the bridge objectives, and thus the enemy was well aware of the presence of the lightly armed airborne troops by the time they had reached their objectives. To make matters worse, few of the re-supply materials during the operations landed on British-held areas. Many of the planners and commanders involved sought to distance themselves from the operation afterwards.

Arnhem

Major John Dutton Frost commanded the 2nd Battalion of The Parachute Regiment during Operation *Market-Garden*, and led the capture of the northern end of the Arnhem road bridge:

"I was wounded on the Wednesday morning, not very badly but extremely painfully, so after a time I was given morphia, and went down to the cellar. Freddie Gough assumed the overall command of the bridge, but every time he used to come and confer all the problems with me. There wasn't anything we could do, we couldn't escape. We had discussed doing a sortie and going northwards, but it was much more important that we should stay in positions at the north end of the bridge for as long as possible so as to give the maximum help we could to any one trying to cross from the south. Even if one had been left with no ammunition at all one might have been able to do something to help them. So there was no way we could possibly move, we were absolutely sealed in by enemy infantry and armour. One time we were being bombarded with self-propelled guns you could actually see firing at us. This had the effect of setting more and more buildings on fire, and there it was. Fortunately the flames were not in such a direction of the wind to completely consume everywhere we were, until the last evening when finally this government building where the brigade headquarters had been (and was an absolute key place) caught fire. And by now there was no water, no means of putting the flames out. So the head doctor came to see me and said: 'I'm afraid unless we can put the flames out our 200 wounded men are going to be burnt alive, including you, sir.' There didn't seem to be much point, at this stage we really almost ceased to be a fighting force due to lack of ammunition etc. So the doctor said: 'Can I go out and try to make contact with the Germans so as to evacuate the wounded?' This he did. The Germans agreed to a truce to get the wounded out and for that time everybody available, including the Germans, including the SS, laboured night and day to get everyone out of the building, by which time it was blazing quite fiercely. And after they had

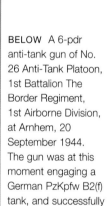
BELOW A 6-pdr anti-tank gun of No. 26 Anti-Tank Platoon, 1st Battalion The Border Regiment, 1st Airborne Division, at Arnhem, 20 September 1944. The gun was at this moment engaging a German PzKpfw B2(f) tank, and successfully knocked it out.

got almost the last man out, including the German wounded and prisoners, the building collapsed. From that time on really our own men were in little groups of people without any coordination, and when the morning came completely superior numbers of German soldiers were able to round them up. I was taken out of the building and laid on the embankment on the other side. The battle had ceased for quite a time while this happened and everyone was moving about quite freely, and then we were put onto half-tracks and stretchers were laid across them and driven into the St Elizabeth Hospital on the western approaches to the town ... Early next morning we were put into ambulances and driven straight into Germany."

RIGHT Four men of the 1st Parachute Battalion, 1st Airborne Division, take cover in a foxhole outside Arnhem on 17 September 1944.

BELOW The Bren Mk 2 machine gun. At the outbreak of the Second World War, the Bren Mk 1 was the standard light machine gun of the British Army. However, many were lost during the fall of France and the need to speed up manufacture resulted in the adoption of a simplified model – the Mk 2. For the lightly armed airborne troops at Arnhem, the Bren was a key source of firepower.

202

GREECE 1944–1945

Following the start of the German withdrawal from Crete and Greece in September 1944, the country entered a phase of political instability, with infighting breaking out between the anti-German partisan forces. A pro-royalist coalition government (which Britain supported and exerted pressure on all parties to form) was instituted in October. However, the armed communist ELAS partisans, who were busy harassing the retreating Germans and were in control of much of the country, withheld their full support. To liberate Athens, on 12 October 1944 Operation *Manna* was launched; the lead elements of 4th Parachute Battalion, 2nd Independent Parachute Brigade Group, landed at Megara airfield west of Athens in dangerously windy conditions on 12 October. The rest of 2nd Independent Parachute Brigade, dispatched to Greece from the landing operations in southern France, landed a few days later, together with elements of 23rd Armoured Brigade; the British forces would come under the name "Arkforce". On 15 October men from the 2nd Commando Brigade entered Athens in pursuit of the German troops, but found the city had already been abandoned. The government in exile in Cairo returned to Greece on the 19th.

Over the course of the next two months, Arkforce harassed the retreating Germans north to the border with Bulgaria, but were soon dragged into the country's internal political turmoil. In December, when the police fired on pro-communist demonstrators in Athens, the situation rapidly deteriorated, and ELAS troops attempted to take control of the capital. British troops managed to stabilize the situation and break the rebellion, and in February 1945 ELAS forces were disarmed, by which time 2nd Independent Parachute Brigade had returned to Italy.

In 1946, following their boycott of the organized elections and the vote on the return of the exiled king from Cairo (which subsequently returned a "yes" vote for the restoration of the monarchy), the pro-communist faction (now called the Democratic Army) resumed their armed struggle, plunging the country into a bloody civil war. British troops attempted to maintain order but the task would eventually prove too onerous, particularly in the light of other global commitments in the immediate post-war period. America now began to provide increased financial and material support for the pro-royalist forces. The civil war continued until a ceasefire was declared in 1949, when many of the Communist fighters fled the country into Albania. Greece subsequently became a member of NATO. British troops were finally withdrawn from Greece in 1950.

The return to Greece

LEFT The formation badge for III Corps and subsequently HQ Land Forces Greece, later known as British Forces in Greece (BFIG). The badge's fig-leaf design reputedly constitutes an oblique reference to the surname of the corps' commander at the time of its adoption, Sir Ronald Adam. The corps fought with the BEF in France and Belgium in 1940 and later moved to Northern Ireland where this badge was adopted. In 1943 III Corps moved to Persia and later to Syria. It transferred to Egypt before crossing to Italy and ended the war in Greece.

Harold Brian "Vic" Coxen was the commanding officer of the 4th Battalion The Parachute Regiment (part of 2nd Independent Parachute Brigade) in Greece in 1944:

"Almost immediately after we had carried out the French [Dragoon] operation and had joined up with the British and

American forces that had carried out that landing, we were pulled out and brought back to Italy. Within three days we had been dropped in Greece, the whole brigade ... We landed on the south coast of Greece to the west of Athens. I had quite a few casualties in my own battalion as the wind was blowing like anything ... The rest of us mooched off on all sorts of vehicles that we could get hold of – we hadn't any of our own – and went into Athens. There was no bother from the Germans, they had left, and the Andartikos [resistance fighters] had not got enough strength to really be a nuisance. They were merely being non-cooperative, but it was perfectly obvious that they were there to take over ... There were of course one or two people of left-wing persuasion in the battalion, there always are. One of them was a little man, whose name I won't give you, who was a journalist and a communist. I said to him after the fourth day we were there: 'What do you think of your communist chums?' And he replied, 'They're a shower of shit, sir.' And he at least was a convert ... The problem of fighting the Andartiko was that he was not in uniform, he was merely armed in civilian clothes with a bandolier around him. All he had to do was take those off and throw it under a bed and you didn't know whether he had been fighting or not. One of my wits reckoned we used to feed them – we used to feed the Greek populace you see ... None of the soldiers liked the Andartikos; they thought they had come over to save Greece and found they were being shot at by those bastards ... How did we secure Athens? Quite simply, we put up a fence of wire around an area and searched every house for arms and weapons. If you found anyone armed, you arrested them and then moved them out. Sometimes you had to fight and sometimes not. You could not shoot into any house until you had been shot at ... One had to move very carefully, and it cost you every now and then. You had people clocked because they had taken a chance; so many of these people were boys of 14 who had been brainwashed."

LEFT Paratroops from 5th Parachute Battalion, 2nd Independent Parachute Brigade, take cover on a street corner in Athens during operations against members of ELAS, 6 December 1944.

ABOVE Sergeant R. Gregory and Driver A. Hardman admire the Caryatids during a tour of the Acropolis in Athens in October 1944.

ADVANCE TO THE RHINE

The River Rhine was the last natural defensive barrier preventing the Allies from breaking through into the plains and industrial heartlands of northern Germany. Following a period of preparation and re-supply in the wake of the failed German Ardennes offensive of late 1944, the forces of 21st Army Group began a sequence of operations to either destroy the Germans in the northern Rhineland sector, or push them back beyond the river.

The first of these was Operation *Veritable*, launched on 8 February, which aimed to clear the German forces (comprising First Parachute Army) from the River Maas in the Netherlands to the River Rhine in a drive starting to the

south of Nijmegen. Canadian II Corps would lead this attack together with the British 15th, 51st and 53rd Divisions, and it would involve a direct assault against a heavily fortified section of the West Wall defences. Simpson's US Ninth Army would support this offensive with an attack 60 miles to the south (Operation *Grenade*). During Operation *Veritable*, 51st and 53rd Divisions were involved in fierce, prolonged fighting in the Reichswald Forest, and movement along the congested roads and in the flooded Rhine Valley was difficult and slow. 43rd Wessex and the Guards Armoured Divisions joined the battle, and the key town of Cleve was captured on 11 February by 15th Division and Canadian troops. The 43rd Division then slowly fought its way towards the heavily fortified town of Goch, creating a salient in the German lines;

Crossing the Rhine

Ian Charles Hammerton was an officer serving with the 22nd Dragoons, 79th Armoured Division, during the advance into Germany:

"I think the word that describes the whole of the Reichswald fighting is 'confused'. There were odd little bits and pieces going on all over the place ... We were up to our eyes in mud, you'd jump off the tank and sink up to your knees in it – it was soft as that. Shortly after that the Germans blew the Rhine dykes and the area flooded ... As we got near to Cleve, we had heavy snow overnight. I remember coming into Cleve, which was just a big heap of rubble ... We got a call during the night to move immediately, as the water was coming up, and we had to drive up onto the higher ground. The Germans had blown another section of the dykes, it was a terrific scramble ... From then on we were constantly on the move in support of little attacks around Cleve. It was horrible going and there was very little cover up there ... Then we were moved up nearer to the river, and before the Rhine crossing quite an amount of time went by. There was a tremendous smokescreen maintained all the way along the western bank of the Rhine. They were the smoke generators that had been used in the UK to fool the Luftwaffe; they were brought up and they sent up this filthy, oily smoke over everything to conceal the movement of troops and so on. We

were not taking part in the actual Rhine crossing, and I can remember the day it happened – seeing the paratroop Dakotas, and the other planes, coming right over our heads and the chaps dropping out, then the gliders. I can remember a considerable amount of flak, and I saw several of the gliders hit, one in particular was carrying a tank and it

broke out and fell through the sky. We crossed over with our feet dry on a pontoon bridge about a day after, and from then on we moved up through Germany ... At this stage of the war, we were pretty anti-German, and we weren't going to stand any nonsense from anybody; we just treated them coldly, as if they didn't exist."

the British 52nd Division joined the assault, and the town fell to a final attack by the 15th and 51st Divisions on the 22nd.

Canadian II Corps (supported by British 43rd and 11th Armoured Divisions) now began Operation *Blockbuster* through the formidable Hochwald defences in a drive south to capture the town of Xanten on the banks of the Rhine. The Canadians eventually broke through the defences on 2 March. The next day, 53rd Division completed the link up between *Veritable* and *Grenade* at the town of Geldern. German forces now began to retreat across the river.

On the night of 23/24 March 1945, Operation *Plunder* (the crossing of the Rhine) was launched by Montgomery's 21st Army Group. The river crossing was spearheaded by the 51st and 15th Divisions under the cover of darkness, supported by Commando troops. The next day an Allied airborne operation (codenamed *Varsity*), the British contribution to which was 6th Airborne Division, landed on 24 March near Wesel on the far side of the Rhine and secured the high ground dominating the river. As at Pegasus Bridge during the D-Day landings, the 2nd Battalion The Oxford and Buckinghamshire Light Infantry was involved in capturing the bridges across the river by means of a "coup de main" force, which suffered severe casualties from heavy German fire; the 1st Battalion was also involved in the operations. The land and air elements linked up later the same day, consolidating the bridgehead, and forcing the German defenders to withdraw northwards towards Hamburg and Bremen. The plains of northern Germany now lay before Montgomery's forces.

RIGHT Churchill tanks of the Scots Guards, 6th Guards Tank Brigade, carrying men of the 10th Battalion The Highland Light Infantry, 15th (Scottish) Division, during the advance to the River Elbe, 13 April 1945.

LEFT The France & Germany Star (1944–1945) medal. The star was awarded for entry into operational service in France, Belgium, Holland and Germany from 6 June 1944 to 8 May 1945. The obverse design bears the "GRI VI" cypher in a circular centrepiece surrounded by an edged band bearing text "THE FRANCE AND GERMANY STAR". The design of the ribbon is attributed to HM King George VI; the colours represent the Union Flag and the flags of France and the Netherlands.

LEFT Men of the 5th Battalion The Dorsetshire Regiment, 43rd Wessex Division, crossing the Rhine in a Buffalo (an amphibious tracked vehicle), on 28 March 1945. The 43rd Division played a key role in the success of Operation *Veritable*.

THE RECONQUEST OF BURMA

Following the heavy defeat they inflicted on the Japanese at Kohima and Imphal, British and Indian troops began a pursuit of the remnants of the Japanese Fifteenth Army as it retreated into Burma from Assam. Slim saw an opportunity for British Fourteenth Army to push into the central Burmese plains, terrain that was well suited to movement of his superior armour and artillery concentrations, with which he could defeat the reeling Japanese forces and safeguard the overland routes of supply between China and Burma. Lord Louis Mountbatten proposed a combined offensive by Fourteenth Army and Chinese forces in the north to capture Mandalay and secure the central plains (Operation *Capital*). A further operation (*Dracula*) would see seaborne and airborne landings to liberate Rangoon in the far south.

The British Fourteenth Army continued to exert pressure on the retreating Japanese Burma Area Army, and by 2 December 1944 lead elements had reached the River Chindwin. The next day the 11th East African, and 19th and 20th Indian Divisions crossed the river. The Japanese Fifteenth Army now retreated to the River Irrawaddy, forcing Slim to modify his original plans for Operation *Capital*. He would now send XXXIII Corps (which included British 2nd Division) on a diversionary attack on Mandalay, which the Japanese would be expecting. At the same time IV Corps would move down the Myittha Valley, hopefully without

Crossing the Chindwin

Norman Leonard Bryant was a British private serving with the 2nd Battalion The Worcestershire Regiment in Burma in 1944–1945:

"We got to Dimapur and went through to Imphal and Kohima. We passed them, leaving the 2nd Division behind, and went on to the banks of the Chindwin. We were right up now, face to face with the Japanese. We were one side of the Chindwin, the Japanese were on the other. Then we sent our patrols over, in November. Then they built a big Bailey bridge and, at the beginning of December, our division crossed the Chindwin. We had no opposition at all, the Japanese fled in front of us ... We went 11 or 12 days without coming into contact with the Japanese at all, marching 10–15 miles every day, until we met them. We had our first skirmish with them, and we lost four or five, and the Japanese lost the same ... I shall never forget that day. We all lay down – we didn't expect it, having been in the jungle for a fortnight without meeting any Japanese, nor to see people getting killed around you. I remember lying down and looking up at the sky. It was a beautiful day, and I thought 'This is not true, I'm in a fantasy. There are people dead, and all this machine-gun fire.' I don't think any of us took it in at first ... We were the first troops to hit the Irrawaddy. We had orders for two companies to go forward to see if we could reach the river. We met some Gurkha patrols, and they said they had had a skirmish with some Japs up the road. So, they were about. We carried on, and never met anybody until we got to this village right on the banks of the Irrawaddy. We had a little skirmish with these Japanese and finished them off and looked across the river. We could see the Japanese on the other side washing their trucks down and bathing, because they didn't realize that there were British troops anywhere near."

ABOVE Private Putterill, Royal Sussex Regiment, 36th Infantry Division, armed with a Bren gun during a patrol, 22 November 1944.

LEFT Two British soldiers on patrol in the ruins of the Burmese town of Bahe during the advance on Mandalay in January 1945.

RIGHT British troops move up after crossing the Chindwin River in the Sittang area, December 1944.

detection, and attack the key town of Meiktila. The town was surrounded by four airfields and lay on the main road from Rangoon to Mandalay – a critical supply and communications route for the Japanese armies in-country. Slim renamed the land advance Operation *Extended Capital*, and speed and surprise were vital to its success.

Extended Capital was launched on 20 December, with XXXIII Corps advancing on a broad front across the River Chindwin and capturing the town of Shwebo on 10 January. The first bridgeheads were established over the River Irrawaddy at the same time by British 19th Division. On 12 February XXXIII Corps moved more troops across the river at Myinmu, while on 14 February troops of IV Corps began to cross it at Nyaungu further south.

By 28 February IV Corps had reached Meiktila and the main attack on the town was launched by 48th and 63rd Brigades, and 255th Tank Brigade. After fierce fighting, the town eventually fell on 3 March, and the British began aggressive patrolling to stave off Japanese counter-attacks until the town could be reinforced. This took place at the end of March. Mandalay was captured on 20 March by XXXIII Corps. The road to Rangoon now lay open, and Slim sent IV Corps down the River Sittang in an advance on the city, while XXXIII Corps would move southwards down the Irrawaddy.

On 1 May 1945 Operation *Dracula* was finally launched, although in a much more modified form than originally planned. Gurkhas of 44th Indian Airborne Division parachuted onto Elephant Point, the location of Japanese gun

positions at the mouth of the Rangoon River, while 26th Indian Division conducted an amphibious landing. This was to be the only major parachute jump by British and Commonwealth forces in the Far East theatre. The following day troops of the 26th Indian Division landed to secure Rangoon itself, and the Japanese forces withdrew eastwards.

Two pockets of Japanese resistance continued, with the 28th Army to the west of the River Sittang, and the remains of the 15th and 33rd Armies in the Shan. However, their ability to move to the offensive had now vanished. At the Battle of the Sittang Bend, fought between 3 and 10 July, mostly in terrain flooded by the monsoon-swollen Sittang River, the remnants of the Japanese Thirty-third Army attacked across the river in an attempt to allow Twenty-eighth Army to break out of its pocket and link up with the rest of Burma Area Army. The attack failed, and the British were able to ambush and pick off the retreating Twenty-eighth Army troops almost at will.

208

VJ Day

The dropping of the two atomic bombs on Hiroshima and Nagasaki (6 and 9 August 1945) quickly altered the course of the war in the Far East. The Japanese surrender was announced by Emperor Hirohito in a radio broadcast to the nation on 14 August (with the next day proclaimed VJ Day by the Allies), although the Instrument of Surrender was not signed until 2 September 1945. The formal capitulation of all Japanese armed forces in South-East Asia, including those in Burma, finally took place at Singapore on 12 September 1945. British troops landed in Malaya and reoccupied Singapore and Hong Kong, beginning the task of restoring order following the Japanese withdrawal.

BUCKINGHAM PALACE

The Queen and I bid you a very warm welcome home.

Through all the great trials and sufferings which you have undergone at the hands of the Japanese, you and your comrades have been constantly in our thoughts. We know from the accounts we have already received how heavy those sufferings have been. We know also that these have been endured by you with the highest courage.

We mourn with you the deaths of so many of your gallant comrades.

With all our hearts, we hope that your return from captivity will bring you and your families a full measure of happiness, which you may long enjoy together.

George R.I.

September 1945.

LEFT The letter from King George VI welcoming home British prisoners of war from the Far East.

The end in the Far East

John Pomeroy Randle was a British officer serving with 7/10th Baluch Regiment on the lower reaches of the River Sittang, Burma in 1945:

"At that stage we weren't going to start risking men's lives, and as the brigadier and the CO never came up we got away with it. It's not something I'm particularly proud of now, but I'm not unproud of it, because once the bomb had dropped we realized it might well be all over and I didn't want to chuck men's lives away on aggressive patrolling just for its own sake – we held our positions ... The brigadier was planning a direct assault river crossing of the Sittang. Again we didn't view this with a great deal of enthusiasm. He said that the Japanese were finished. Well, we didn't entirely go along with that, and later on when they surrendered we discovered that the brigadier was wrong, that the Japanese had been reinforced and they would have

RIGHT The Burma Star (1941–1945) medal. Qualifying service in the Burma campaign counted as from 11 December 1941. For land operations the award was made for services in Burma, and for services on land in Bengal or Assam from 1 May 1942 to 31 December 1943, and from 1 January 1944 onwards, in those parts of Bengal or Assam east of the Brahmaputra. Those who qualified for both the Burma and Pacific Stars were awarded the first star earned with a clasp on the ribbon to denote that qualifying service for the second star had been rendered. The obverse design bears the "GRI VI" cypher in a circular centrepiece surrounded by an edged band bearing the text "THE BURMA STAR". The design of the ribbon is attributed to HM King George VI. The ribbon colours are said to symbolize the British Commonwealth Forces (red) and the sun (orange).

RIGHT The Pacific Star (1941–1945) medal. The star was awarded for operational services in the Pacific theatre of war from 8 December 1941. For land service eligibility was restricted to operational service between specific dates in territories invaded by Allied or enemy forces. These included, amongst others, Hong Kong, Malaya, Borneo and Sarawak, Solomon Islands (British and Mandated Australian Territory), Sumatra, Timor, Java and New Guinea. The obverse design bears the "GRI VI'"cypher in a circular centre piece surrounded by an edged band bearing text "THE PACIFIC STAR". The design of the ribbon is attributed to HM King George VI. The green and yellow represent the forests and beaches of the Pacific; the red the armies; the dark blue the naval forces and merchant navies and the light blue the air forces.

given us a bloody nose ... At the time, my company was up defending the divisional gun box and for once I was eating European food. I went into the gunners' mess and I remember the adjutant of the mess saying 'Morning, John. Have you heard the news? The Yanks have dropped a massive bomb, 10,000 tonnes or something like that.' And I said, 'Well that's good news.' We all were a bit sceptical, thinking perhaps it was one of those newspaper hypes. Then we heard they had dropped another one, and then we began to realize that this was something outside all our normal experience of warfare. The full significance didn't really appear, though it sounded good news. Gradually we began to hear that the Japanese were thinking of surrendering and that the war was coming to an end ... Just about a week after the bomb the division moved south, and again we were dug in and patrolling ...

When VJ Day came, we were in the line in a bloody awful wet place near the banks of the Sittang. The rain was pissing down, and there was a terrific feu de joie ... Everyone was firing, the guns were firing star shells, and all the rest of it. Brigade HQ said: 'What's going on? What are you firing at?' And all I said was, 'What fire?' Then we settled down and I was able to move my company into a Buddhist monastery ... Then we were ordered to go down and cross the Sittang by ferry, and to arrange the surrender of the Japanese 18th Division."

BELOW *Burma – 14th Army: The battle of the Sittang Bend, July 1945. Men of The Queen's Own (Royal West Kent) Regiment making an armed patrol*, by Leslie Cole (oil on canvas, 1945).

PRISONER OF THE JAPANESE

In the Far East, over 190,000 British, Commonwealth, Dutch and American servicemen became prisoners of war of the Japanese, whose government had signed but never ratified the 1929 Geneva Convention. In addition, 130,000 Allied subjects found themselves in civilian internment in the wake of Japan's victories in 1941–1942. Often they were held in very harsh circumstances in generally quite primitive camps or "civil assembly centres" where their captors demonstrated minimal concern for their welfare. Harry Sidney George Hale of 1st Battalion, The Royal Scots was captured when Hong Kong fell in 1941. He describes his initial movements into captivity at the Shamshuipo barracks following the British surrender:

"I suppose it was the end of January, beginning February. I got taken across by ferry on the Kowloon side and then had to march two to three hours from the ferry up to Shamshuipo Barracks, where we were halted outside the gates, were examined by the Japanese, searched, and then allowed into the barracks proper ... I was quickly initiated into the food situation – it was cold rice, cooked early in the morning and then put into baths ... there was no salt and quite a number of people just couldn't swallow it. They just took a mouthful and then vomited it up. You used to get about a cupful."

Sickness and disease, such as diphtheria, dysentery and beri-beri, were the constant companions of those held in the cramped and insanitary conditions of the camps, where medical intervention was minimal and malnutrition rife. Death became a familiar presence to many prisoners, as Harry Hale recalls:

"At that time we were losing five or seven a day with dysentery. They just lay on a rush mat on a board ... until they died. They were rolled up in the mat, tied up, put in a wooden crate and carried out with no ceremony. A few of their mates went out with them and the padre, but this was going on five or six times a day ... Originally they started playing the Last Post, but then they had to drop that because it had such a depressing feeling on the friends that had witnessed their mates being carried through the camp."

Mental toughness and resilience of spirit became prerequisites for survival, particularly for those who would go on to endure over four years of confinement, often in the face of extreme brutality meted out by their guards or in efforts to gain intelligence from prisoners. For civilian internees, which included many elderly men and women as well as young children, the privations and hardships of captivity were hard to deal with. Servicemen were generally better equipped and prepared to cope with their predicaments, although uncertainty over their fate from one day to the next was a constant concern, as Harry Hale recalls:

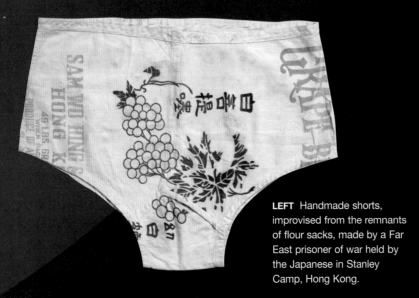

LEFT Handmade shorts, improvised from the remnants of flour sacks, made by a Far East prisoner of war held by the Japanese in Stanley Camp, Hong Kong.

"We never had any doubts from the time we surrendered in Hong Kong that we would win. The only thing that worried us was that we should get out of it in time to celebrate the winning, and what the Japanese were going to do with us. They told us in the latter months of the war that if the British and Americans ever landed on Japan then all the POWs would be shot either in the front line or executed out of hand. We had no doubts about that."

LEFT *Orderly On His Rounds in X Ward, Changi Gaol, Singapore, with POW's Suffering from Starvation and Beri-Beri*, by Leslie Cole (oil on canvas, 1945).

RIGHT Liberated POWs at a Rangoon jail share a last meal of rice before being evacuated, 3 May 1945.

The Japanese military code at that time did not regard the surrender of fighting men to the enemy as an acceptable option, and they decided to use the Allied prisoners of war as a labour force in support of their war effort. Most notoriously, over 60,000 prisoners were eventually employed on the construction and maintenance of the Burma–Siam railway. Large numbers were also sent to work, under similarly harrowing conditions, on such tasks as airfield construction on the Moluccas, coal mining and ship building in Japan, and copper-mining in Formosa. Some 20–25 per cent of the total number of these prisoners perished as a direct result of the conditions they endured. In 1943 Harry Hale was moved from Shamshuipo camp to Nanking and then to Hakodate POW camp in Japan, to work in the coal mines. He describes the latter stages of his journey, and the attitudes of Japanese civilians to the Allied prisoners:

"They laid us onto trains and we came up through one of the middle islands, south of Tokyo and Yokohama. We were herded onto the trains. They made us pull the blinds down and we weren't allowed to look out of the windows, though of course men did look out and we were able to see the devastation that had been done to Japan. Mile after mile of just rubble and huts burned to the ground ... We eventually arrived in Tokyo station and we were taken from the train into the cellars and whilst in there we experienced heavy air raids ... Then they took us from the tunnels underneath up onto the Tokyo railway station platform, indicated the train we were supposed to get in and started to herd us in, when we got rushed by a big mob of Japanese civilians, men and women. They set about us with poles and sticks, anything they could lay their hands on."

The surrender of Japan in August 1945 brought about the liberation of the prisoners, many of whom were severely malnourished and in need of medical attention, and a long process of readjustment to liberty and civilian life. Indeed,

the surrender terms imposed on Japan required her forces to ensure the well-being of all prisoners and civilian internees in their hands until such time as Allied forces took over. Many prisoners remarked on the improvement to their conditions in the immediate lead up to the announcement of the surrender. Harry Hale recalls how he was informed about the war's end:

"The Japanese commandant and higher ranking officer stood on the platform and started to make a speech that, through unfair tactics by the Americans, who had fought the war unfairly and dropped a bomb, the war was finished; and now we would all be good friends and we would all shake hands and the war was over. But he stressed that the Americans had fought the war unfairly. He said that we would be retained in camp under Japanese guard for our own protection because they didn't know what the Japanese civilians would do to the British and American POWs in their near vicinity ... The British flag, which had been concealed about the body of one of the men in the camp, was run up the flagpole along with an American flag. We sang 'God Save the King' and the American anthem ... Quite a number of men, myself included, broke down and cried ... That night a terrific lot of shouting was heard from the outside, and lo and behold there were two British Commandos and an American."

In the aftermath of the war, many prosecutions for war crimes against prisoners were conducted throughout the former Japanese-occupied territories. A debate continues to this day as to whether Japan has adequately compensated former prisoners of war for the hardships they endured in captivity during the Second World War.

ABOVE Emaciated British prisoners in a Japanese prisoner-of-war hospital at Nakom Paton, Thailand, in 1945.

THE END IN ITALY

Following the fall of Rome in 1944, and the launching of the battle for Normandy, the Italian theatre became less important in terms of the Allied overall strategy. British Eighth Army troops continued to play a key role in the drive north up the peninsula, clashing with the Germans across a series of defensive lines (including the Dora, Albert and Heinrich Lines) as they retreated up the country. The last and most formidable barrier before the natural barriers of the River Po and the Alps comprised the Gothic (or Green) Line, which stretched between Pisa on the Tyrrhenian and Pesaro on the Adriatic. The Allied assault began on 25 August 1944, and by mid September British troops had broken through parts of the line to the Lombard plains, before the onset of winter brought major operations to a halt. The main offensive to defeat the German forces in Italy was delayed until April 1945, with Eighth Army advancing through Lombardy, capturing Bologna and advancing to the Po. German resistance collapsed, and the surrender of all their forces in Italy came into effect on 2 May 1945.

GERMANY FALLS

Following the breaching of the Rhine barrier, British Second Army began its drive for the key northern cities of Bremen and Hamburg. The Germans were fighting on two fronts, with the Soviets pressing hard to the east, having advanced deep

212

VE Day

Stephen Dale was a German Jew who emigrated to Great Britain in 1939, and served with the Pioneer Corps between 1942 and 1944. He subsequently served with Special Operations Executive in Italy, where he was captured and imprisoned in Oflag 79 prisoner of war camp, Germany, before being liberated in 1945:

"It was pretty clear that it would be a momentous day, that victory in Europe was an accomplished fact. We arrived in London. During the day it was announced that everything had been signed ... Around Piccadilly and Leicester Square there were, it seemed, millions of people milling around, climbing up lampposts, onto bus shelters ... People were being very friendly, embracing each other, being cheerful, with lots of bantering going on. I was berated on several occasions for walking around with a miserable, long face. And it was perfectly true. Naturally I was very happy that the war was over, but it was also a moment for reflection. It was great that the killing had come to an end in Europe, but for me it was a depressing moment, because I suddenly felt all the awful things that had happened to me and my family. They came to the surface. I couldn't join in these celebrations, which of course were perfectly justified."

RIGHT A crowd celebrates in front of the Ministry of Health building in Whitehall, London on 8 May 1945.

into German territory in March. British troops reached Osnabrück on 4 April, and by the 19th they were on the River Elbe – the agreed halt point for joining up with the Soviets. British forces now headed north to occupy the Baltic coast (which they reached on 2 May) and thence to liberate Denmark and Norway. Berlin fell to the Red Army on 2 May, and on 3 May 1945 Hamburg came under the control of British Second Army. On 8 May (Victory in Europe Day) the surrender of all German armed forces, signed by General Alfred Jodl, became effective.

ABOVE The 1939–1945 Star medal. This was originally designated the 1939–1943 Star, and was awarded for service in the Second World War between the dates 3 September 1939 and 2 September 1945. In general terms, qualification for the award of this Star was for the Army six months' service in any operational command. Airborne troops qualified if they had participated in any airborne operations and had completed two months' service in a fully operational unit. The obverse bears the "GRI VI" cypher within a circular centrepiece surrounded by an edged band bearing the text "THE 1939-1945 STAR" surmounted by a crown. The design of the ribbon is attributed to HM King George VI, and the colours represent the Royal and Merchant Navies, the Army and the Royal Air Force.

LEFT Corporal T. Fenn, of Mottingham, London; Private E. W. Jones of Esher, Surrey; Private W. J. Leaman of Ashburton, Devon; Private A. Clark of St Johns, Deptford, London; and Private G. C. Foreman of Warminster, Wiltshire, celebrate the end of the war in a gondola on the Grand Canal, Venice, June 1945.

THE LIBERATION OF BERGEN-BELSEN

Bergen-Belsen concentration camp was located near Celle in Lower Saxony, Germany. A POW camp had been present on the site since 1940, and in the early war years it housed Soviet prisoners of war, many of whom died in cramped and unsanitary conditions. In April 1943 part of the camp was given to the control of the SS organization, which began to use it as a detention camp for Jews. Throughout 1944 and early 1945 the camp saw large influxes of prisoners, notably women and those too sick to work in other Nazi camps. In January 1945 the camp ceased to be used for prisoners of war and instead became a concentration camp, under the command of SS-Hauptsturmführer Josef Kramer. As the Soviets advanced in the east, many detainees from other concentration camps were moved to Bergen-Belsen, which brought overcrowding to new levels and caused the deaths of many thousands of internees through disease, malnutrition and exhaustion; their bodies were buried in mass graves on and near the site. On 15 April 1945, British troops liberated the concentration camp of Bergen-Belsen, where thousands of bodies remained unburied and typhus was rife; the buildings were subsequently burned to the ground, and the camp moved to a nearby location. This camp was used as a displaced persons camp by the Allies in the immediate post-war perod. The total number of people who died at Bergen-Belsen is estimated at around 50,000. Kramer and the camp guards who were caught (many of them women) were subsequently tried in Hanover at the Belsen Trial in September 1945. Kramer was sentenced to death and executed on 13 December 1945.

ABOVE The bodies of victims at Bergen-Belsen concentration camp.

Michael Lewis was a British NCO cameraman with the Army Film and Photographic Unit who was present during the liberation of Bergen-Belsen:

"We drove up in a jeep through dense pine woods to a wired wooden gate, and that place was Belsen. There were people standing behind the wire at the entrance to the gate pressing their faces against the wire, eating us up with their eyes, the uniforms that we wore – British uniforms. They had heard that we were coming. They were not political prisoners. This was a Concentration Camp and they couldn't believe their eyes at that khaki colour and our British voices ... We drove inside and it was said that when we got there the number of dead which were lying everywhere, was round about 10,000. We stayed there for about two weeks. There were pits there, as far as I can remember after all this time, that were as large as lawn tennis courts, what depth I could only guess. They were crammed with bodies, from babies to old men through all ages. There were piles of bodies, usually without clothes. There was a stench of human excrement, a stench of death and the death of all human

dignity and hope, and they lay there thin and starved. It was a terrible sight ... The massive scale of death and stench and what had happened to people – I was too overwhelmed by feelings to think clearly about it. The rations which the British Army had brought in had to be doled out carefully. These people had been starving, they couldn't eat too much. They were given a little bully beef, and some other food, and even then it was too much for them and they couldn't manage it. I was told later that round about another 13,000 had died."

Martin Addington was a British gunner serving with the Royal Artillery. He describes his unit's approach to the camp:

"We were advancing with the Yanks, US Seventh Army, when we were told that we would be approaching a big Concentration Camp. Funnily enough we knew we were on it because of the deathly smell we kept smelling – the death smell. It was terrible, you can't explain the smell. I suppose you could get near it if you went into a slaughterhouse and smelled the dead carcasses that had been hanging up for a few years. That would give you an idea of the smell, and it was utter silence when we went in there. To see the poor figures crawling about and scratching, and those that did have the strength coming up to you and asking for food or a cigarette, with flea-bitten rags on, that's all they had ... All ages, men, women, kids."

RIGHT *One of the Death Pits, Belsen. SS guards collecting bodies,* by Leslie Cole (oil on canvas, 1945). Cole was a war artist with an honorary commission as a captain in the Royal Marines. He travelled widely recording the aftermath of the war in Malta, France, Greece, Germany and the Far East. He did not return to Britain until the spring of 1946, having witnessed the horrors of Belsen concentration camp and Japanese prisoner-of-war camps in Singapore. After the war he taught at the Central School of Arts and Crafts and Brighton School of Art.

LEFT Former guards at Bergen-Belsen are forced to lie in one of the empty mass graves by British soldiers following the camp's liberation, April 1945.

ABOVE Josef Kramer, the sadistic camp commandant of Bergen-Belsen, photographed under British armed guard and in irons at Belsen before being removed to the POW cage at Celle, 17 April 1945.

1945–1989

Paratroopers wait on board the ferry *Norland* before their landings at San Carlos Water, 21 May 1982. Within days they would launch one of the most famous actions of the Falklands War, the capture of the settlements at Darwin and Goose Green.

AN ARMY OF OCCUPATION

The division of Germany in 1945 into four military occupation zones brought about the formation of the British Army of the Rhine (BAOR), whose principal elements from 1948 comprised 7th Armoured Division, 2nd Infantry Division and 16th Parachute Brigade (the 6th and 11th Armoured Divisions were added in the early 1950s). From 1949, the BAOR would form a key part of NATO's land forces, tasked with countering any Soviet invasion. In the immediate aftermath of the war, the role of British forces was to maintain law and order in the north-west of the country, which had seen large influxes of ethnic Germans who had both fled and been expelled from Poland, the Soviet Union, Czechoslovakia and Hungary as the Red Army advanced. British troops also controlled one of the three sectors of West Berlin (and would do so until 1994) that were blockaded by the Soviets for ten months in 1948, leading to the Berlin Airlift. The BAOR would remain in Germany manning the Cold War "front line" until 1994, when the British Army, Royal Air Force and civil elements stationed in Germany were re-titled British Forces Germany.

INDONESIA 1945–1946

On 17 August 1945 Indonesian independence was declared in Jakarta. Unable to send sufficient numbers of her own troops to the area, the Netherlands requested British assistance, and British troops began to arrive in late September. Fighting broke out between the nationalists and Dutch settlers and repatriated internees, who were backed up by Japanese troops ordered by the British to help fight the independence movement. On 25 October, some 6,000 men of the 23rd Indian Division, under the command of Brigadier A. Mallaby, entered Surabaya. Serious fighting broke out on 28 October and the British positions were soon surrounded. The British decided to take Surabaya by force, and in November secretly landed 24,000 men of the 5th Division supported by 24 tanks. There followed a battle that lasted three weeks during which 200,000 of the city's population fled and 16,000 Indonesian and 2,000 Commonwealth and British troops were killed. The British troops stationed in Indonesia had three tasks: to round up the Japanese Army as prisoners of war, to release and repatriate Dutch and other Allied prisoners of war, and to maintain law and order. The Dutch soon realized the immense struggle they would face in attempting to restore colonial rule in the region. British and Commonwealth troops would be withdrawn from Indonesia in late November 1946.

218

Occupation duties

John Charles Lattimer served in the Royal Artillery during the Second World War. Between 1945 and 1946 he served in Munster, Germany with 351 Town Major Unit:

"Military Government was housed in the former German Armed Forces West building which was virtually undamaged and also housed the only cinema in the city … The place was overrun with black marketeers, prostitutes, criminals, deserters and whatever, who disappeared in daylight. One carried side arms at all times out of doors, but the Military Police made raids and tried to quell a large amount of the nefarious activities, and so slowly things did improve … The Cold War was just beginning to ice over in those days and Germans coming to our office from the Eastern Zone spoke of large Russian forces near our Zone frontier; we told them that we knew and that our defences were in place … One had a job to keep a straight face when civilians came in the office and when in front of your desk, started to raise their arm and say 'Heil Hitler'. But we just shook our heads and asked their problems … The displaced persons were a real headache and defied all instructions to stay in their camp near the canal and nightly raided outlying farms and houses, leaving murder, rape and robbery and general panic among the population. We had mobile patrols out and issued chimney flares to such places, and they still evaded our every attempt to foil them; they were taking revenge on the Germans … We'd got our hands full in Munster. The military courts were just that, no juries or solicitors, and the sentence was proscribed more or less and in every case 'Summary' … On the whole the Germans caused us very little trouble. They could see that we were helping them in their desperate plight that Hitler had left them in and appreciated the fact that the Russians weren't there or even the Americans, who some referred to as 'Gangsters', as some did indulge in openly looting, 'spoils of war' that were openly 'mailed' home to the United States …

ABOVE British and Russian soldiers on the balcony of the Chancellery in Berlin in July 1945.

WARNING
IT IS AN OFFENCE FOR
ALLIED SOLDIERS TO
SELL OR BARTER W.D.
N.A.A.F.I. OR P.X. GOODS
WARNUNG
ES IST DEN ALLIIERTEN SOLDATEN
VERBOTEN MILITÄREIGENTUM
ZIGARETTEN, SCHOKOLADE v. SEIFE ZU
VERKAUFEN ODER ZU TAUSCHEN

ABOVE At the beginning of the military occupation of Berlin it was official policy to discourage fraternization between soldiers and the German population. This British notice warns both soldiers and civilians not to indulge in such activities

RIGHT The formation badge of the 1st Corps Royal Signals. The corps was with the BEF in France in 1940 and afterwards was involved in the defence of the UK. It took part in the North-West Europe campaign and ended the war in Germany. Post-war, 1st Corps District administered Rhine Province and Westphalia. The basic sign was retained when the formation became part of the BAOR.

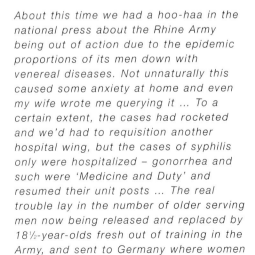

About this time we had a hoo-haa in the national press about the Rhine Army being out of action due to the epidemic proportions of its men down with venereal diseases. Not unnaturally this caused some anxiety at home and even my wife wrote me querying it ... To a certain extent, the cases had rocketed and we'd had to requisition another hospital wing, but the cases of syphilis only were hospitalized – gonorrhea and such were 'Medicine and Duty' and resumed their unit posts ... The real trouble lay in the number of older serving men now being released and replaced by 18½-year-olds fresh out of training in the Army, and sent to Germany where women pounced on them like flies round a jam pot. The youngsters had no older guidance and sex for a bar of chocolate or a few cigarettes was like all their Christmasses coming at once, until they 'caught a dose'. Of course in a month or two and with our Redcap Raids at night time rounding up in 3-tonners any couples we found without 'papers' and taking them for 'exams', it died down again and we handed back the hospital wing."

RIGHT "You're no match ... for VD" – the slogan on a book of matches produced by the Universal Match Corps, St Louis, USA. Sexual diseases were a problem for servicemen of every nationality.

THE PALESTINE EMERGENCY 1946–1948

During the middle years of the Second World War, Jewish extremist groups had resumed their terrorist activities against British security forces both in Palestine and beyond its borders. One of their most notorious acts was the murder of the British Minister Resident in the Middle East, Lord Moyne, who was assassinated in Cairo in November 1944. Illegal Jewish immigration in the immediate post-war period continued to be an obstacle to any political settlement. As a result, significant numbers of British troops were heavily involved in security duties in Palestine, in what Britain soon came to admit was an "unworkable mandate".

At 0700hrs on Monday 22 July 1946, six members of the Jewish Irgun organization set out, disguised as Arabs, to bomb the King David Hotel in Jerusalem, which housed the Military Headquarters for Palestine as well as the offices of the Palestine government. On reaching the side entrance to the hotel, the terrorists overpowered the guards and placed timed explosives in the empty restaurant alongside some structural pillars that supported the hotel. During their withdrawal they were fired upon, and two were wounded. Telephone calls were made to the hotel, the editorial office of the *Palestine Post* newspaper and the adjacent French Consulate, stating that a bomb had been planted in the hotel, but the authorities appear to have ignored the warning, and when the explosion happened 25 minutes later the entire southern wing of the hotel was destroyed. Ninety-one people were killed.

In November 1947 the United Nations formally accepted the idea of the partition of Palestine into Jewish and Arab sectors, and the British mandate in Palestine ended on 14 May 1948. After the British withdrawal the 1948 Arab-Israeli war broke out.

RIGHT A wounded soldier is carried from the ruins of the King David Hotel on a stretcher, having been hauled out from underneath the wreckage on 23 July 1946, the day after the attack.

The bombing of the King David Hotel

Captain Ridely Hugh Clark, MC, served in the 2nd Battalion The Oxfordshire and Buckinghamshire Light Infantry (part of 3rd Brigade, 1st Division) during the Palestine troubles in the aftermath of the Second World War. He describes his posting to the Middle East:

"Towards the end of September (1945) we heard that we were definitely on the move and this time it was to Palestine. There was a lot of unrest in Palestine at the time. At the end of the First World War the British had been granted a Mandate to control the country. As I understand it, the Jews were allowed a specified number of immigrants each month, but so many were escaping from Germany after the war and getting into the country that the Arab population were trying to control the numbers by armed opposition. Our job was to go in and try to keep the peace and also to control the number of immigrants. It was going to be a no-win situation ... The Regiment had a busy time out on search and curfew duties. The security situation varied, sometimes we were allowed to go out on our own and at other times we had to be in threes and carry our weapons ... On 22 July terrorists blew up the King David Hotel in Jerusalem. I was commanding the duty company and had to take them out to enforce a cordon round the hotel. We were out on that duty for a week or so and encamped in the grounds of the YMCA, which was just across the road from the King David. Watching the rescue teams digging out the dead bodies was a horrible sight. There were about 100 killed. The first night on curfew, the Company Sergeant Major was so mad and worked up by the killing of innocent civilians that I took charge of his pistol for the night, as I was sure that he was going to shoot someone."

RIGHT The explosion of a second bomb at the King David Hotel in Jerusalem, 22 July 1946. The hotel housed the headquarters for all armed forces in Palestine as well as the offices of the Palestine government. The attack on the hotel was the biggest blow struck against British rule in Palestine by fighters of the Jewish Irgun organization.

ABOVE The post 1945 formation badge of HQ Palestine and Transjordan (British Troops in Palestine). The badge was worn by British troops in Palestine up to the end of the British Mandate in 1947.

THE MALAYAN EMERGENCY 1948–1960

By 1945, the Communist Malayan People's Anti-Japanese Army was 7,000 strong. Its members had fought alongside the British during the Second World War, but they now sought to force the British from Malaya and to initiate a communist revolution, using terrorism and political agitation. By 1948 the CMPAJA had been reconstituted as the Malayan People's Anti-British Army, although its members, many of whom were ethnic Chinese, were usually referred to as "CTs" or "Communist Terrorists" by British troops. Widespread murder and intimidation took place of people working for European-owned enterprises such as rubber plantations and mines, and CT bands

RIGHT A British soldier relaxing next to a basha (shelter) during a jungle patrol in Malaya, 1955.

222

A jungle war

Ian S. Gibb served as a platoon commander with 1st Battalion The Seaforth Highlanders in Malaya from 1948 to 1950. He describes his experiences during the early stages of the Malayan Emergency:

"On the day the Emergency was declared the British had precisely two British infantry battalions on the spot. There was the King's Own Yorkshire Light Infantry in Penang and my own battalion the 1st Battalion The Seaforth Highlanders. There were also about half a dozen Gurkha battalions and two or three Malay Regiment battalions ... This mixed bag of forces was spread throughout the 55,000 square miles of the country ... At our level we hardly knew the strategic layout of our enemy. In fact we hardly knew the strategic layout of our own forces ... To find our enemy in the jungle was like looking for a needle in a haystack ... I was in charge of thirty men, a platoon. It was a platoon commander's war. It was very basic ... Later there was to be much more control, much more organization, more troops with helicopters and other sophisticated instruments of warfare. At the beginning there was very little ... We carried rifles, light automatics and Bren guns, packs on our back, with a ground sheet and tins of food from our compo rations. That was all. The enemy had much the same ... And so this was to be a deadly game of hide and seek for days, for weeks, for

months ... There are wild animals in the Malayan jungle: tiger, pig, elephant, crocodiles, wild buffalo, bear and deer. It was a fairly rare occurrence to catch sight of many of these ... It was the smaller things that tended to be unpleasant. Snakes, hornets, red ants, leeches, all in abundance ... National Servicemen formed a high percentage of the troops involved. Often they were from towns, large and small spread throughout the British Isles. With sound training and good leadership they were excellent ... Obviously for some the jungle could be, and was, at least at times, a very frightening place. Each man of course had his own personal horror or dislike, for some it was snakes, for others leeches and for yet others the bandits themselves, and some merely took it in their stride without any apparent concern ... Any casualty always affected me. I felt both sad and partly responsible. As junior commanders are constantly near the front of a patrol day after day we ourselves should have been very vulnerable. Usually because we were moving we were shot at first by the enemy. Mostly at very close range. Mostly with automatic and rifle fire. Mostly unexpectedly. ... The tension of awaiting an almost certain close-range firefight in dense jungle was not a happy situation to be in ... One bright morning moving through a rubber estate a young National Service soldier behind me was hit through the chest and neck. It was

only one bullet and it went in fairly high in the chest. I had him in my arms and bright red frothy blood was pouring from his mouth and his face was going purple through suffocation. I had one hand on a pulse and one hand with a handkerchief scooping the blood from his mouth and holding his head down, desperately trying to get the blood to pour out. But in seconds the pulse weakened, a few moments later it flickered, and then it stopped for good. What a waste. I felt defeated and drained of all emotion."

conducted raids from their bases in the dense jungles of the peninsula. The result was a security crackdown, and a series of innovative anti-guerrilla operations and measures conducted by the British Army and Commonwealth units over the next 12 years. Although it took from 1948 to 1960 to finally defeat the communist insurgents, the Malayan Emergency can be seen to have been a considerable achievement for British arms. The British Army ultimately defeated the Communist Terrorists through its willingness to live and fight in the jungle for long periods, by taking the fight to the insurgents and trying to beat them at their own game. More than 100,000 British soldiers served in Malaya between 1948 and 1960 (including a large Gurkha contingent, and 22 SAS Regiment), many of whom were National Servicemen.

ABOVE A cap belonging to a member of the Malayan People's Anti-British Army.

RIGHT Men of 22 Special Air Service Regiment in Malaya, November 1957. During the Emergency 22 SAS was formed from the Malayan Scouts.

THE KOREAN WAR 1950–1953

The seeds of conflict in Korea had been sown by the division of the country in 1945 along the 38th Parallel. The Japanese had annexed Korea in 1910, and Japanese forces that found themselves north of the 38th Parallel in 1945 had surrendered to Soviet troops. Those in the south surrendered to the United States forces present in the country. In 1948 a stand off developed between America and the Soviet Union, as two separate republics were declared in both the north and south (both of which laid claim to the whole country) – the Democratic Republic of Korea in the north, and the Republic of Korea in the south. On 25 June 1950 North Korean forces began offensive operations to capture the southern capital Seoul. They advanced in force and quickly overcame the South Korean forces they encountered in the Uijongbu Corridor.

The United Nations condemnation of North Korea's act of aggression was swift, and forces were immediately sent to the south, in the form of US Eighth Army under the command of General Douglas MacArthur, who had received the Japanese surrender in Tokyo Bay in 1945. However, the North Korean offensive quickly captured Seoul and pushed the limited US forces present down into a defensive pocket in the far south-east of the country, based around Pusan.

LEFT The second-pattern formation badge of the 1st Commonwealth Division. The division was the first completely integrated Commonwealth division, and was formed in Korea on 28 July 1951. It comprised 25th Canadian Brigade, 28th British Commonwealth Brigade and 29th British Infantry Brigade with divisional troops drawn from various Commonwealth countries. The division was disbanded in November 1954.

A far-off place

Ronald "Wellsey" Wells undertook his National Service between 1950 and 1952, serving with the Gloucestershire Regiment in Korea. He describes his journey out by boat in October 1950:

"I have a vivid memory of the crowds at the dock when the ship sailed. People were cheering and lots were crying ... We were told it would take four weeks for the ship to reach Japan, so here we were on a floating hotel ... Our officers decided we should do some drill and training while we were en route, but the ship's captain put a stop to all that. He said he could not have a load of troops stamping about on different parts of the ship, so all we got was Physical Training etc. in the mornings ... I was up on deck lying in the sun, when I fell asleep. That cost me three days in sick bay with heat stroke. It was only having an understanding officer that I was lucky not be put on a charge for self-inflicted wounds ... Things took a turn for the worse in Korea, with heavy fighting breaking out and the United Nations' forces were coming under heavy fire with many losing their lives. Rumours began to go around the ship that maybe some of us were going to be taken off at the next port, which was Singapore, and flown the rest of the way to Japan and then on to Korea where our services were urgently required. Before any of this happened I had my 19th birthday. Try to imagine what it was like to be such a young age and going to fight in a war in a place I had never heard of ... Before we flew a lot of us were transferred from The Royal Ulster Rifles to The Gloucestershire Regiment, so in my first six months in the army I had served in four different regiments."

RIGHT Members of the 1st Battalion The Royal Fusiliers disembark from the troopship *Empire Halladale* at Pusan, Korea, in July 1952.

British and Commonwealth servicemen from all three branches were among the first UN troops to arrive in theatre, with land forces in the form of 27th Infantry Brigade disembarking at Pusan on 28 August 1950. Among the first British troops to arrive were men of the Argyll and Sutherland Highlanders and the Middlesex Regiment, and they were soon involved in the fighting in the breakout from Pusan, which forced the North Korean forces to retreat. The overall organization for British and Commonwealth forces in Korea would later be renamed 27th Commonwealth Infantry Brigade, with Australian, Canadian, New Zealand and Indian units making up the order of battle.

In September 1950 US forces conducted an amphibious landing at Inchon and recaptured Seoul at the same time, trapping large numbers of North Korean forces in the south. It was now the turn of the South, with the backing of the UN, to invade the North, and an offensive began in October that saw the North Korean capital of Pyongyang overrun and its forces pushed almost to its northern borders with China and the Soviet Union. At this point, the Chinese intervened, and the forces of the Chinese People's Liberation Army (under the guise of the Chinese People's Volunteers) first brought MacArthur's offensive to a halt, before breaking through his lines and forcing the UN troops to retreat once more to the 38th Parallel. The fighting was conducted during the onset of the savage Korean winter.

Further British reinforcements, in the shape of 29th Independent Infantry Brigade, arrived in Korea in November

8th King's Royal Irish Hussars in Korea

Edward "Ted" Beckerley served as a Cromwell tank driver in the Reconnaissance Troop of the 8th King's Royal Irish Hussars (29th Independent Brigade) during the Korean War. His force, "Cooper Force", was supporting the Royal Ulster Rifles when the Chinese struck on New Year's Day 1951. He was subsequently captured and imprisoned in Pyuktong Camp near the border with China:

"The Ulsters were heavily engaged on the night of the 1/2 January and suffered quite a few casualties. Our tanks came into action at first light on 2 January and we were able to give a very good account of ourselves during the day, succeeding in holding the Chinese off during the hours of daylight … The Chinese fire was intense, mortars, machine guns, and rifles, and there were millions of them. We carried several Ulster riflemen on the back of each tank, and they must have had a really dreadful time of it. In addition to pouring fire on us, the Chinese kept trying to board our tanks … and the lads on the back of the tanks were kept busy trying to repel them … God knows what happened to those chaps. I only know that when we had to leave our tank, there was no sign of any of them. One by one our tanks were put out of action … I had lost all sense of time, but it seemed like many hours after the start of our attempt to fight our way out of that valley, when a small mortar landed immediately above my head and destroyed one of my periscopes … With my visibility now limited, it wasn't long before I slid off the road and had one track in the ditch at the side of the road … I was unable to get the track out of that ditch, but the ditch was being used by Chinese medics to tend to their wounded. There was hell going on all around us … and I kept

RIGHT A British Centurion tank of the 8th King's Royal Irish Hussars, carrying infantrymen of the 1st Battalion The Royal Northumberland Fusiliers, climbs the steep bank of the Imjin River on return from a patrol. The new Mk III Centurion, mounting a 20-pounder gun, proved to be the best British tank of the war, winning admiration from friend and foe alike.

LEFT Trooper Sam Fox, of A Squadron, 8th King's Royal Irish Hussars, in his tank turret north of the Imjin River, while awaiting orders to advance, 7 June 1951.

British and Commonwealth servicemen from all three branches were among the first UN troops to arrive in theatre, with land forces in the form of 27th Infantry Brigade disembarking at Pusan on 28 August 1950. Among the first British troops to arrive were men of the Argyll and Sutherland Highlanders and the Middlesex Regiment, and they were soon involved in the fighting in the breakout from Pusan, which forced the North Korean forces to retreat. The overall organization for British and Commonwealth forces in Korea would later be renamed 27th Commonwealth Infantry Brigade, with Australian, Canadian, New Zealand and Indian units making up the order of battle.

In September 1950 US forces conducted an amphibious landing at Inchon and recaptured Seoul at the same time, trapping large numbers of North Korean forces in the south. It was now the turn of the South, with the backing of the UN, to invade the North, and an offensive began in October that saw the North Korean capital of Pyongyang overrun and its forces pushed almost to its northern borders with China and the Soviet Union. At this point, the Chinese intervened, and the forces of the Chinese People's Liberation Army (under the guise of the Chinese People's Volunteers) first brought MacArthur's offensive to a halt, before breaking through his lines and forcing the UN troops to retreat once more to the 38th Parallel. The fighting was conducted during the onset of the savage Korean winter.

Further British reinforcements, in the shape of 29th Independent Infantry Brigade, arrived in Korea in November

8th King's Royal Irish Hussars in Korea

Edward "Ted" Beckerley served as a Cromwell tank driver in the Reconnaissance Troop of the 8th King's Royal Irish Hussars (29th Independent Brigade) during the Korean War. His force, "Cooper Force", was supporting the Royal Ulster Rifles when the Chinese struck on New Year's Day 1951. He was subsequently captured and imprisoned in Pyuktong Camp near the border with China:

"The Ulsters were heavily engaged on the night of the 1/2 January and suffered quite a few casualties. Our tanks came into action at first light on 2 January and we were able to give a very good account of ourselves during the day, succeeding in holding the Chinese off during the hours of daylight … The Chinese fire was intense, mortars, machine guns, and rifles, and there were millions of them. We carried several Ulster riflemen on the back of each tank, and they must have had a really dreadful time of it. In addition to pouring fire on us, the Chinese kept trying to board our tanks … and the lads on the back of the tanks were kept busy trying to repel them … God knows what happened to those chaps. I only know that when we had to leave our tank, there was no sign of any of them. One by one our tanks were put out of action … I had lost all sense of time, but it seemed like many hours after the start of our attempt to fight our way out of that valley, when a small mortar landed immediately above my head and destroyed one of my periscopes … With my visibility now limited, it wasn't long before I slid off the road and had one track in the ditch at the side of the road … I was unable to get the track out of that ditch, but the ditch was being used by Chinese medics to tend to their wounded. There was hell going on all around us … and I kept

RIGHT A British Centurion tank of the 8th King's Royal Irish Hussars, carrying infantrymen of the 1st Battalion The Royal Northumberland Fusiliers, climbs the steep bank of the Imjin River on return from a patrol. The new Mk III Centurion, mounting a 20-pounder gun, proved to be the best British tank of the war, winning admiration from friend and foe alike.

LEFT Trooper Sam Fox, of A Squadron, 8th King's Royal Irish Hussars, in his tank turret north of the Imjin River, while awaiting orders to advance, 7 June 1951.

going until the ground levelled out a bit, so that I could get out of that bloody awful ditch. The medics scrambled out of the way, but I crushed several Chinese wounded soldiers. That memory will be with me until I die … We came round a bend and saw, on a piece of fairly level ground, two of our tanks burning. One of these tanks had been our troop second in command's … he was killed by a mortar bomb which burst on the top of his tank, in front of his face, while he was observing the action. Another of our tank commanders was killed by having his head out of the turret; a bullet went through his head.

His wireless operator told us later that he had clapped his hands to his head and dropped into the turret; when they looked at him they saw that he had clasped his head after the bullet had gone through … A Rifles captain told us that we would have to make it on foot from here, and took off with a group of his men. We never saw them again. We set about destroying our tank. We removed the armoured covers above the fuel tank filler caps, pulled the pins out of a couple of hand grenades, and dropped these onto the fuel tanks. Then we took off, after the rest of the crew, up the hill."

LEFT The cap badge of the 8th King's Royal Irish Hussars. The 8th had a long and illustrious heritage, stretching back to the 17th century. In 1958 the 8th King's Royal Irish Hussars and the 4th Queen's Own Hussars were amalgamated to form the Queen's Royal Irish Hussars.

LEFT The Korea Medal (1950–1953), the British Commonwealth campaign medal for the war. The obverse shows the head of Queen Elizabeth II, while the reverse depicts Hercules fighting the Hydra.

1950 at Pusan. In December 1950 all the troops deployed to Korea were renamed British Commonwealth Forces in Korea.

The opening months of 1951 saw a renewed offensive by the North, with Seoul falling once again, and the UN forces counter-attacking to retake it in March. Both the British 27th and 29th Infantry Brigades were heavily involved. A series of "Spring Offensives" then followed from the North in April and May 1951, the strategic goal of which was the re-capture of Seoul. During the first offensive in late April, the Battle of Imjin River took place. Led by the Chinese Sixty-third Army, the North launched an attack on forces of 29th Independent Infantry Brigade that were stationed on the Imjin River, guarding the key crossing points and protecting the flanks of the South Korean and American forces stationed either side of

The "Glosters" at Imjin River

Francis Edward Carter fought with the 1st Battalion The Gloucestershire Regiment in Korea from October 1950 to April 1951. He took part in the fighting on the Imjin River, where he was captured.

"The 21st and 22nd of April turned out to be lovely warm days; it was a treat to be out on the hillside, but something was brewing. We were seeing more and more Chinese troops in broad daylight ... As soon as it was daylight we were ordered to withdraw to new positions higher up the Lamaksan Ridge ... We were moved in a hurry – we had to leave everything – only essential kit was to be taken. ... Whilst we were working our way to the top through some small scrub trees, the two leading platoons came under fire from some Chinese troops dug in about 50 yards from the summit. We hit the deck and started to return their fire, working our way to their flanks; for about 10 minutes it was a regular old firefight, then everything went quiet. We waited, and then advanced cautiously to where they were dug in; they were gone, not a sign, vanished over the top. We followed up and started to dig in ... We then settled down for the night to await events – they were not long in coming ... Just before midnight the bugles started to blow all around our position, and we could hear them moving forward through the bush towards us. They came out of the bush in lines of about

20 men, wave after wave. I was firing nearly as fast as my No. 2 could fill the Bren mags ... By now the whole company was involved, they were all around us. Our artillery OP started to call for support from our 25-pounders and they were dropping the shells 50 yards in front of our positions to try to stop them ... I changed the barrel on the Bren, burning my hand on it in the process, as it had got so hot. You are supposed to change the barrel on a Bren gun every 200 rounds, but that was the one and only time I changed it all night ... 0300hrs they came at us again en masse, bugles blowing and screaming. How I kept on firing I just can't remember ... I can remember ducking down as they ran by our trench on to Company HQ, only to be driven back once again by our sections higher up the hill. By now we were beginning to take casualties ... the Chinese were learning – they started to crawl forward on their stomachs and they were getting harder to see and to hit. It was getting near to dawn and we were still alive ... At 0800hrs we were ordered to break out with what was left of the Company, and make our way to Gloster Hill where the rest of the Battalion were situated ... I left with seven other chaps. The fire from both sides of us was terrific – it's a wonder none of us was hit on the way down. When we arrived at the bottom we found that it was impossible to get to Gloster Hill as the Chinese were on the

road between the Battalion and us, so we decided to work our way south to our own rear in the hope of getting out in one piece. We managed to make about five miles to the rear, diving for cover every time a Chinese patrol was spotted ... they were everywhere ... As we made our way to the sound of the guns I was beginning to think that we might just make it – we had just one more small hill to climb over. As we went up the last rise the Chinese spotted us and started to fire at us. We all hit the deck and waited – coming towards us was a patrol of about 30 soldiers. We could see that we were in a hopeless situation so we took the bolts out of our rifles and threw them away and then stood up waiting for them to come to us, expecting the worst. When they saw this they started running towards us – they were all smiles. 'Good fight, Johnny', they said as they shook our hands. This I could not understand; I felt mentally drained at this point and sat down on the ground. I think the past 24 hours had finally caught up with me."

RIGHT Centurion tanks and men of the Gloucestershire Regiment advancing towards Hill 327 in Korea in February 1951, in their push to the Imjin River. The stubborn defence of the "Glosters" in April at the Imjin River would be critical in blunting the first Chinese and North Korean Spring Offensive.

them. The Chinese 187th and 188th Infantry Divisions, each about 9,000 strong, crossed the river on 22 April, and came up against the men of the 1st Battalion The Gloucestershire Regiment at a strongpoint called Hill 235, which would later become known as "Gloster Hill". Here the "Glosters" conducted a heroic stand, which lasted for three critical days. Many men of the regiment were captured by the Chinese and North Koreans, ending up in captivity in the North for the rest of the war, and many others were killed. However, the stubborn resistance offered by the "Glosters" allowed UN forces to regroup in the rear, and halt this first spring offensive in its tracks. Centurion tanks of the 8th King's Royal Irish Hussars were also heavily involved in the fighting. A second Chinese and North Korean offensive in May also ground to a

RIGHT The cap badge of the Gloucestershire Regiment, worn until 1958 when the Wessex Brigade badge was adopted. The emblem of the Sphinx was awarded for the regiment's service in Egypt in 1801.

229

LEFT A pack of North Korean cigarettes given to British POWs during the Korean War.

230

halt, and UN forces were then able to conduct a counter-offensive. By June 1951 it had pushed the Chinese back to the north of the Imjin River and just beyond the 38th Parallel. In July, the Commonwealth troops in theatre were reorganized once more, and were re-titled 1st Commonwealth Division.

The war then entered what was effectively a phase of stalemate. With the exception of a brief UN offensive in September and October 1951, two North Korean and Chinese ones in June and July 1952, and a final attempted push by the North to break through in March 1953, which saw the Duke of Wellington's Regiment in action defending a hill known as "The Hook", the stalemate continued to the war's end in July 1953. Bombing raids on the North's supply depots and its logistical infrastructure continued, while both sides strengthened their defences along the Parallel; meanwhile, the ordinary infantryman conducted routine patrols and sat waiting for the enemy's next offensive. A new type of soldier was attached to the Commonwealth forces in late 1952, known as a "Katcom" (an acronym of "Korean Attached to the Commonwealth Division").

Over 1,200 Commonwealth soldiers lost their lives during the war, including almost 700 British soldiers. One notable aspect of British Army service during the time of the Korean War was that the National Service period increased from 18 months to two years. The British troops who served in the war comprised a mixture of regular army soldiers, conscripted National Servicemen (who fell into the 18–20 age group), and reservists. British troops were rotated in and out of theatre approximately every 12 months. Commonwealth forces would remain in Korea until 1956.

Prisoners of the North

Francis Edward Carter of the 1st Battalion The Gloucestershire Regiment was captured by Chinese forces at the Imjin River in April 1951, and was marched to a camp near the village of Chongsong. It was here that Carter and his fellow soldiers would spend the next 2½ years as POWs. He describes the immediate events following his capture:

"After a while the Chinese soldiers started to hand out safe conduct passes to allow us to travel to the rear of their lines safely. We looked at them, wondering what to do with them, when they decided for us – we had to go with them. They started off in the quick kind of walk that only the Chinese can do. We had to go with them because we were out in the open and never knew when an American plane would come over ... We had just arrived at the highest point in the valley when I heard a lot of machine-gun fire behind us. Turning round I was horrified to see a flight of black American Corsair dive-bombers coming up through the valley machine-gunning everything in sight ... After the planes had gone I looked round to see who was still alive. One of our chaps had been killed and another had a hole in his thigh where a bullet had gone right through, but he could still walk ... It

RIGHT At "Freedom Village" near Panmunjon, Korea, 1953, Private William Cox of the Gloucestershire Regiment is given an issue of cigarettes and magazines by Miss P. F. Hill of the British Red Cross after being kitted out with new clothing following his release from North Korean captivity. Private Cox was captured during the Imjin River battle in April 1951. He had previously spent five years as a prisoner of the Germans during the Second World War.

BELOW Ex-prisoners of the North Koreans waiting on the quayside at Kure docks to board the *Empire Orwell* for their return to Britain, 19 September 1953.

was early evening when we rounded a corner and came upon a large bunch of our chaps sitting on the side of a hill. There must have been at least 200 of them; they all looked tired and worn out. Amongst them were a few faces I was very happy to see again – mates from my own Company. I think they were relieved to see us as well. 'What's the matter?' they asked, 'Couldn't you run fast enough?' There was still a bit of humour left in some of them ... By this time I was starting to get hungry. I couldn't remember the last time I had eaten ... There followed a nine-week march to the camp, based near the village of Chongsong ... The village was completely empty of all civilians; there was no barbed wire to keep us in, only guards stationed at vantage points around the camp ... 'You cannot escape from here. Even if you do, you do not look like the people of the area', said the Camp

commandant. A few of the lads who had been prisoners in Germany during the war were saying it would be easy to get out, but the Chinese were proved right in the end ... The camp was pretty rough for the first six months. To begin with we all had lice, which we had picked up from the houses we had slept in on the way up. It was a regular daily routine to go through the seams of our clothes to crush the lice and their eggs ... A few of our lads were going down with dysentery, myself included, although I wasn't as bad as some ... The American POWs were at the north end of the camp and we were not allowed to go into their half of the camp or mix with them. Most of them had already spent their first winter in the camp, and were in a terrible state compared to us. Most of them had been overrun on the Yalu River and the Hungnam Reservoir when the Chinese had first come into the war ... We kept on

pressing the Chinese to allow us to go into the American side and help them, and in the end they relented. I remember my first time there – it was terrible – I did not think any human being could sink so low as some of these, they were just lying there listless with dull eyes, not wanting to do anything for themselves; we literally had to kick some of them into life to make them move and start walking ... I was worried as to whether my mother had heard if I was alive or dead (she was not informed for nine months after my capture). I would get periods like this, I think we all did. Morale would be up one day and down the next – it wasn't too bad if you had something to occupy your mind, then you didn't have the time to think of anything else ... I grew up quickly in that camp, I was only 20. I learned a lot about life."

ABOVE A wounded British lieutenant receives aid from a 3rd US Division medic near Uijongbu, April 1951.

RIGHT Two men of the 1st Battalion The Black Watch relax before moving off on patrol in 1952. On the left is Private Jim McHale, and on the right is Corporal Kim Man Kyogh – a "KATCOM" soldier fighting alongside British troops.

RIGHT Troops of the 8th King's Royal Irish Hussars take time out to bathe and wash clothes in the Imjin River, 7 August 1951.

LEFT Men of the 1st Battalion The Duke of Wellington's Regiment drink beer at a makeshift pub, "The Supporting Arms", soon after their gallant defence of "The Hook" in June 1953.

RIGHT A soldier of the 1st Battalion The Gloucestershire Regiment indicates the route of the Chinese attack on D Company in the Battle of the Imjin River (April 1951). This picture was taken five weeks after the battle.

THE MAU-MAU UPRISING 1952–1956

The Mau-Mau was a secret anti-British movement that originated among members of the Kikuyu tribe, the dominant ethnic group in the country. The tribe waged a campaign of terrorism against white, Asian and Arab settlers, as well as against fellow Kenyans who refused to become Mau-Mau. Its overall aim was to drive settlers out of Kenya and take control of their land. The British colonial government responded with harsh measures, employing the Royal Air Force, locally recruited Kikuyu "Home Guard" units, the King's African Rifles, the Kenyan Police Force and regular British Army units. The rising had largely been suppressed by 1956, but not before the Mau-Mau had killed over 2,000 people and the security forces over 10,000 Mau-Mau. However, one of the consequences of the uprising was that a process of constructive dialogue had begun between the colonial authorities and moderate Kenyan nationalist leaders, which led to the country's independence in 1963. The cost of suppressing the revolt was a key factor in Britain's decision to withdraw from her colonial possessions in Africa.

Among the first units sent to Kenya were the 1st Battalion The Lancashire Fusiliers; the 1st Battalion The Devonshire Regiment; the 1st Battalion The Royal East Kent Regiment (The Buffs); and the 1st Battalion The Black Watch (all of which formed part of 39th Independent Infantry Brigade). The service of the Devonshires in Kenya would turn out to be the last operational task to be carried out by the regiment in its long history. In 1958 it was amalgamated with the Dorset Regiment to form the Devonshire and Dorset Regiment. From 1954, 49th Infantry Brigade was also stationed in the country, bringing about a significant increase in the British forces that would remain until the end of the rebellion.

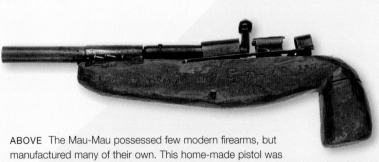

ABOVE The Mau-Mau possessed few modern firearms, but manufactured many of their own. This home-made pistol was captured from a Mau-Mau band led by "General Marwe" (his *nom de guerre* translates as "Hard as Stone") during an attack made on a Home Guard post.

The Devonshires in Kenya

Lieutenant-Colonel John K. Windeatt, OBE commanded the 1st Battalion The Devonshire Regiment during counter-insurgency operations against the Mau-Mau in Kenya, April 1953–February 1955:

"The problem facing the security forces was to bring the Mau-Mau gangs to battle. Once the gangs realized that the security forces were becoming stronger and more active, they either withdrew into the Aberdare and Mt Kenya forests, or dispersed into the Kikuyu Reserve and in the farms, leading a normal existence until concentrating to perpetrate some outrage ... In general terms the Battalion was either operating in the forests or carrying out sweeps, searches, following up cattle thefts and training the home guard in the Reserve and the European farming areas – less arduous than forest patrols ... Patrol commanders frequently had a real problem in accurately pinpointing their positions when in the forest ... A patrol might move for hours without getting a proper glimpse of the sky or the horizon, during which several streams

ABOVE Suspected Mau-Mau terrorists being searched by British soldiers. These suspects had been rounded up in Kanyuki during Operation *Scaramouche*.

might be crossed, some of which were on the map, others not marked ... Patrol bases, normally a platoon strong, were sometimes established deep inside the forest ... In order to stand a chance of a kill in these brief encounters it was essential that the leading man of the patrol was thoroughly alert, had really quick reactions, and was a good shot ... It was essential therefore that the leading man of the patrol was constantly changed in order to maintain a high degree of alertness. Owing to the fact that the denseness of the forest forced patrols to move in single file, it was very seldom that anyone except the leading man was able to open fire ... In the autumn of 1953 the press got hold of an alleged atrocity incident ... Before starting operations in the Aberdare Forest, the Commanding Officer offered £5 to the patrol that killed the first Mau-Mau ... The regimental badge was printed at the head of the article which suggested that men in the Devonshire Regiment were paid so much a head for every Mau-Mau killed and that harmless, defenceless Africans were being murdered for the reward ... The War Office ordered a Court of Enquiry thoroughly to investigate all charges which had been levelled against units in Kenya ... The Battalion and all British battalions were exonerated. The hostile press comments had roused all ranks who felt that they were being stabbed in the back by the people at home ... Too many people imagined the Aberdare Forest was like the New Forest, not realizing that the Aberdare Forest was uninhabited. Any African killed in the Aberdare Forest was a Mau-Mau. There was no killing of harmless Africans."

ABOVE A British soldier looks at the bodies of dead Mau-Mau insurgents, c.1954. The Mau-Mau had suffered over 10,000 dead by the end of the uprising.

RIGHT A double-edged Simi knife favoured by the Kikuyu tribe of Kenya, and seized from a Mau-Mau insurgent.

THE SUEZ CRISIS 1956

On 26 July 1956, President Nasser of Egypt nationalized the Suez Canal, removing it from the control of the predominantly British- and French-owned Suez Canal Company. The Canal was a vital shipping route for raw materials to Britain, notably oil from the Persian Gulf, and a historical link that connected the home islands with the sub-continent of India. British forces had only recently withdrawn from their 72-year-long military occupation of Egypt, and now its Middle East HQ was based in Cyprus, itself the scene of an emergency between 1955 and 1960 in the struggle of the EOKA movement to gain independence from Britain.

France and Israel joined Britain in moving to retake the Canal, with Israel invading Egypt on 29 October 1956 and capturing the Sinai peninsula (lying between Israel and the Suez Canal) with a combined airborne and armoured assault. Britain and France began an air war on 31 October, aimed at destroying the Egyptian Air Force. On 5 November, British paratroopers (from 16th Independent Parachute Brigade Group) dropped on Gamil airfield. Having secured the site, they advanced to Port Said to the north-west of the Canal. Meanwhile, French paratroops secured Port Fouad on the north-eastern side of the Canal, and also took control of

Port Said

Captain Roger T. Booth commanded a platoon of the 1st Battalion The West Yorkshire Regiment (3rd Infantry Division) during the follow-on landings of what was originally known as Operation *Musketeer*, and later called Operation *Revise*, in mid November 1956. He takes up the story after the division arrived by boat at night in Port Said:

"We took up our positions in the city ... Now we had time to study the French and they had time to study us. A Foreign Legion parachute battalion near us had the air and absorbed swagger of established killers. Some 30 per cent of them were German ex-Panzers and Wermacht and perhaps even SS. They had generally not stopped fighting somewhere since the 1940s. On greeting one with the conventional salute they would thump their rubber boots together and say 'You wish to see my captain?' with the accent of a bad English actor in a bad English war movie. They clearly regarded us as boy scouts ... The Egyptians now had time to study us. After all we were not invaders from Mars. We had governed their country before and only comparatively recently had left the Canal Zone ... Our sand-coloured vehicles bore the white identifying letter 'M'. Posters and graffiti appeared saying 'GO HOME FILTHY M' and better 'YOUR KING IS A WOMAN' ... Life now assumed the routine of military occupation with patrolling, curfews and a mixture of civilian normality and

military presence ... Pride and resentment returned to Egyptian youth at night when sniping started and grenades were thrown ... I made the acquaintance of one of the French journalists ... He was highly experienced and had covered the Algerian War ... Our military posture bewildered him. British vehicles frequently had grenades thrown at them. Soldiers would dismount, ring the doorbell of the offending house and enquire of the householder

'Excuse me, do you mind if we go upstairs? Someone has just thrown a grenade at us from the roof.' French reactions were inevitably more severe. In Port Fouad solely occupied by the French on the opposite side of the canal, few Arabs could be seen. They were all indoors. A canal pilot who had a flat there claimed a French Foreign Legion officer had said to him 'If you want anyone killed, just let us know.'"

parts of Port Said – considered vital for securing landing sites for armour and infantry to follow. British reinforcements, in the form of the 3rd Commando Brigade of the Royal Marines with tanks of the Royal Tank Regiment, landed in Port Said on 6 November to secure the city. They encountered stiff resistance from Egyptian troops, who gradually withdrew. The harbour having been secured, troops from the British 3rd Infantry Division, including men from the West Yorkshire Regiment, began landing in the port from 11 November to begin security and patrol duties. However, international pressure soon brought a halt to the combined Anglo-French

RIGHT The formation badge of 3rd Infantry Division (the "Iron Division"). Immediately after the war the division was sent to Palestine, and was then disbanded in June 1947. The division was reformed in the UK in November 1951, and formed part of the follow-up forces during the Suez operation.

operation. UN peacekeepers were sent to the zone, and the British and French forces were forced to withdraw from Egypt on 22 December. Israel too was forced to renounce its gains, and Egypt's boundaries reverted to their former status.

LEFT Smoke rises from oil tanks hit during the initial Anglo-French assault on Port Said, 5 November 1956.

RIGHT A recently captured prisoner is led away on the march by two British soldiers in Port Said, November 1956.

ADEN 1962–1967

238

ABOVE Private Terence Bulmer, aged 19, keeps a vigilant look out as he walks down a street in the Crater district of the city of Aden in 1965, the scene of recent rioting. He is from the 1st Battalion The King's Own Yorkshire Light Infantry. Behind him is a private of the Prince of Wales's Own Regiment of Yorkshire.

The Aden Protectorate territory was a small British colony with a mountainous interior, which bordered on the Yemen. In the late 1950s increasing Arab nationalism following the Suez crisis of 1956 fuelled political unrest in Aden. The Aden Protectorate–Yemeni frontier had always seen periods of significant trouble and unrest, but the scale and frequency of cross-border raids rose sharply in 1957, causing Britain to increase its infantry and ground force presence. Yemeni claims to the Protectorate, and growing Soviet material support for the Yemeni Army, also led to British military action in the areas of the Yemeni border. In the middle phase of the confrontation the British began to rely on RAF bombing raids to punish rebellious tribes in remote areas. British political attempts to create a federal state of South Arabia failed to quell the growing unrest, and an Egyptian-led coup d'etat in Yemen in 1962 further increased tension in both Yemen and in Aden. The border tribe of the Radfan was amongst the most troublesome to British forces, and a major campaign was launched against them in 1964. Among the British troops to see service in the 14 months of the Radfan operations were men from the East Anglian Regiment, the King's Own Scottish Borderers, the Royal Scots, the Parachute Regiment, 22 SAS, 45 Commando, and 12 Squadron Royal Engineers, together with several batteries of the Royal Artillery. British forces finally withdrew from Aden in November 1967.

The Radfan campaign

Brigadier David Baines, MBE served with the Royal Artillery during counter-insurgency operations in the Aden Protectorate, February 1957–November 1967. He describes the activities during the Radfan campaign of 1964:

"Geographically the whole area was dominated by the peaks of the Jebel Radfan massif. Though only 60 miles from Aden it was very rugged country with sheer cliffs rising to 6,000 feet. The ground was so cut with wadis and gorges that one mile on the map was about three on foot. In summer the average midday temperature was 115°F. In this arid and savage country, the Danaba Basin and the Wadi Taym were comparatively fertile and intensively cultivated. There were no tracks passable even to a Landrover. The method of warfare used by the Tribesmen was traditional. Coming down in small groups from the hills they ambushed and shot at convoys and travellers, and then escaped to mountain villages, fortified and sited for defence. In late 1963 attacks on the Dhala Road increased at an

BELOW A company commander of the 1st Battalion The Royal Susex Regiment receives information on an infantry wireless set from one of his forward patrols during an operation in the Radfan mountains.

RIGHT A Royal Anglian Regiment fighting patrol covering a track in Aden, 1965.

alarming rate, and in January 1964 the FRA [Federal Regular Army, a local force with British officers] moved in brigade strength into the Radfan by foot, camel, and helicopter supported by two sections of J Battery ... Operation Nutcracker continued for 6 weeks, with the gunners firing over 3,000 rounds ... The lessons learned were no doubt those known to scores of mountain gunner officers from the North-West Frontier of India, with several new ones thrown in – map reading from the barest of maps with no heights marked; the essential need for picquets on the high ground; the total lack of local water when every man needs a dozen pints a day; observer parties existing on Arab rations; continual mechanical defects in guns and vehicles to be overcome ... On 14 April 1964 a special Radfan Force was constituted with the aim of preventing the tribal revolt spreading, reasserting authority and stopping attacks on the Dhala Road and Thumeir ... The

schizophrenic nature of the artillery commander's task in South Arabia was well illustrated on 21 April, when Battery Headquarters had to man three 25-pounders at Aden on the Queen's birthday parade. As all his officers were upcountry, the Battery Commander attended the parade himself in No. 3 Dress, cross belt, dress sword and spurs. With no time to change he went straight from the parade to an 'O' group for the Radfan operation, attracting certain remarks on the Royal Horse Artillery's idea of dress for war. However, as he had just spent four months in the Radfan on Operation Nutcracker, and almost no one else present knew where it was, he was not perturbed! ... The first major operation in the campaign was an assault onto the high ground between Danaba Basin and Wadi Taym ... An SAS patrol was in trouble on the edge of the Wadi Taym, where they were lying up before marking a DZ for a parachute drop on the night of the 30th.

Discovered by a shepherd, the patrol was soon surrounded by over a hundred tribesmen, and J Battery guns, under continuous fire themselves, responded to direct-fire calls from the SAS passed through Force HW until dusk, when the dissidents were so close to the patrol that further support was impossible. Eventually the patrol broke out, having lost its troop commander and radio operator with several others wounded ... As is usual in war the infantry managed to rotate their companies in action, but the gunners had no relief ... The final stages of the campaign up to 12 June secured the Wadi Misrah and Jebel Huriyah ... Clearing up and intense patrolling continued, but the hard fighting was over and the tribes began to submit to the political authorities. I Battery (Bull's Troop) and 170 Imjin returned to their normal stations, having fired over 3,000 and nearly 2,000 rounds respectively."

THE INDONESIAN CONFRONTATION 1962–1966

In December 1962, the Brunei Revolt took place. Pro-Indonesian rebels under the leadership of Yassin Affendi took control of the towns of Seria, Tuton, Limbang and Bangar in Brunei and Sarawak. The rebels' intention was to capture the Sultan of Brunei and win support for the integration of Brunei (then part of the large island of British Borneo) into the Indonesian President Ahmed Sukarno's proposed "Greater Indonesia" (comprising Malaya, Indonesia and the Philippines). They also hoped to prevent the British-proposed Federation of Malaysia (which in 1963 would see Malaya joined with Singapore and parts of

North Borneo). British forces (including men from the 2nd King Edward's Own Gurkha Rifles, Royal Green Jackets and Queen's Own Highlanders) were quickly deployed to Brunei, and the rebels fled into the jungle. The British Army carried out mopping-up operations, which continued until May 1963, to track them down.

From 1962, attacks began to escalate on soft targets in British Borneo by Sukarno-supporting Indonesian irregulars and the Indonesian regular army, particularly along the lengthy international border area between Indonesian Borneo (Kalimantan) and the British north of the island (comprising

Claret patrols

Brigadier Christopher Bullock, OBE, MC, served in Borneo between August and December 1965, aged 24. He commanded Support Company, 2nd Battalion The 2nd King Edward VII's Own Gurkha Rifles. His unit was tasked with conducting covert operations (involving "Claret" companies) against Indonesian Army lines of communication across the Sarawak/Kalimantan border. Here he describes the difficulties and hazards of operating in rainforests and swamps and his part in a typical Claret patrol operation:

"One of the main difficulties of this type of operation was getting to the right target area. There were no maps and wading through deep swamp for

ABOVE A Wessex helicopter of No. 845 Royal Naval Air Squadron picks up a British Army patrol in Borneo, August 1964.

four or five days was a grave disadvantage ... We had to be able to go without resupply for 12 days, which meant that we could only carry those bare essentials to sustain ourselves, remembering that half our load would be weapons and ammunition. In the end we dispensed with the heavy Army tinned rations and lived on a diet of sardines, dry biscuits, rice and a form of dried sprat known as 'Ikan Bilis' ... We also carried one bottle of rum per man, a Gurkha custom determinedly retained and a large jar of Marmite per seven men to ward off the vitamin deficiency disease 'beri beri' ... Despite paring everything, the average man's load was 80 pounds with signallers and machine gunners carrying well in excess of this ... Apart from my gunner officer and his two signallers all the rest were Gurkha ... If the soldiers felt discomfort and fatigue, they never showed it on their impassive faces. On they plodded, weighed down by their massive packs, but still alert and searching for sight and sound of movement ... We had been marching for three days now and were still no wiser as to how near we were to our target area. Already two of the men bitten by the scrub typhus mites were feeling ill, plus the usual crop of twisted ankles and backs caused by slips and falls. I was far from easy as to our present situation. The company on this type of operation was like a pendulum which had to hit the enemy whilst swinging forward; if not the

effect of appalling terrain, monsoon weather, illnesses and lack of proper food led to a falling off in their alertness and confidence. In this sort of warfare alertness was vital, for it was the ability to hear or see the enemy first that literally made the difference between life and death ... After about 10 minutes the halt sign came down followed by the signal for me to go forward. Accompanied by my orderly and signaller, I walked along the column occasionally exchanging a smile with a soldier on the way. Gurkhas take quite a long time to get to know, but once one has succeeded in gaining their trust, they remain the closest and most loyal of comrades. Since they give their comradeship so sparingly, many of their critics label them as lacking in rapport and disinterested, which could not be further from the truth. To become accepted by Gurkhas is difficult, but once accepted a Gurkha is the most devoted and indefatigable of comrades ... I believe the Borneo war saw them at the peak of their operational effectiveness."

RIGHT A boat patrol from the Queen's Own Highlanders searches the jungle for rebels in hiding and for arms and ammunition around Seria during the Brunei Revolt, January 1963. Following their landing to free European hostages held by rebels at the police station in Seria, the Highlanders patrolled by boat and on foot in an attempt to round up the remaining members of the rebel army.

the regions of Sarawak, Sabah and Brunei). Incidents also occurred on the Malayan peninsula. The British Army began to conduct a series of top secret "Claret" operations (cross-border raids conducted by companies of British, Gurkha, Australian and New Zealand troops) to wrest the initiative away from the rebels and to harass them. 22 Special Air Service Regiment played a key role in these operations.

Helicopter support from the naval air squadrons of the Royal Navy's Fleet Air Arm was also essential for inserting and withdrawing ground troops in the difficult terrain of the island. In 1965 Indonesian support for the confrontation collapsed when a coup took place; in August 1966 a ceasefire was signed and the conflict between Indonesia and Malaysia was declared over.

NORTHERN IRELAND – THE EARLY TROUBLES

ABOVE A Company, 1st Battalion The Gloucestershire Regiment, moves up to the Diamond, Londonderry to control a riot between Protestant and Catholic women in 1970.

LEFT A British L3A1 anti-riot baton round (commonly referred to as a "rubber bullet"), manufactured in 1973. These were first used in Belfast by the British Army in August 1970, and almost 56,000 rounds of this type were fired up until 1975. The initial British rubber bullet, using rubberized plastic around a metal core, was 6in. (150mm) long, 1.5in. (38mm) in diameter, and about 4oz (145g) in weight. It was fired from a modified and lengthened Very pistol named the L67. The instructions for firing the round stated that it should be fired at the ground so as to ricochet into the target, for, if fired directly, the round could cause serious injury. A new type of projectile named the "plastic bullet" or "plastic baton round" was introduced in 1972. It was initially used alongside the rubber bullet, but eventually replaced it.

ABOVE 2nd Lieutenant Robin Martin and Rifleman Andy Walker of the 1st Battalion The Royal Green Jackets engage in a friendly conversation in the doorway of a house in Belfast. This photograph was taken in December 1969 during the first few months of the British Army's deployment to Northern Ireland. The friendliness would soon disappear.

RIGHT 2nd Lieutenant Peter Hall of 1st Battalion The Royal Green Jackets at a road barricade on a wet winter's day in Belfast, December 1969. A rifleman stands on guard in the background.

NORTHERN IRELAND: THE TROUBLES RETURN

The British Army's involvement in the Northern Ireland conflict began in August 1969 with the deployment of the 1st Battalion The Prince of Wales's Own Regiment to the Bogside area of Londonderry. Trouble had been brewing on the streets of Ulster for some years, as the initially peaceful civil rights movement of the Catholic minority in the Six Counties gradually disintegrated into unrest and disorder. The Royal UIster Constabulary and its armed "B Special" auxiliaries could not contain the growing violence, and this led to the British government's decision to deploy regular army troops on the streets of the North. Initially welcomed by the Catholic minority as their protectors, the increasingly tougher crackdown by the Army brought a swift change of opinion, and attacks by the Provisional Irish Republican Army spiralled.

The events of 30 January 1972 were a major turning point. Thirteen civilians were shot dead on "Bloody Sunday" by soldiers of the 1st Battalion The Parachute Regiment during a demonstration. This radically polarized opinions and opened the door to major sectarian and armed conflict by a myriad of both republican and loyalist groups, such as the

LEFT The cap badge of the Royal Welch Fusiliers. This type was worn from 1920 until 1958, when the Welsh Brigade badge replaced it; the unit reverted to the regimental cap badge again in 1969. Before the older spelling of the unit was re-adopted in 1920, the inscription on the badge read "Royal Welsh Fusiliers". The Prince of Wales's plume was first borne by the regiment during the reign of King George I, when it went under the name of "The Prince of Wales's Own Royal Regiment Welch Fuzileers". The 1st Battalion The Royal Welch Fusiliers deployed to Belfast in March 1975 – a typical tour of duty for British troops. They stayed until June of that year, and were tasked with keeping order on the Ballymurphy, Springfield and Whiterock estates.

Patrolling the streets

Scott Farrell Strichen served as a private in the 3rd Battalion The Royal Regiment of Fusiliers between 1973 and 1977, during which time he was sent to Northern Ireland on security duties. Having taken the ferry across to Belfast and then moved on to Lurgan, he describes his initial experiences in the province:

"From Lurgan, I was then passed on to Dungannon to rejoin my company, where at last I felt safe. As soon as I got there, I was assigned to 3 Platoon, drew my kit out, flak-jacket, helmet, riot stick, rounds etc. and was then put on guard in one of the sangars (watch towers) in the middle of a snow storm that had blown up. The sangar swayed all over the place, worse than the ferry across. Hello Northern Ireland. After my first stint on guard duty I had my first patrol around Dungannon to show me the ropes ... The place was deserted and I wondered what the hell we were doing out there ... Our area for that patrol was around the central part but Dungannon isn't that large a place so we'd covered it again and again, taking care to vary the route. Habits and routines were dangerous, as you became complacent if you didn't

ABOVE A sentry watches the activities of passengers during car searching by men of the 1st Battalion The Royal Welch Fusiliers at the Hump, Strabane in October 1973.

RIGHT Corporal Les Smart, a member of the 3rd Battalion The Light Infantry, patrolling the "Peace Line" in Belfast, 1977. This was a physical barrier erected in 1969 between the Protestant Shankhill and Catholic Falls Road areas of Belfast, in order to keep the two communities apart.

watch it ... It all seemed such a terrible mess, especially not knowing anything politically or historically, and of course the Army weren't exactly forthcoming with an objective argument, and how could I be objective about the place and the situation when I was on the receiving end of abuse? If you don't know why people are doing that to you, then of course you will react. It took a lot of getting used to, women and kids swearing or spitting at you, in my case it was because of my naïve belief that we were there to stop the sectarian violence that was at a peak in the mid 1970s, so I couldn't understand the shunning and abuse ... One night we received a call that a bomb had been planted on the Ponderosa, a large Catholic estate in Dungannon. It was a Friday night and most of the people were out so we had to evacuate all the kids and some old residents. There was an old lady in a wheelchair so I and another bloke had to help her out of the house and into the ambulance that had been called. I was smiling at her and making friendly noises as we got her into the back. Then she turned to us and called me, or us, 'British bastards!' Well, this really threw me. It hurt as well. Things were being turned on their head; after all, hadn't we just taken her away from a dangerous area? Yet she still hated us ... Nerves were a bit frayed to say the least and there were always incidents that we heard on the grapevine of someone getting caught with a booby-trap or shot or someone being caught by a mob. These things tended to keep us on our toes but you can't look out for everything."

Provisional Irish Republican Army, the Irish National Liberation Army, the Ulster Defence Association and the Ulster Freedom Fighters. As a result, the number of British troops stationed in the province rose dramatically, and so began the darkest period of the Troubles, a time during which the violence was at its peak and the number of shootings rocketed. By the mid 1970s the RUC and the locally recruited Ulster Defence Regiment (which had replaced the "B Specials", and which would be later merged into the Royal Irish Regiment), took more of a leading role in security matters. Although the terrorist attacks continued, the violence became more marginalized from mainstream Northern Irish society. The British Army too had begun to learn how to cope better with the challenges it faced in the

province, improving troop training prior to deployment and modifying protective equipment and vehicles, as well as increasing resources and manpower for the "secret war" against the terrorists. However, the violence would continue, often in spectacular form, until a political settlement was reached in the early 1990s, when a sense of what promised to be a lasting peace returned to the troubled north.

At the height of the Troubles in the early 1970s, over 20,000 troops were stationed in the north, but this was gradually scaled down as the RUC took more of a leading role in the fight against the terrorists and in security duties. Among the most famous operations conducted by the Army was Operation *Motorman*, following the Provisional IRA's detonation of 22 bombs within Belfast city centre on 21 July

Bomb disposal

Colonel Stephen George Styles served as a technical staff officer dealing with unexploded bombs in Northern Ireland between 1969 and 1972:

"I was told quietly by the Director of Ordnance Services in London that he'd got a 'jolly good posting' for me next. I was to go to Northern Ireland. That was about 1968 ... There was no thought at that time that anything was going to erupt ... On 13 September 1969, I got off the ferry to see the smoke rising from Shankhill and The Falls ... I had to start up, organize and run the anti-terrorist-side of work in the North, building it up as the situation developed ... Which incident stands out in my mind? I suppose you

could say the first, or the last, or any of the hundred in the middle. I remember most of them very, very distinctly, and each of them has something quite unique. For instance, we had one particular spate of terrorist attacks against small hotels in Botanic Avenue in Belfast ... One of the rules of my organization was that if they came across something unusual, they were ordered to get in touch with me immediately and ask for a second opinion ... This day, there had been a small explosion in Botanic Avenue, and the young man who went to the scene was immediately called to another hotel about 100 yards further down the road, where the terrorists had burst into the

LEFT A Queen's Lancashire Regiment team use a dog to search a railway embankment near Newry in 1977. Dogs proved most useful in sniffing out explosives and other items of terrorist equipment in Northern Ireland.

lobby and left a bomb on the carpet. It hadn't gone off ... He called me and asked for a second opinion. I went down myself with a reserve squad ... It was a different type of bomb, and we evacuated the area ... We managed to get an X-ray of the bomb, and we saw that it had a timer inside it, and that the timer had in theory closed the switch, and in theory the thing should have exploded. That's not unusual – on many occasions a small piece of dirt could get between the contact switches and in fact stop the current flowing. If you jogged it or moved it or pushed it in any respect, you could dislodge that tiny particle and the thing could go off ... At the vital moment when, in his armoured suit, the young officer was lying behind his protective sandbags with this bomb on a pole some two or three feet in the air, a Siamese cat came down the stairs, and it got under the bomb and started playing with it, tapping it from one side to the other. I was standing way back, and my immediate reaction was to pick up an ashtray from one of the tables and throw it at the cat – then I stopped myself. So I made a noise like a dog. That scared it off. I'll always remember that Siamese cat ... The danger of the job only really occurs to you after the event ... The thought that you are going to get blown to smithereens doesn't go through your head; you are going to try your best, and you are going to do it safely, and that is the attitude that always occurs."

1972. The Army's response was swift, and on 31 July 1972, 27 battalions were involved in breaking down the "no-go" area barricades of the Catholic Bogside in West Belfast and Creggan in Londonderry.

The British Army lost over 400 soldiers in the Troubles, with many thousands more injured and disabled. Its role was to try to prevent unrest and disorder, and to separate the warring factions in the province. The execution of search and patrol missions, the imposition of curfews, and the gathering of intelligence were the key tasks of the soldier on the ground. Troops could be sent as part of the garrison units, which served for a period of between 18 months and two years. Others were on rolling tours (under the long-running Operation *Banner*), which were of much more limited duration, and were generally involved in higher risk and more intensive operations. Units sent to the province came under the control of the 3rd, 8th and 39th Infantry Brigades covering three separate areas of Northern Ireland. Specialist troops – such as the Explosive Ordnance Disposal (EOD) units of the Royal Army Ordnance Corps and search and sniffer-dog teams of the Royal Engineers – played a critical role in the conflict. Over 4,000 terrorist devices were dealt with by the EOD units during the Troubles, for the loss of some 20 technical officers. The personnel of the Army Air Corps, the Royal Military Police, the Royal Electronic and Mechanical Engineers and the Women's Royal Army Corps all gave vital support both to these units and the infantryman on the ground.

RIGHT An ammunition technical officer (ATO) uses a "Wheelbarrow" (a remotely controlled bomb disposal machine) to deal with a car bomb on Great James Street, Londonderry, 28 August 1982.

BELOW A typical incendiary device of the type used during the Provisional IRA bombing campaign in 1993. The plastic box in which it is contained measures 13.5cm x 11cm.

THE FALKLANDS 1982

In 1982 Britain went to war with Argentina over the Falkland Islands, a remote outpost some 8,000 miles from Britain with a population of fewer than 2,000 people. The Galtieri Junta's invasion force had invaded and captured the islands on 2 April 1982. Pictures were beamed around the world of a small detachment of Royal Marines being marched along with their hands in the surrender pose, or lying prostrate on the ground under armed Argentine commando guard. The British people's sense of outrage was acute, and their government's reaction was swift. A large, combined-arms task force was assembled under the codename Operation *Corporate*.

The principal ground-force elements spearheading this operation comprised over 4,000 soldiers of the 2nd and 3rd Battalions The Parachute Regiment, 3 Royal Marine Commando Brigade, and the Medium Recce Troup from B Squadron, The Blues and Royals (whose AFVs comprised four Scimitars, four Scorpions and one Samson). These lead elements sailed from Britain between 5 and 9 April, making their way down to the Falklands via Ascension Island. A second force – 5th Infantry Brigade, whose infantry elements comprised 2nd Battalion Scots Guards, 1st Battalion Welsh Guards and 1st Battalion The 7th Gurkha Rifles – set sail on board the recently requisitioned *Queen Elizabeth 2* and other vessels on 12 May. These units were supported by troops from

ABOVE Dusk at San Carlos on 2 June 1982, following 5th Infantry Brigade's landing on the Falkland Islands.

Darwin and Goose Green, 28 May 1982

The South Atlantic Medal, 1982.

Peter John Richens was company sergeant-major of B Company, 2nd Battalion The Parachute Regiment, at the time of the Falklands War. His unit sailed on the *Norland*, and landed on the Falklands in Royal Marine landing craft at San Carlos Water. He describes his unit's approach to the fighting at Goose Green:

"We did our approach march, in a big battalion snake, to our assembly area, where we went firm. We had the coldest night that anyone has ever suffered … We had to keep under cover, and our whole company was in and around a garage and a Landrover … The next day we had our final briefings for our assault on to Darwin and Goose Green. It was to be a six phase night attack, and it was emphasized that everything had to be done and dusted by first light … Towards the end of the

BELOW The battlefield at Darwin after the heavy fighting between men of the 2nd Battalion The Parachute Regiment and Argentine forces on 28 May 1982. The battlefield is littered with debris, including helmets and blood-stained field dressings. It was during this action that 2 Para lost 17 men including their commanding officer, Lieutenant-Colonel "H" Jones.

day, one of our radio operators was tuning through the channels to find the World Service, which we did frequently, to be horrified to hear the Defence Secretary in Parliament saying that British paratroopers were five miles from Goose Green. If we heard that, the rest of the world heard that, and I'm sure the Argentines heard that. That spread through the Battalion like wildfire, and it didn't help anybody's morale … We went off to the start line with A Company being the left forward company, and B Company (my company) the right forward company … We didn't get the artillery support we were promised, and when we crossed the start line, 2 Para was on its own, the fire support and firepower was only what the battalion could give at that time … It was very rough at sea, so we didn't have the Harrier air support we were promised. We were on the start line for an hour or so … We went off. A target appeared to our front. Fortunately, it was a scarecrow. I think he had quite a few rounds put into him, which relieved a bit of jumpiness with the lead sections. We came across our first trenches, and took those sections out. It was very difficult, very slow. Fighting at night is very thorough, you can't take chances … It's difficult when fighting at night to take prisoners. In the heat

of the battle, there's a lot of firing going on, you're taking trench by trench, pitch black, it's a very difficult situation … Colonel Jones was very keen to get us moving … He was getting very annoyed, very impatient that we weren't making the ground we should have been. He said if we didn't get our arses in gear, he would pass D Company through us, and they would do a better job than us … We just couldn't make the pace we thought on the briefing. Daylight came, the terrain was very open – hills, ditches, no trees, no cover … In an extended arrowhead formation, we went through to meet our enemy … Unfortunately, B Company was caught in the open … We were opened up by the enemy, in very well prepared trenches … The company was split, nothing we could do about it. There was a lot fire, and we just had to go firm. They had snipers … We must have been in there for about 6 hours … We heard the tragic news that Colonel Jones was killed … The Milan eventually got to us, we were very short of ammunition. They fired the rounds into the enemy positions, and that was the whole turning point of that stage of the battle for us … We carried on, and ended up at the bottom end of the settlement of Goose Green … We saw a lot of Argentines coming into the settlement, but all

ABOVE The cap badge of the Parachute Regiment.

249

they wanted to do was put their hands up and surrender to us. It got a bit silly in the end … All we could do was break their rifles, take their ammunition, and tell them to clear off into the settlement. We just couldn't handle the amount of prisoners. They weren't awkward, they just gave up."

BELOW The funeral of British soldiers killed in the battle for Darwin and Goose Green.

the Royal Artillery and Royal Engineers, as well as medical, transport, mechanical, ordnance, signals and other elements.

The vanguard of the task force landed at San Carlos Sound on 21 May 1982, to all intents unopposed. Within days offensive operations had begun, with men from the 2nd Battalion The Parachute Regiment (supported by guns of the 29th Commando Regiment, Royal Artillery) launching a night assault beginning at 0200hrs on 28 May to capture the settlements of Goose Green and Darwin. This move was vital for securing the bridgehead to enable re-supply operations and the follow-up landings of 5th Infantry Brigade. During the Goose Green battle 2 Para lost its commander, Lieutenant-Colonel Herbert "H" Jones, who was posthumously awarded the VC. He had been leading A Company in an attack on an enemy trench on Darwin Hill when he sacrificed his life in an effort to sustain the 2nd Battalion's attack momentum. The battle continued throughout 28 May, with the Paras employing Milan anti-tank and Blowpipe missiles on the Argentine positions. The exhausted Paras (who had resorted to using Argentine weapons when their ammunition ran out) eventually reached Goose Green on the evening of 28 May. Over a thousand Argentine prisoners gave themselves up. The Paras had defeated a force over three times their size.

The arrival at San Carlos of 5th Infantry Brigade on 30 May brought the total number of British troops to about 8,000 in the islands. During transfer by boat from San Carlos to Fitzroy, the men of the 1st Battalion Welsh Guards

250

The Welsh Guards at Fitzroy Cove

LEFT Wreaths laid by relatives at the memorial at Fitzroy Cove to the Welsh Guards killed in the Falklands War. The relatives were given the opportunity to visit the area after the war ended.

ABOVE RFA *Sir Galahad* on fire at Fitzroy Cove during the aftermath of the Argentine air attack of 8 June 1982.

On Tuesday 8 June five Argentine A-4 Skyhawk planes hit two British supply ships, *Sir Galahad* and *Sir Tristram*, as they waited to disembark men and equipment at the British-held position in Fitzroy, near Port Stanley. The *Sir Galahad* was carrying explosives and men from the 1st Battalion Welsh Guards. The *Sir Galahad* was badly damaged by the bombs and a flash fire broke out on the decks of the ship. Thirty-nine Welsh Guards were killed, with 115 more service personnel injured, of which 75 suffered minor wounds

and 40 of them serious. The most famous victim was Simon Weston, who suffered extensive burns in the attack. Simon's lengthy physical and psychological recovery was documented in five major BBC television documentaries, and he was awarded an OBE in 1992. Eight other servicemen were killed, comprising five members of the *Sir Galahad* crew, two men from the Royal Engineers and one member of the Royal Army Medical Corps. The *Sir Tristram* was hit by strafing fire, with two crew members killed, and two unexploded bombs became lodged in her insides; she too caught fire. Also caught up in the attack was one of the landing craft from HMS *Fearless*, which was hit in Choiseul Sound with the loss of six Royal Marines and Royal Navy personnel, and the frigate HMS *Plymouth*, which was attacked and lightly damaged in Falkland Sound. The *Sir Galahad* was later towed into deep water and sunk by the British submarine HMS *Onyx* as a war grave, while the *Sir Tristram* was repaired and returned to service as a Royal Fleet Auxiliary vessel in 1985. The *Sir Tristram* was eventually decommissioned in 2005.

ABOVE The cap badge of the Welsh Guards, The Welsh Guards were raised on 26 February 1915 by order of King George V, taking their place alongside the English Grenadier Guards and Coldstream Guards, the Scots Guards and the Irish Guards.

suffered heavy casualties when the landing ship *Sir Galahad* was hit during an Argentine air attack.

The net gradually closed around the Argentine forces stationed in and about Stanley, the capital of the Falklands, but there was one more key engagement to be fought – the Battle of the Mountains. During the late evening of 11 June, 3rd Battalion The Parachute Regiment began their attack on Mount Longdon, a strong defensive position riddled with caves, rocks, dug-outs and trenches with over 300 Argentines in situ. During the lengthy attack on Mount Longdon, Sergeant Ian McKay of 4th Platoon, B Company, 3 Para, was killed while storming an Argentine machine-gun nest on the ridge. He too was awarded a posthumous VC. It took 3 Para until morning of the 12th to clear the hundreds of individual positions, during which they were subjected to heavy artillery fire.

With Mount Longdon secured, the second phase of the battle began, after a day's delay to re-stock ammunition supplies and conduct reconnaissance. On the night of 13/14 June, 2 Para attacked and seized Wireless Ridge, while the Scots Guards moved from their positions on Goat Ridge and assaulted Mount Tumbledown, securing the mountain at 0800hrs on the 14th. Meanwhile, 1/7th Gurkhas attacked Mount William and the Welsh Guards took Sapper Hill, all ably supported by heavy artillery fire from Royal Artillery field units and Royal Navy frigates. The road to Stanley now lay open. The British victory in the Battle of the Mountains

252

The Battle of the Mountains

Lieutenant-Colonel Alan John Warsap, of the Royal Army Medical Corps, served as regimental medical officer with 2nd Battalion Scots Guards, part of 5th Brigade, during the Falklands War. On 2 May 1982 he sailed on the *QE2* before transferring to the *Canberra*, and landed at San Carlos Water. He describes the events from the landings leading up to the Battle of the Mountains:

"Men were overloaded with mortar bombs, and heavy MG ammunition, and small-arms ammunition, and their food, and so on. The weights carried by the men were simply stupendous ... Quite a few people had put far too much clothing on ... One or two people even overheated. In fact, my first casualty after arrival was heat exhaustion ... It was impossible to dig deep trenches except in a few spots due to the ground water, all you could do was dig down a little and build up a peat wall. It really was a damp and soggy place ... The Welsh Guards moved off to try to walk from San Carlos to the Goose Green area, but I believe they had to turn back from this, because with the weights they were carrying, and the soft ground, long distances were simply not

RIGHT The aftermath of the Battle of the Mountains. Walking wounded of the Scots Guards move toward a Scout helicopter for evacuation.

LEFT Preparations for the assault on Tumbledown, the final battle before the fall of Stanley. Under fire, 2nd Battalion Scots Guards digs in below Goat Ridge. In the distance an Argentine shell ignites a British phosphorus grenade in a white puff of smoke. A Scorpion light tank of the Blues and Royals can be seen in the middle distance on the right.

possible ... The amount of material that the Guards were given to carry was so much greater, and if the Marines had the same weight, the same thing would have happened to them ... The plan was to sail from San Carlos Sound by night, round the south coast, and up round the enemy's position to approach Stanley from the south and west. We were the spearhead of this movement ... I have heard that in the attack on Tumbledown Mountain, the commanding officer was very keen that tradition should be followed, with piping into battle, and I believe in the attack Piper Roger, or one of his comrades, played his pipes ... We moved out from Bluff Cove towards our forming up positions prior to attack on 13 June ... The 2nd Scots Guards would take and hold Goat Ridge and

Tumbledown Mountain with simultaneous actions by the Welsh Guards and the Gurkhas in 5th Brigade, in concert with the actions of the Marine brigade on the other flank ... All the action took place at night, certainly all the infantry fighting ... After Bessel's diversionary attack, and after G Company were in position, the left and right flank companies of the Scots Guards had the unenviable task of taking the remaining 8/10ths of Tumbledown ridge ... The Argentines inflicted heavy casualties on our men, in particular the first platoons that attacked them ... In effect, due to the heavy fire, there was no casualty evacuation, it could not be done – it was dark, it was cold, there was snow ... Very few casualties were evacuated off the mountain that night ... As dawn

approached the left flank secured their objectives on Tumbledown, and the last third was taken by an attack by the right flank ... The Gurkhas took Mount William, and the Welsh Guards took Sapper Hill ... The sacrifice made by the Scots Guards was the main price that had to be paid for that night's victory. They had to take the Argentine caverns and dugouts in hand to hand fighting, the various platoon positions they came across as they moved along the feature from west to east. Bayonets were used when grenades ran out ... In the end, it was men creeping from rock to rock, and lobbing grenades, and being prepared to close with the enemy that really took the mountain that night."

brought about the Argentine surrender, which came into effect on 14 June.

The SAS, under the command of the then Lieutenant-Colonel Michael Rose, was heavily involved throughout Operation *Corporate*, conducting reconnaissance on landing sites for the main task force, conducting raids and ambushes, and coordinating air strikes. Among the most notable operations, 22 SAS Regiment together with 42 Commando took part in the capture of South Georgia on 25 April, and conducted a raid on Pebble Island airfield, home to a mobile radar station, on 14 May. The regiment lost 19 men when a helicopter crashed into the sea just after take-off on 18 May.

The Falklands campaign was characterized by the difficult terrain and weather – a factor made worse by the loss of vital helicopter airlift capability for the infantry when the *Atlantic Conveyor* was sunk on 25 May. The *Atlantic Conveyor* was carrying a total of 11 Chinook and Wessex helicopters, and their loss resulted in the famous "yomp" and "tab" crossings of East Falkland by the Royal Marines and Paras. Snow, ice, strong winds, and driving rain played havoc with soldiers both on the approach to and in battle, in the lead up to the southern hemisphere winter. Marching long distances under load across peat tracks, the difficulty of digging trenches in the boggy ground which constantly filled with water, and the inadequacies of issued clothing and equipment when faced with prolonged exposure to the elements, all made the campaign a hard one for the fighting men. There were even cases of trench foot.

The road to Stanley

Peter John Richens was company sergeant-major of B Company, 2nd Battalion The Parachute Regiment:

The Falkland islanders were so pleased with what we'd done for them, they just couldn't do enough for us … The Brigadier wanted the Commandos to take the surrender in Port Stanley, but it was a red rag to a bull. We were the first ashore, we were the first to go into action, and we were going to be the first ones into Port Stanley, and that was the end of it …

We had to look for accommodation, we had to sort all the POWs out … Our companies were allocated houses. The majority of the occupants had vacated their houses and moved into the centre of the town … After a good clean up, we marched in threes, by companies, to the cathedral, where we had a church service … Port Stanley was in a shambles, with litter strewn over the place – absolute chaos … The Falkland islanders in Port Stanley were not used to a lot of people being about, and they were very, very

pleased with what we'd done for them, but it got to the stage when they asked 'When will you be going?' I think we could understand that. Being on an island, without many people in their community, it was difficult for them. We'd done our job, and we wanted to clean up and clear off … Before we left, we had two days on a support ship, to clean up, make some calls home … On the way back to Ascension Island on the Norland, we had a sports day, on Airborne Forces day. It was a good shot in the arm for us, where we could really relax."

LEFT Soldiers from 3rd Battalion The Parachute Regiment with the battalion flag in Stanley following the Argentine surrender on 14 June 1982.

ABOVE A soldier of the 3rd Battalion The Parachute Regiment is welcomed home, having arrived back in the UK at Brize Norton.

LEFT Argentine rifles piled up beside the road leading to the airfield at Stanley after the surrender, during which thousands of Argentine soldiers were taken captive before being shipped back home. As a consquence of the Argentine defeat, the government of General Galtieri fell, and democratic rule returned to Argentina in 1983. In 1986 Galtieri was tried and imprisoned for incompetence and his part in the Falklands War. Although full diplomatic relations were resumed between the United Kingdom and Argentina in the 1990s, the latter still maintain its claim to the "Malvinas". The United Kingdom keeps a garrison on the Falkland Islands, consisting of naval, land and air elements, which continues to protect the South Atlantic Overseas Territories to this day.

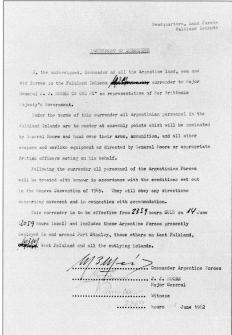

ABOVE The instrument of surrender, signed at 2359hrs on 14 June 1982 by General di Brigada M. B. Menendez on behalf of the Argentine forces, and Major-General Jeremy Moore for the British. In the opening paragraph the word "unconditionally" was crossed out before the word "surrender" by General Menendez. Although it was technically already 15 June in London, the time of surrender was backdated three hours to synchronize it with local time in the Falklands, to prevent confusion among the Argentine soldiers who might have thought that they were supposed to keep fighting until the 15th.

1990–2006

British infantry storm a trench system during a live-fire exercise in the Persian Gulf, 1990. The lead soldier carries a PRC-349 radio, used by section commanders and their second in command.

A TIME FOR CHANGE

The collapse of communism and end of the Cold War brought profound changes for the British Army. There was no longer a need for large numbers of troops to be stationed at home and on the Continent to defend against a potential massive Soviet assault. Troop numbers, particularly those under NATO control in Germany, were reduced following the withdrawal of former Soviet forces from the east. In 1991 a process of review called "Options for Change" began. Overall, the "peace dividend" of the end of the Cold War saw defence spending fall and British armed forces cut by a third between 1990 and 1998. The increasing prospects of a lasting peace settlement in Northern Ireland also contributed to this. Not without controversy, several infantry regiments were amalgamated, while others saw their battalions reduced by one. The Options for Change review also saw the British Army's presence in Germany reduced to three armoured brigades and a divisional HQ.

In May 1991 the NATO Defence Planning Committee called for the creation of an Allied Rapid Reaction Corps (ARRC). This headquarters force, which commanded a multinational, corps-sized grouping of rapidly deployable combat elements, would serve to meet the new challenges facing the organization in the post-Soviet period. The British Army would play a leading role in the ARRC, contributing most of its staff and infrastructure support, as well as filling the posts of Commander and Chief of Staff with British generals. Among the key Army units that might be assigned to ARRC in times of need were 1st (UK) Armoured Division and 16 Air Assault Brigade.

258

The Gulf War 1991

ABOVE A column of Challenger tanks in the desert during the Gulf War of 1991.

LEFT The formation badge of 7th Armoured Brigade, worn on the right sleeve from c.1990 to 2000. Apart from Operation *Desert Storm*, units and individuals from the brigade served in Bosnia between 1994 and 1996, and from April to October 1997, as part of SFOR on Operation *Lodestar*. The brigade was deployed to Kosovo on Operation *Agricola 3* in February 2000, and was based in Pristina.

Captain Hamish de Bretton-Gordon served with the 14th/20th Hussars, 4th Armoured Brigade, 1st Armoured Division, during Operation *Granby*:

"It was a relief to get the orders to attack. We'd been out in the desert long enough to have seen it and done it, and want to get home ... For the initial 12 hours of the fighting you were still unsure, but after that you realized that it was going to be OK ... The American intelligence was telling us that a lot of the Iraqis' kit was still there and all working, and going through the breach, everyone was waiting for the artillery to come in, and it never came in ... It was only during the first attack we did that we had any

RIGHT The crew of a Challenger tank in their vehicle. The Challenger was developed from the Shir Iran tank, which used Chobham armour (a multi-layered armour made from ceramics, aluminium and other materials, with significantly better performance than conventional armour plating). When the Shah of Iran was deposed in 1979, a number of Shir Iran 2Ds (FV 4030) were in production. These vehicles with some further modifications became Challenger FV 4030/4s, the first of them coming into service in 1983. The 14th/20th Hussars was the first regiment to receive these new tanks. The Challenger saw action for the first time in the Gulf War of 1991.

incoming fire ... There was quite a lot of small-arms fire coming at us, but as we were standing off at about 1200–1,500 metres, it never really had any effect at all. The only tank fire we had was from a T-55. We had swung around from our line of axis through 90 degrees and were attacking a position 1,500 metres to our south. From about 10 o'clock as we looked at it, there was a T-55 that fired a round that landed about 50 metres in front of one of the tanks. That tank reversed, and another round came and landed where it was, but luckily someone further down the line picked it up and hit it, and took it out ... Through the TOGS [Thermal Observation and Gunnery System] we could pick up the Iraqi infantry moving round and getting out of trenches, and co-axial machine-gun fire was fired at them, mostly at extreme range. It was also used a lot for target designation, that was the most important job. And for general indication. Somebody would be trying to explain where something was, or which mound, and he'd say 'Right, I'm going to fire in that direction' ... The Iraqis would get up and walk around when the firing stopped. Perhaps they were trying to surrender. Another possible explanation was that the Iraqis would fire one round and then jump out of their tanks into their fire trenches, because they knew they'd be acquired and be knocked out ... We had a few ammunition casualties, negligent discharges, people treading on cluster bombs, that sort of thing – but during the actual battles, none at all ... The only time one of the tanks got knocked out was from a Rarden cannon by one of the infantry who were following us by G+3. I think the infantry in particular were getting a bit upset because they weren't having much to do, and seeing all the tanks firing, so the last night of the fighting they were joining in themselves and were firing over our heads. A friend of mine fell in a tank scrape, and the back of the tank was sticking up in the air, and someone started firing at him from behind. He got a 30mm shell through the back."

THE GULF WAR 1991

In August 1990, Iraq invaded Kuwait. The threat of invasion had been present for some time, and despite the best efforts of shuttle diplomacy in the first half of the year, as well as Saddam Hussein's hollow promises that he had no intention of invading his smaller neighbour, Iraqi armour and infantry poured over the border on 2 August. The Kuwaiti forces were heavily outnumbered and quickly overwhelmed, and the royal family fled to Saudi Arabia.

Whilst Saddam had always been known for his unpredictable behaviour, the reasons for the invasion lay principally in the dire economic straits his country found itself in. This followed the end of the costly, attritional Iran–Iraq War, which had dragged on for eight long years between 1980 and 1988. Kuwait was rich, and its oil reserves could help kick-start the Iraqi economy and help repay its war debts, as well as giving Saddam even more control of one of the developed world's most valuable assets – oil. One can surmise that Saddam, a dark master of social control, was also keen to keep potentially troublesome elements of his own people tied up in another conflict, and thus far away from himself. Control of Kuwait could also give Iraq better access to the waters of the Persian Gulf.

The dangers of a dirty war

Anne Selby was a British NCO serving with Women's Royal Army Corps and Royal Army Ordnance Corps in the Territorial Army during the Gulf War, 1991. She describes the events after landing in Riyadh, during her unit's deployment to the Gulf:

"We were taken upstairs to this huge, cavernous room, and were told to put our kit down. These officers just loomed up from nowhere, and a sepulchral voice said 'Welcome to Saudi Arabia, ladies and gentlemen. We do not have an alert at the moment, but if the sirens go off you will be required to kit up. You were issued with pyridostigmine bromide NAPS (Nerve Agent Pre-treatment Set) tablets. We require you to take them now.' And we were told to get our water bottles out, and they stood over us while we took them. We were told that we'd be told when to take them throughout the day, and we all dutifully swallowed the tablets ... We were part of Laundry Platoon, attached to a hospital ... The sirens went off ... We'd all had the training to get this stuff on, and we were all under stress to get this kit on. Have you ever seen a noddy suit? It comes in two parts, a jacket and trousers. The trousers have two straps that come from the back, down the front, and they cross at the front, then you take them through and fasten them round the back. Then you have your respirator. The suit has a hood that

LEFT Two British soldiers in NBC (nuclear-biological-chemical) clothing and equipment, pose with their SA80 rifles during the Gulf War of 1991.

RIGHT A Fuchs amphibious NBC reconnaissance vehicle, used by Coalition forces to detect, identify and report nuclear, biological or chemical contamination on the battlefield during the Gulf War.

you pull over and tighten. Then you have two sets of gloves, a white set and black rubber set. Then you have a set of overboots to go over your boots. You're literally encased. You have got to get this kit and your respirator on in seconds. We'd all practised like mad of course ... I managed to get my trousers on and couldn't find the ties, and so I gave up. I put my hood and gloves on. I made the mistake of trying to put my boots on after my gloves ... When you've got the gas mask on, everyone sounds like Darth Vader. All you could hear was heavy breathing, gasping, groaning, swearing, things being dropped. Then the all clear sounded. When I looked up, it was the funniest thing of my life. There

were people in various stages of NBC undress. The young TA lad next to me was just stood there, respirator in hand, with none of it on. He looked like a rabbit caught in the headlights. Just staring. The warrant officer turned around and shouted 'What a f***ing shambles!' ... I had my trousers on back to front. ... I think our main fear was from this silent deadly thing, to do with the nerve agents ... Of course Saddam had set fire to the oil wells ... We were breathing in this crap from the burning oil wells, showering in it, it was coating your food, it was swimming in your cup of tea ... it was sinking through your skin ... It was like we were being poisoned to death."

ABOVE The SA80 rifle. The SA80 weapon system (comprising this rifle and a heavy-barrelled light support weapon) was developed in Britain during the 1970s as a small-calibre replacement for the 7.62mm L1A1 rifle. The position of the ejector port meant the rifle could only be fired from the right shoulder. The rifle was adopted for British service in 1985, as the L85A1, and was the subject of much subsequent controversy, particularly in the wake of the 1991 Gulf War, when doubts about its reliability in harsh battle conditions were raised. Between 2000 and 2002 around 200,000 L85A1 rifles were upgraded to L85A2 status, a process that addressed several design faults.

The condemnation of the international community came swiftly, via the United Nations, and a military coalition was formed, led by the United States. Within a matter of days the lead elements of a military task force were sailing for the Persian Gulf and Saudi Arabia. America would provide the lion's share of men and *matériel* in the fighting that was to follow, though troops and equipment from countries such as the United Kingdom, France, Syria, Egypt, Pakistan, Saudi Arabia, Argentina, Canada and Morocco also played their part. Britain was the first NATO country to commit forces to the theatre; its land-force contingent was 1st (UK) Armoured Division, including 4th and 7th Armoured Brigades. 22 SAS Regiment was also heavily involved from August 1990 onwards. Britain's involvement would come under the codename Operation *Granby*, and 1st (UK) Armoured Division would come under the control of US VII Corps.

The coalition response was planned in two phases. Operation *Desert Shield* would see the build up of forces in the Persian Gulf and in Saudi Arabia (which had to be sensitively handled) as a deadline of 15 January 1991 approached for Saddam to withdraw his forces back to the original border. If he failed to do so, Operation *Desert Storm* would begin, with the full might of the Coalition brought to bear in forcing Iraq to comply with the resolutions of the international community. The date passed without withdrawal, and the Coalition launched a massive six-week air campaign to take out key weapons systems, installations and troop formations, in preparation for an armour and infantry invasion of southern Iraq and Kuwait.

Among the key dangers facing the troops on the ground were the potential strength of the Iraqi Army, particularly its well-armed and well-equipped Republican Guard, and the threat of chemical weapons – mustard gas, nerve agents and biological weapons – being employed. Saddam had used gas against his own people at Halabja, and had a developed an extensive Scud missile arsenal, which could potentially deliver nuclear-biological-chemical warheads over distances of up to 300 miles. The British Army, in particular, took the threat very seriously and issued protective clothing and special tablets to troops. Some veterans have claimed that such precautions did more harm than good, and that along with the environmental hazards encountered, such as depleted uranium on the battlefield and ingesting the by-products of burning oil heads, they may have possibly contributed to the condition known as Gulf War Syndrome. The veterans' demand for recognition and compensation continues.

When the land campaign (Operation *Desert Sabre*) began on 24 February 1991, US 1st Infantry Division created a breach in the Iraqi border defences, and 1st (UK) Armoured Division

262

The aftermath of war

A letter to Sergeant Pete Smith dated March 1991 from a member of the 1st Battalion The Staffordshire Regiment, during Operation *Granby*:

"Well, we cried havoc and they let us loose. It was, I must say, my kind of war, with very little coming this way, but a f***ing lot coming that. Actually apart from about 5 or 6 battles that we got involved with, the bastard tanks got into the en posn [enfilade position] before us, and we got stuck with the flaming EPW [enemy prisoners of war]. And what a sight. On talking to the EPW they had been conscripted ten days before and dumped in the front, whereupon their officer legged it back to Baghdad. They didn't cause many problems, although they were not able to tell us where the anti-personnel mines were, but we soon found out. One of the trucks found one and then the rotten bastards made me ride around in the APC until I'd cleared a route. Some bloody mate. (Actually the pressure of the tracks set them off and we couldn't feel anything) ... I nearly got to fire my .50-cal. one night in an ambush, but would you believe it C Coy and Milan got in first again. The above action was where young Moult was killed, the bastards had started to surrender, but as it got dark one of them fired an RPG 7, which got him in the upper chest. I think C Coy showed tremendous restraint because apart from killing the bastard who fired it they took the rest prisoner ... We have eventually ended up north of Kuwait City blocking their main escape route to Basra. By the time we got here there were only a few minor skirmishes. The place is a complete wreck – tanks, bodies, APCs, bodies, AA guns, and more bodies – and yes our first task, clean up! Primarily the bodies ... All in all we didn't do too bad, only two dead and about 4 or 5 injured, but upon reading this it wasn't as easy as it sounds, and I must admit I wouldn't want to do it again."

LEFT Iraqi prisoners of war, 1991.

RIGHT *"Death Squad"* by John Keane (1991). Four soldiers carry a body bag across the desert.

passed through them, its mission being to defeat the Iraqi tactical reserves in order to protect the American right flank. The Iraqi defences quickly collapsed, with thousands surrendering, and 1st (UK) Armoured Division began its move towards the Kuwaiti coast, completing the left hook that would cut off the Iraqi forces there. On 26 February nine British soldiers (including three from the Queen's Own Highlanders) lost their lives in a "blue on blue" (friendly fire) incident, when their Warrior vehicle was destroyed by an American A-10 aircraft. On 27 February, elements of 1st (UK) Armoured Division fought a battle in poor weather against the Iraqi Medina and Adnan Divisions, eventually emerging victorious after two days' fighting. By the evening of the same day, all Iraqi forces had surrendered.

THE FORMER YUGOSLAVIA

In 1991, Yugoslavia erupted into civil war. Following the death of Josep Tito in 1980, long-standing ethnic, religious and cultural tensions had resurfaced, with the principal groups of Serbs, Croats and Muslims each fearing the ambitions and potential actions of the other. The declarations of independence by Slovenia and Croatia in June 1991 brought the intervention of the JNA (the Yugoslav army) in Slovenia, but this turned out to be something of a brief sideshow. The JNA's intervention in Croatia, and the declaration of independence by the Serbian minority population in the Krajina region, were catalysts for the conflict proper,

The Cheshires in Bosnia

Richard Forde-Johnston was a British captain serving as Regimental Signals Officer with 1st Battalion The Cheshire Regiment in Bosnia between November 1992 and May 1993:

"We were an armoured infantry battalion, recently converted ... I had very mixed feelings about Bosnia, partly through fear of the unknown ... I had to establish the full communications plan for an entire battalion group, with an emphasis on rural communications to a base in Split ... Overall I was very positive and looking forward to it. The Cheshires were due for amalgamation at that time – but we'd been under the threat of amalgamation for so long, so we put that aside ... There was a feeling of this being a 'last fling', and morale was high ... it was good to put our training into action, and something of a change from deployment to somewhere like Northern Ireland ... We drove up into the mountains from Split to Vitez. I realized I was driving into a war zone when the convoy pulled over, and the convoy commander said 'Right chaps, let's get the body armour on, the helmets on, and the weapons loaded up from here on in.' ... The roads were pretty poor. One of my abiding memories is of bouncing around in the back of Landrovers as we went upcountry, the roads getting progressively worse ... We moved around quite a bit ... I went up to Sarajevo. We did a recce about

halfway through the tour; there had been a proposal that the Cheshires might take over some of the duties in Sarajevo with Warriors. We found it wasn't actually practical, the vehicles were too large for the streets, too vulnerable. It was interesting to see it. My abiding memory is of stopping at traffic lights at crossroads, not because of the lights, which mostly weren't working anyway, but because of the firefight going on in the next block, and having to wait until it had finished or died down. And the bizarre sight of shells landing on suburbs a few hundred metres away. The odd sniper shot, the awareness of the need to keep one's head down especially going up Sniper Alley. And the difficulty we had of getting out that night. This was just after the murder of the Bosnian vice-president by a Serb soldier while under protection of the French battalion at the airport. They were fairly touchy and suspected us of trying to smuggle Muslims out in the protection of the Warrior. A T-55 rolled out onto the road and effectively the door was closed on us, as behind us the airfield had erupted into a firefight again. We were stuck in this nasty situation, with lots of cocking of weapons ... We had about four or five Warriors at this stage, and two Scimitars. ... The most dangerous situation in Bosnia I found myself in was when we took some food and supplies to an isolated mountain village. We came upon a roadblock, protecting a Muslim

HQ up the road. Mines were on the road in front of us, and RPGs were being pointed at us. As we were talking, a truck went past, mounted with a 12.7mm machine gun, and five very recognizable Croats in Croatian Army uniforms with balaclavas on their heads – it happened in slow motion before my eyes. Within seconds all the Muslims on the roadblock had opened up with us in the middle. Two mortar rounds impacted on a house about 50 yards away. It was quite nasty. I remember climbing out of the top of the cupola despite the crossfire, to retrieve my camera, which I'd left on the deck. Such is the stupidity of risking your life for a very cheap camera. We reversed very quickly out onto the main road and scuttled back to Vitez to make a report on the situation, which actually deteriorated over the next couple of days into general fighting around that area."

ultimately leading to the bloody collapse of multi-ethnic Bosnia in 1992. The war lasted until 1995, and would be noted for its savage and brutal nature, particularly in the form of mass murder (as at Srebrenica in 1995) and untold episodes of ethnic cleansing.

The international community's response was to form UNPROFOR in 1992. Its peacekeeping and protection role was taken over by (the NATO-led) IFOR, SFOR and EUFOR in 1995, 1996 and 2004 respectively. The UK's contribution to UNPROFOR was tasked with providing armed escort to United Nations humanitarian aid convoys. The first British Army unit sent to Bosnia in late 1992 was the 1st Battalion The Cheshire Regiment, under the command of Colonel Bob Stewart, and it operated in the volatile and dangerous area

265

LEFT The cap badge of the Cheshire Regiment. This example was worn from 1922 until 1958 when the regiment changed to the Mercian Brigade badge. However, in 1969 the old regimental badge was re-introduced. The origins of the acorn and oak leaf emblem, the ancient symbol of permanence and strength, traditionally have two explanations. One theory is that the acorn and oak leaves were derived from the Arms of First Colonel of the Regiment, Henry Howard, 7th Duke of Norfolk. The second possibility was that King George II awarded the emblem to the regiment, when the Grenadier Company saved him from enemy cavalry near an oak tree during the Battle of Dettingen on 27 June 1743.

RIGHT "Juliet", the Warrior IFV used by Colonel Bob Stewart, commander of 1st Battalion The Cheshire Regiment makes its way over an unsafe bridge at Malankovici in Bosnia. The Warrior is painted in the high-visibility white colour scheme used to identify UNPROFOR vehicles in Bosnia.

RIGHT The arrival of British forces in Bosnia. Civilians cluster around a British soldier of 1st Battalion The Cheshire Regiment at Travnik in November 1992.

around Vitez. Equipped with 45 white-painted Warrior IFVs, and wearing UN blue helmets, the Cheshires' duties included protecting convoys of food and aid into remote areas, and responding to emergencies and crisis incidents (as at Ahmici, the site of a massacre in 1993). The Cheshires' tour ended in May 1993 when they were relieved by Prince of Wales's Own Regiment of Yorkshire. Many other British Army units would go on to serve tours of duty in the former Yugoslavia in the years that followed.

THE KOSOVO WAR 1999

Throughout the 1990s, tension had been rising in Kosovo, a semi-autonomous region of the former Yugoslavia, which had a predominantly Muslim-Albanian population. However,

the Serbs considered Kosovo the cradle of their culture and it was the location of some of their most holy Orthodox sites. Widespread violence erupted in 1998, as the predominantly Serb police and military authorities cracked down on Albanian unrest, and fought openly with the irregular Kosovo Liberation Army (or UCK). The ugly head of ethnic cleansing in the Balkans reared itself again, and a massacre took place at Racak in January 1999. NATO intervened militarily between March and June 1999, with an air campaign, which included attacks on the Serbian capital Belgrade. A peace agreement was signed on 10 June 1999, which led to Operation *Joint Guardian*, the deployment of a British rapid reaction force under the command of Lieutenant-General Mike Jackson.

Kosovo 1999

This initial entry force included men from the 1st Battalion The Parachute Regiment – part of 16 Air Assault Brigade. On the day that NATO troops deployed into Kosovo (12 June) an unauthorized Russian advance party of 200 airborne troops, based in Bosnia, deployed to secure Pristina airport, provoking a minor diplomatic incident. However, the Russians soon withdrew. By 20 June, all Serb forces had left Kosovo, and the multinational stabilization force (KFOR) took over control of the province. The UK's contribution to KFOR at its peak strength was by far the largest of all the 39 nations.

LEFT A Yugoslavian-manufactured PMR 3 anti-personnel fragmentation stake mine, which was recovered by D Squadron, Household Cavalry Regiment during their tour of duty with Kosovo Force (KFOR) in Kosovo 1999 between 12 June and 29 October 1999. This type of mine has two modes of operation, either by pressure or by pull. The mine can cause extensive damage to light vehicles and kill and maim personnel over a large effective radius. The mine is 125mm high without the fuse, and 80mm in diameter.

RIGHT On the Kacanik Pass, Kosovo, 12 June 1999, a paratrooper from the 1st Battalion The Parachute Regiment leads a column of soldiers up the road. (Kevin Capon)

LEFT Paratroops of the 1st Battalion The Parachute Regiment take cover as they prepare to embark on the Puma helicopters of No. 33 Squadron RAF on the road to Pristina, Kosovo, 12 June 1999. (Kevin Capon)

FACING THE CHALLENGES OF THE FUTURE

In July 1994, the first Permanent Joint Headquarters (PJHQ) was formed, under a Chief of Joint Operations, to better coordinate the deployment of British forces overseas (its "permanent" nature was as opposed to being established ad hoc for a particular operation). A Joint Rapid Deployment Force was also to be created for immediate deployment at the PJHQ's request, and would become operational in 1996; this would evolve into the Joint Rapid Reaction Forces in 1998. A Joint Force Logistics Component was also provided to PJHQ.

In July 1998, a Strategic Defence Review (SDR) was presented to parliament by the then Secretary of State for Defence, George Robertson. The origins of the SDR lay primarily in the disappearance of the Soviet Union and the Warsaw Pact, and with it the major direct threat that British

Sierra Leone 2000

In May 2000, members of the rebel Revolutionary United Front in Sierra Leone were holding some 300 members of the United Nations force and one British officer captive. Operation *Palliser* was launched, and some 1,000 British troops (including the 1st Battalion The Parachute Regiment) were sent to the country to protect British nationals there, to secure the airport while evacuations took place and to assist the UN mission. On 17 May, the Paras were involved in a brief but intense firefight near the airport, where four rebels were killed. The operation ended in June, but in a few months the regiment would be back in the country to solve another hostage crisis. In August 2000, 11 soldiers from the Royal Irish Regiment, who had been assisting with training the Sierra Leone government army, were taken hostage by a group known as the West Side Boys. Although five of the soldiers were subsequently released unharmed, the British Army launched Operation *Barras* to free the rest of them on 10 September. The mission involved some 150 paratroopers of the 1st Battalion The Parachute Regiment; it is reported that the SAS also took part. The mission was a difficult one, as the element of surprise had to be complete or else the hostage takers would begin executing their captives, who were being held in densely forested jungle next to a creek. There were also numerous rebels in the area. The British forces were landed by helicopter in the immediate vicinity of the camps, and within 20 minutes the hostages were freed, though a fierce firefight continued for some time before the area was finally secured. About 25 rebels were killed, and their leader, Foday Kallay, was captured. One paratrooper lost his life in the operation.

269

LEFT Land Rovers mounted with .50-cal. machine guns and 7.62mm general purpose machine guns, returning from a local protection patrol in the surrounding villages to Benguema, home to the British Short Term Training Team. (Photograph by Kevin Capon. Crown copyrght/MOD. Image from www.photos.mod.uk)

ABOVE A British lance-corporal instructs a soldier from the Force Reconnaissance Unit in the use of the Clansman radio. Soldiers from the 1st Battalion The Light Infantry, part of the Short Term Training Team 7, were working as part of the British commitment to the troubled West African republic of Sierra Leone, assisting in the training of the Sierra Leone armed forces at the Benguema Training Centre 30 miles south of the capital, Freetown. One thousand Sierra Leone Army recruits undertook a six-week intensive training programme every six weeks. The training covered fitness, shooting, map-reading and general soldiering skills. On completion of the training the soldiers joined regular battalions within the Sierra Leone armed forces. (Photograph by Kevin Capon. Crown copyrght/MOD. Image from www.photos.mod.uk)

forces, and indeed the Western Alliance, had faced since the end of the Second World War. However, tensions that had been simmering in various parts of the world could soon also erupt into conflict. The key thrust of the SDR was the need to reshape and modernize Britain's armed forces to meet the challenges of the 21st century, in which political instability and change could produce any number of new, asymmetric threats – ones that might defy conventional military thought and expectation. They might also undermine Britain's skill and ability in executing combined-arms warfare, sometimes more simply known as "not fighting fair". This might include the use of weapons of mass destruction.

One key conclusion of the SDR was the need to take British armed forces to the source of any crisis, as opposed to waiting for the crisis to come to them, thus nipping it in the bud. The result was a promise of more container ships and transport planes, and an expanded and improved support and service "tail". Medical support was singled out for particular improvement.

Another element was the recognition of the need to coordinate the activities of the three services more closely. A direct result of this was the 1999 formation of the Joint Helicopter Command, which brought together control of the battlefield helicopters of the Royal Navy, the Army and RAF. The 6,000-strong 16 Air Assault Brigade was formed in 1999 from the amalgamation of 24 Airmobile and 5 Airborne Brigades. It was to serve as the Army's primary rapid reaction formation, under control of the Joint Helicopter Command. It comprised parachute and airborne assault troops, parachute artillery, engineers, helicopters (from both Army Air Corps and the RAF), and service, support and intelligence elements.

Afghanistan

The British Army's participation in operations in Afghanistan from 2001 was split into two distinct phases. The first was Operation *Veritas*, the UK's contribution to Operation *Enduring Freedom* – the US-led coalition to destroy al-Qaida forces and elements inside Afghanistan. The second involvement came with Operation *Fingle*, the UK's contribution to the International Security Assistance Force (ISAF), which aimed to provide and maintain security in the capital Kabul during the ongoing political stabilization process. The UK was the lead nation during ISAF's first six months of existence from 18 February 2002, and initially contributed 1,800 troops, including engineers and logistics personnel. In August 2003 ISAF came under NATO control. In July 2005 preliminary plans were announced to support the expansion of ISAF by establishing a British-led Provincial Reconstruction Team in the province of Helmand, in southern Afghanistan. 16 Air Assault Brigade provided the initial contribution to this high tempo and demanding operation, with the 3rd Battalion The Parachute Regiment deploying in early 2006. It included a force of eight Apache Attack helicopters, provided by 9 Regiment, Army Air Corps – the first time the new Apaches were deployed on an operation. The air deployment of 16 Air Assault Brigade using Lynx and Chinook helicopters was considered vital given the country's poorly developed road infrastructure.

RIGHT A British soldier of ISAF aims his L110A1 5.56mm-calibre Minimi Para light machine gun in Helmand Province, Afghanistan, June 2006. This Belgian-manufactured weapon, which features a shortened barrel and telescopic stock, provides key firepower to infantry sections of the British Army.

BELOW The ISAF formation badge.

LEFT 16 Air Assault Brigade's formation badge. 16 Air Assault Brigade was formed on 1 September 1999 with the amalgamation of 24 Airmobile and 5 Airborne Brigades. It is a unique formation within the British Army, bringing together both aviation and parachute capabilities. A rapidly deployable brigade, it is designed to open or secure points of entry for other land or air forces.

Efficiency improvements and better coordination were also promised with the creation of a tri-service Chief of Defence Logistics. The role of Chief of Joint Operations was also given more responsibility as a result of the SDR. A joint Army–RAF Nuclear-Biological-Chemical Regiment was formed in 1999, to provide reconnaissance and detection for land-based operations. Joint training and exercises were also to be increased across all branches of service.

The SDR recognized the value of the 1996 Joint Rapid Deployment Force, and the concept was developed into the Joint Rapid Reaction Force (JRRF). The aim of the JRRF was to pool the capabilities and talents of the branches of service, by creating joint forces that could be delivered rapidly to the point of need, and with sufficient "punch" to make them

effective on the field of operation. The JRRF was declared operational in 1999, and would see service in Kosovo (1999), East Timor (2000) and Sierra Leone (2000).

A new deployable Army brigade added to the existing three armoured and two mechanized brigades. The resultant 12th Mechanized Brigade was part of 3rd (UK) Division, and featured among its combat elements the lineages of the Kings Royal Hussars, the Light Dragoons, the 1st Battalion Grenadier Guards, the 1st Battalion The Royal Anglian Regiment, and the 1st Battalion The Staffordshire Regiment. The number of tank regiments was reduced from eight small to six large ones, and the numbers of tanks per regiment increased from 38 to 58.

The Territorial Army and reserves also underwent significant reorganization, driven by the desire to integrate

The invasion of Iraq 2003

On March 2003, a US-led coalition invaded Iraq. It had been claimed that Saddam Hussein was stockpiling weapons of mass destruction. British participation in the invasion (and subsequent operations in Iraq) came under the codename Operation *Telic*. Britain provided over 30,000 troops for the operation, by far the largest participant after the United States; the key elements comprised 1st (UK) Armoured Division, 16 Air Assault Brigade, and 102 Logistics Brigade. On 20 March British forces began a drive up from Kuwait towards Baghdad. 7th Armoured Brigade defeated the Iraqi 51st

Mechanized Division at Basra on 21 March, while 16 Air Assault Brigade occupied and secured the southern oilfields. Basra and the surrounding area were eventually secured by British troops (including the 3rd Battalion The Parachute Regiment, who cleared the old town on foot) in early April. Part of 1st (UK) Armoured Division then pushed north from Basra towards Al Amarah on 9 April to reinforce US units there. Although President Bush declared that "major combat actions in Iraq" had ended on 1 May 2003, the country disintegrated into what was tantamount to a state of civil war, with increasingly brutal attacks being carried out by Sunni, Shia,

Saddam-loyalist and anti-American armed factions. Following the end of hostilities, the British 3rd Division took over control of southern Iraq in July 2003, with units rotating regularly in and out of theatre from then onwards. In 2004, the first Victoria Cross since 1982 was awarded, to Private Johnson Beharry of the 1st Battalion The Princess of Wales's Royal Regiment. Following a rocket-propelled grenade attack on the Warrior IFV he was driving, Private Beharry rescued several wounded colleagues despite being seriously injured himself, before driving them to safety in the burning vehicle.

ABOVE The formation badge of 16th Signal Regiment, Royal Signals, which took part in Operation *Telic* in 2003.

ABOVE The formation badge of 1 Mechanized Brigade, part of 3rd (UK) Division.

ABOVE The formation badge of the 1st Battalion The Royal Welch Fusiliers, worn on the shoulder during their tour of Iraq in 2004.

LEFT Members of the 1st Battalion The Royal Green Jackets await the landing of their helicopter transport in Iraq in October 2003.

274

the activities of Britain's reserve forces more closely into those of the regular units. Improved training and specialist skills for reservists were seen as critical in this process too. However, the TA saw a 30 per cent reduction in its strength.

The SDR was to be no quick fix; indeed, its original remit was to look 20 years into the future. Its recommendations, particularly those involving procurement, would take many years to implement fully, some well into the second decade of the 21st century.

The terrorist attack on the World Trade Center in New York on 11 September 2001 led to a fresh strategic defence review, entitled "A New Chapter". The Secretary of State for Defence Geoff Hoon announced to parliament in July 2002 that a review would be undertaken of the capabilities and fighting concepts of the British armed forces, and how suited they were to dealing with the new forms of threat that Britain now faced. The overall conclusions and goals of the original 1998 SDR were considered still valid, a reason why this second review was not branded as a completely new one. The key thrust of the "New Chapter" review was the awareness of the need for a global deployment of British expeditionary forces – and potentially several simultaneous, possibly lengthy deployments – as opposed to focussing too closely on Europe, the Mediterranean and the Gulf, or large-scale, conventional war-fighting. The role of special forces would be critical in this, as would intelligence gathering and improved mobility and firepower. "A New Chapter" also addressed the problems that the Army faces in the 21st century of recruiting talented individuals in a highly dynamic and competitive job market, where employees no longer necessarily contemplate "a job for life". The review also recognized the valuable role that the Reserve Forces, both volunteer and regular, played in recent operations, and proposed the establishment of Reaction Forces from the Volunteer Reserves for home defence and security.

LEFT A commemorative reproduction of the "Iraqi Most Wanted" playing card deck. The cards were first issued by the Defense Intelligence Agency and US Central Command in Iraq in April, 2003. The pack includes 52 wanted Iraqi personalities plus two jokers with Arab titles, Iraq military ranks and the famous Hoyle joker.

Iraq 2003

Daniel Hardingham was a British NCO serving on detachment to 3rd Close Medical Support Unit, Royal Army Medical Corps during the invasion of Iraq in 2003. Between March and July 2003, for Operation *Telic I*, he was posted as a signaller to H Battery (a support battery) of the 7th (Parachute) Regiment, Royal Horse Artillery.

"We went over the border on 22 March 2003. In all honesty I slept until we got to the border. I remember waking up and feeling the heat from the oil wells, the Iraqis had managed to set fire to some of the oil heads ... You could feel the heat of the oil heads through the skin of a Land Rover ... We set up an A2 position there ... The camp never came under attack, but there was always a threat of attack over the border ... There wasn't much fuss made when the 'active war' ended on 1 April. There was quite a lot of speculation as to what we'd be doing next. We found out we'd be moving up to a place called Al Amarah, two hours north of Basra, near the Iranian border ... We drove through a lot of villages, my first real look at the Iraqi people, lots of kids running out trying to get run over, waving their hands. In

RIGHT Members of 3 (UK) Division Headquarters and Signal Regiment on security patrol in Basra during Operation *Telic II* in September 2005.

LEFT The Iraq Medal (2003). The Iraq Medal was awarded in recognition of campaign service related to operations in, and in support of, Iraq, the opening qualification date being 20 January 2003. Qualifying service is service on, or in support of, Operation *Telic* within the Joint Operational Area. The obverse design bears the crowned head of Queen Elizabeth II, while the reverse design bears the symbol of the "Lamussu" (a sculpture dating from the Assyrian period) above the single word "Iraq".

contrast the adults were extremely wary of us, some wouldn't look at us, some would turn their backs on us. Others were just like the kids. They weren't hostile, they just didn't quite know where to put themselves initially. It was a new experience for everybody, not just us, but them as well ... I was sent up to guard a rebroadcasting centre in an old Iraqi army camp. There were quite a few incidents there. The camp was near to a small village. We used to get a lot of kids coming up, checking us out, asking for water, asking for food, wanting to play football. We'd do our best to keep them entertained and out of the camp, but there was a lot of ordnance around. On one occasion a piece of unexploded ordnance went off and killed six of the children up there. The locals' immediate response was to take them straight to us. The lads did what they could and sorted them out. One even got the Queen's Commendation for Bravery. He wasn't the only one to deserve it. The kids had been throwing this UXO about, and it had gone off."

Acknowledgements and credits

Marcus Cowper and Nikolai Bogdanovic would like to thank all the staff of the Imperial War Museum for their helpfulness, courtesy, and cooperation during the researching and writing of this book. Special thanks are due to Liz Bowers, Gemma Maclagan, Margaret Brooks, Alan Jeffreys, Hilary Roberts, Emma Golding, Simon Robbins, and Alan Wakefield, and to Alison Worthington.

The authors are also indebted to the Trustees of the Imperial War Museum for allowing access to and reproduction of the following materials in their collections.

DEPARTMENT OF ARTWORK

Page	Reference no.
11	IWM ART LD 1143
12	IWM ART LD 1755
13	IWM ART LD 3465
35	IWM PST 1244
37	IWM PST 2734
42	IWM PST 5034
44	IWM ART 1917
47	IWM ART 1145
48–49	IWM ART 1460
56	IWM ART 324
59	IWM ART 798
62	IWM PST 7679
68	IWM ART 2955
70	IWM ART 1273
71	IWM ART 323
73	IWM ART 2473
77	IWM ART 2988
81	IWM ART 2757
83	IWM ART 2626
84	IWM ART 2708
85	IWM ART 215
86	IWM ART 2926
93	IWM ART 538
95	IWM ART 2628
97	IWM ART 2267
99	IWM ART 2501
100	IWM ART 5220
104	IWM ART 2242
111 (top left)	IWM PST 13486
111 (top right)	IWM PST 7686
111 (middle)	IWM PST 7670
111 (bottom)	IWM PST 13494
112	IWM PST 7808
119	IWM PST 7687
125	IWM ART 2277
151	IWM ART 2788
152	IWM ART LD 3465
156	IWM ART LD 5840
157	IWM ART LD 3926
159	IWM ART LD 3475
165	IWM ART LD 3395
169	IWM ART LD 3807
177	IWM ART LD 3771
195	IWM ART LD 5459
196	IWM ART LD 5915
209	IWM ART LD 5617
210	IWM ART LD 5618
215	IWM ART LD 5105
263	IWM ART 16432

DEPARTMENT OF EXHIBITS

Page	Reference no.
24	EPH 4206
25	FIR 11542
26	OMD 60
28	FIR 7246
29	OMD 93
34	EPH 9325
37	EPH 4542
38 (top)	OMD 5381

Page	Reference no.
38 (bottom)	INS 7239
41	EPH 2026
45	WEA 477
46	FIR 8100
49	EQU 3915
51	MUN 3273
57	UNI 12268
61	WEA 800
67	EPH 927
72	UNI 12240
73	FIR 8255
75	FIR 8083
78	UNI 12450
87	FEQ 382
88	UNI 459
89	INS 4958
93	FIR 9220
94	EQU 421
95	UNI 11617
100	WEA 1066
112	OMD 982
115	OMD 73
116	INS 7213
122	INS 5289
125 (left)	INS 5319
125 (right)	EPH 4593
127	FIR 10911
128	INS 7203
135	EPH 4244
136	INS 5317
138	INS 4856
139	INS 6062
143	INS 5245
144	CUR 17083
145	INS 4084
147	INS 5382
149	PHO 201
150	ORD 134
152	INS 5110
154	INS 5261
156	INS 6096
157	WEA 2227
160	FIR 6191
162	INS 7224
165	OMD 166
170	FIR 10762
174	INS 5536
176	INS 4079
179	INS 7092
180	INS 5814
185	OMD 1074
186	INS 5148
188	UNI 5484
189	FIR 6099
198	INS 5116
201	FIR 8008
202	INS 5285
205	OMD 269
208 (top)	OMD 2550
208 (bottom)	OMD 6319
210	EPH 617

Page	Reference no.
213	OMD 149
219 (centre)	INS 5275
219 (bottom)	EPH 1831
221	INS 6061
223	UNI 9447
224	INS 6903
227	INS 4822
228	OMD 1634
229	INS 5717
230	EPH 3357
234	FIR 10612
235	WEA 846
237	INS 5356
232	MUN 1925
244	INS 5627
247	MUN 64
248	OMD 2738
249	INS 7377
251	INS 7817
258	INS 516
261	FIR 10772
264	INS 5618
267	MUN 4843
270 (left)	INS 7826
270 (right)	INS 7836
272 (left)	INS 7847
272 (centre)	INS 7841
272 (right)	INS 7842
274 (left)	EPH 4079
274 (right)	OMD 5757

PHOTOGRAPHIC ARCHIVE

Page	Reference no.
6	HU 93414
7	HU 93558
8	Q 79501
9	Q 4665
10	Q 9248
14	NA 12703
15	SE 564
16	B 15107
17	MH 32582
18	BF 491
19	TR 24500
20	MH 30554
21	FKD 856
22–23	Q 72044
25	ZZZ 7150 D
27	Q 82958
29	Q 82941
30–31	Q 2756
32	Q 66157
33	Q 67397
34	Q 115124
35	Q 70032
37	Q 60695
38 (left)	Q 80449
38 (right)	Q 70451
40	Q 56313
41	Q 53322

Page	Reference no.
42	Q 23838
43	Q 69484
45	Q 51749
46	Q 114867
48	Q 669
50	Q 13315
51	Q 37880
52 (top)	Q 56325
52 (bottom)	E AUS 19
53	CO 1015
54 (left)	Q 17374
54 (right)	Q 17390
55	HU 63277B
57	Q 2879
58	Q 62996
59	Q 31576
60	Q 13679
61	Q 13637
63 (top)	Q 102928
63 (left)	Q 103670
63 (right)	Q 23586
64	Q 90445
64–65	Q 90443
65 (top)	MH 33675
66 (left)	Q 67941
66 (right)	Q 70247
67	Q 107237
69 (top)	Q 70168
69 (bottom)	Q 70189
71 (left)	Q 114057
71 (right)	Q 739
73	Q 58863
74	Q 104057
75	HU 59331
76	Q 5211
77	Q 5100
78	Q 15681
79	Q 67818
80	Q 2275
81	Q 2831
82	Q 2978
83	Q 5935
85 (left)	Q 8879
85 (right)	Q 5709
87	Q 12616
88	From the papers of Canon C. Lomax [87/13/1]
89	Q 5575
90	Q 47963
90–91	Q 6432
91	Q 6284
92	Q 7854
94	Q 67556
95	From the papers of Canon C. Lomax [87/13/1]
96	Q 9271
97	E AUS 3883
98 (middle)	Q 12484
98 (bottom)	HU 75737

ACKNOWLEDGEMENTS AND CREDITS

Page	Reference no.	Page	Reference no.	Page	Reference no.	Page	Reference no.
101	CO 3230	148	E 9754	192	B 6727	233 (top right)	BF 10277
102	Q 25946	149	E 12690	193 (top)	B 5962	233 (bottom)	MH 31873
103	From the papers of	150	E 14578	193 (bottom)	B 5998	234	MAU 865
	Major Sir Owen	153	E 18474	194 (top)	B 9614	235	MAU 431
	Morshead, GCVO KCB	154	E 18972	194 (bottom)	B 9743	236	MH 23509
	DSO MC [05/50/1]	155	E 19690	196	MH 6005	237	MH 23512
105 (main)	Q 31488	157 (top)	A 13229	197 (top)	E 18980	238 (top)	ADN 065 524 021
105 (inset)	Q 47894	157 (bottom)	A 14355	197 (bottom left)	MH 22844	238 (bottom)	ADN 065 355 064
106	HU 76248	158	H 17365	197 (bottom right)	TR 2913	239	TR 24802
107	Q 70742	159	D 12870	198	TR 2566	240	R 28937
108–109	Q 31389	161 (top)	H 22626	199	TR 2368	241	TR 18614
110	Q 3705	161 (bottom)	H 1904	200	BU 1109	242 (left)	TR 32959
113	Q 16850	162	NA 1345	201	BU 1167	242 (top)	HU 43396
114	HU 88578	163	TR 939	202	NA 20515	243	TR 32997
115	HU 88589	164	NA 2550	203	TR 2516	244	MH 30548
116	Q 107775	166	E 21337	204	BU 2449	245	MH 30550
117	Q 107763	167 (top)	E 12385	205	BU 3426	246	MH 30551
118	HU 89852	167 (middle)	MH 2240	206 (top)	SE 729	247	HU 47328
119	HU 56369	167 (bottom)	E 12434	206 (bottom)	SE 2138	248 (left)	FKD 349 C
120–121	NYP 68075	168	TR 1244	207	SE 2758	248 (right)	FKD 355
122	N 59	169	NA 4275	208	MH 27887	249	FKD 116
123	N 241	171 (left)	A 19320	211 (top)	SE 3986	250	FKD 3144
124	F 4799	171 (right)	NA 6230	211 (bottom)	HU 4569	251	FKD 359
126	E 1579	172	TR 1372	212	TR 2876	252	FKD 319
127	E 1766	173 (top)	NA 6720	213	TR 2891	253	FKD 317
128	E 2182	173 (bottom)	NA 7137	214	BU 3760	254 (left)	FKD 364
129	E 2172	175 (top)	JAR 2161	215 (left)	BU 4094	254 (right)	FKD 893
130	E 1296	176 (bottom)	SE 7910	215 (right)	BU 3749	255 (main)	FKD 366
130–131	E 2535	177	SE 24	217–218	FKD 851	255 (centre right)	FKD 429
132	E 3039 E	178	EA 20832	218–219 (main)	BU 8635	256–257	GLF 1425
133 (top)	E 3025 E	179	MH 7877	219 (top right)	HU 56718	258–259	GLF 472
133 (bottom)	E 3020 E	180–181	IND 3697	220	E 31968	259	GLF 470
134	E 5113	182 (top)	NA 14851	221	E 31969	260	GLF 400
135	E 5512	182 (bottom)	TR 1522	222	MAL 309	261	GLF 854
137	E 3660	183	TR 1799	223	D 87941	262	GLF 401
139	E 3464	184	NA 15399	225	MH 32581	265 (top)	BOS 104
140 (top)	E 6509	185	NA 15298	226	MH 32779	265 (bottom)	BOS 33
140 (bottom)	E 6804	186	TR 180	227	BF 10317	271	Afghan Tour 347
141	E 6751	187	TR 1662	229	KOR 649		11/6/06
142	KF 114	188	H 39070	230	BF 11159	273	HQ MND (SE) 03
143	HU 2766	189	B 5288	231	BF 11040		053 234
144–145	K 2204	190	MH 13229	232 (top)	KOR 659	275	HQ MND (SE) 03
146	HU 2781	191 (top)	B 5090	232 (bottom)	KOR 616		053 009
147	FE 20	191 (bottom)	MH 13231	233 (top left)	BF 11052		

INDEX

283

THE IMPERIAL WAR MUSEUM

The Imperial War Museum is the national museum of the experiences of people who have lived, fought and died in conflicts involving Britain and the Commonwealth since 1914.

The Imperial War Museum is the museum of everyone's story: the history of modern war and people's experience of war and wartime life in Britain and the Commonwealth. It is an educational and historical institution responsible for archives, collections and sites of outstanding national importance.

The Museum's five branches include the award-winning Imperial War Museum London; the Second World War cruiser HMS *Belfast*; the Churchill Museum and Cabinet War Rooms, housed in Churchill's secret headquarters below Whitehall; Imperial War Museum Duxford, a world-renowned aviation and heritage complex; and Imperial War Museum North, one of the most talked-about new Museums in the UK.

IMPERIAL WAR MUSEUM LONDON

This London branch of the Imperial War Museum houses exhibits ranging from tanks and aircraft to photographs and personal letters; they include film and sound recordings, and some of the 20th century's best-known paintings. Visitors can explore six floors of exhibitions and displays, including a permanent exhibition dedicated to the holocaust and a changing programme of special temporary exhibitions.

CHURCHILL MUSEUM and CABINET WAR ROOMS

The Cabinet War Rooms were the secret underground HQ used by Winston Churchill and his staff during the Second World War. The rooms now house the world's first major museum recording and illustrating the life and achievements of Churchill through extensive original material and cutting edge computer technology.

HMS *BELFAST*

Europe's last surviving big-gun armoured warship from the Second World War. HMS *Belfast* was launched in 1938 and played a leading part in the Battle of North Cape and the Normandy landings. Today this huge and complex warship provides a unique insight into naval history and the harsh, dangerous conditions, which her crew endured.

IMPERIAL WAR MUSEUM DUXFORD

This historic heritage complex has a unique collection of some 200 aircraft including biplanes, Spitfires, Concorde and Gulf War jets. It is also home to the American Air Museum and one of the finest collections of tanks, military vehicles and artillery in Britain. Throughout the year visitors can experience a wonderful range of events from world-class Air Shows to Flying Proms.

IMPERIAL WAR MUSEUM NORTH

Opened to visitors on 5 July 2002, IWM North is one of the most talked-about new museums in the country. It is on the banks of the Manchester Ship Canal in Trafford, in a spectacular award-winning building designed by Daniel Libeskind. Created to give northern audiences access to the national collections, IWM North focuses on how war shapes lives.

IMPERIAL WAR MUSEUM COLLECTIONS

The Imperial War Museum has an incomparable collection covering all aspects of twentieth and twenty-first century conflict involving Britain and the Commonwealth. The collections include works of art and posters, film and video, photographs, oral history recordings, objects ranging from aircraft to toy bears, a huge range of documents, maps, diaries and letters, and a national reference library.

www.iwm.org.uk